How to Lead

How to Lead

3rd edition

Jo Owen

Prentice Hall
is an imprint of

Harlow, England • London • New York • Boston • San Francisco • Toronto
Sydney • Tokyo • Singapore • Hong Kong • Seoul • Taipei • New Delhi
Cape Town • Madrid • Mexico City • Amsterdam • Munich • Paris • Milan

PEARSON EDUCATION LIMITED

Edinburgh Gate
Harlow CM20 2JE
Tel: +44 (0)1279 623623
Fax: +44 (0)1279 431059
Website: www.pearson.com/uk

First published in Great Britain in 2005
Second edition 2009
Third edition 2011

Pearson Education is not responsible for the content of third-party internet sites.

ISBN: 978-0-273-75961-4

British Library Cataloguing-in-Publication Data
A catalogue record for this book is available from the British Library.

Library of Congress Cataloging-in-Publication Data
A catalog record for this book is available from the Library of Congress.

Ten cartoon illustrations by Roger Beale and five by Laserwords
Typeset in 10/14 Plantin by 30
Printed by Ashford Colour Press Ltd, Gosport, Hampshire

Contents

Acknowledgements		vii
About the third edition		ix
Leadership skills index		xi
Introduction		xiii

Part 1 The foundations of leadership — **1**

1	Focusing on people	3
2	Being positive	33
3	Being professional	67

Part 2 The practice of leadership — **91**

4	Leading from the middle	93
5	Focusing on people	101
6	Being positive	141
7	Being professional	181

Part 3 Mastering leadership — **207**

8	Leading from the top	209
9	Focusing on people	219
10	Being positive	241
11	Being professional	263

Part 4 The leadership journey — **287**

12	The leadership journey	289

| *Index* | | 303 |

Acknowledgements

Creating this book has been a personal journey of discovery, in the course of which I have met many old and new guides to help me along the way. I would not have even started the journey without the inspiration of the staff and participants of Teach First: if they are the leaders of the future, our future is in good hands. Since its creation nine years ago, Teach First has become one of the top five graduate recruiters in the UK: a great example of leadership in action. I hope this book helps all the Teach First participants on their journeys towards leadership. I would not have had the courage to start the book without the gentle support of my agent, Frances Kelly, and of Richard Stagg and Caroline Jordan of Pearson.

In the course of researching *How to Lead* I have drawn on the time and support of many people. A vast array of staff and participants at Teach First, Future Leaders and Teaching Leaders have been a live laboratory for testing the ideas in *How to Lead*. I am also hugely grateful to the several thousand people whom I have interviewed on video or talked to informally, or who have replied to question-naires. Readers of the last two editions have pitched in with practi-cal ideas, challenging questions and personal experiences. My only regret is that I cannot include all the material which I have been offered. Finally, my thanks go to the 100-plus organisations which I have worked with over the years. I certainly have learned much from them: I hope they got something in return.

Leaders, like authors, learn to take responsibility. So blame for the failings of the book lie with me, not with the wonderful support I have received from so many current and future leaders.

About the third edition

The reaction to the first two editions of *How to Lead* showed great hunger for discovering about leadership as it is for mortals. The basic idea of this book is that anyone can learn to lead, and that everyone can learn to lead better. Leadership is like sport or music: we may not be global megastars, but we can all improve with practice and guidance. We can at least be the best of who we are.

The third edition follows the previous two with a relentless focus on the practical skills of leadership. This edition adds three more practical elements to the first two editions, in response to the feedback I have received from readers over the years.

First, this edition shows how you can manage your leadership career better by finding the right context. This is essential for all leaders. The same leader can flourish or flounder depending on whether they have the right context for using their unique, signature strengths.

Second, this edition explores how leadership varies across public, private and voluntary sectors. Traditionally, most leadership books are based on private sector examples. This is massive myopia. Having set up four national charities, I am acutely aware of the challenges that voluntary sector leaders face. They have minimal resources compared to the private sector: that does not make their task easier. And public sector leadership is not easy street either: huge constraints and intense scrutiny are just a couple of the challenges they face. Each sector can learn from the others. Having said that, the basics of leadership remain the same across all sectors: set a direction, motivate people, be decisive, demonstrate honesty and integrity. The principles of leadership are universal, but how you apply them is unique to your context.

Third, I have responded to reader requests to summarise key points in simple checklists which you can copy, take away or hand out to colleagues. You will find 30 of these checklists split between this edition of *How to Lead* and its sister book, *How to Manage* (third edition). These cover all the topics which leaders have to master, including: driving performance, managing time, setting and controlling budgets, dealing with crises and delegating. And to make it even easier for you to use the checklists, they're available to download from the book's companion website at **www.pearson-books.com/howtolead**

As with the first two editions, you cannot read this book and finish it as a leader. But it will help you put structure on the random walk of experience; it will help you make sense of the nonsense around you; it will help you accelerate your learning; and it can be your private coach on your road to leadership.

Leadership skills index

1. Discovering your leadership style   6
2. Persuading people   14
3. Managing upwards   25
4. Staying positive   37
5. Learning to be lucky   41
6. Solving problems   46
7. Making the most of your time   59
8. Learning to learn leadership   70
9. Learning the informal rules of survival   77
10. Using business etiquette effectively   85
11. Motivating different sorts of people   103
12. Creating loyal followers   115
13. Evaluating people formally   122
14. Giving informal feedback   124
15. Coaching for sucess   128
16. Dealing with an awkward squad   135
17. Managing conflicts   138
18. Managing crises   146
19. Running projects   151
20. Leading change   158
21. Acquiring power: 10 laws of power   166
22. Building networks and trust   177
23. Talking and presenting   186
24. Listening   190
25. Writing   193

26. Reading actively: business literacy 196
27. Reading numbers: business numeracy 198
28. Meeting 200
29. Communicating effectively 205
30. Building a leadership team 224
31. Hiring and firing 228
32. Leading leaders 232
33. Working with the board 237
34. Creating a vision 244
35. Communicating the vision 247
36. Identifying and using the levers of power 252
37. Crafting a leadership agenda 258
38. Living your leadership style 268
39. Creating the values of the organisation 278
40. Making the values real 282
41. Finding your context 292

Introduction

Leadership is too often shrouded in mystery. To become leaders we are urged to become a combination of Genghis Khan, Nelson Mandela, Machiavelli and Ghandi. A few people feel that they are already that good. The rest of us feel slightly small when measured against such giants.

The mystery deepens when you try to define what makes a good leader in practice. We can all recognise a good leader in our daily lives. But no leader seems to conform to a single template.

Some academics and consultants decided to solve the mystery of leadership. They had time on their hands – they were on safari. By way of a warm-up exercise they decided to design the perfect predator. Each took responsibility for one element of the predator. The result was a beast with the legs of a cheetah, the jaws of a crocodile, the hide of a rhino, the neck of a giraffe, the ears of an elephant, the tail of a scorpion and the attitude of a hippo. The beast promptly collapsed under the weight of its own improbability.

Undeterred, they turned their attention to designing the perfect leader. Their perfect leader looked like this:

- creative and disciplined
- visionary and detailed
- motivational and commanding
- directing and empowering
- ambitious and humble

- reliable and risk taking
- intuitive and logical
- intellectual and emotional
- coaching and controlling.

This leader also collapsed under the weight of overwhelming improbability.

The good news is that we do not have to be perfect to be a leader. We have to fit the situation. The polar bear is the perfect predator in the Arctic but would be useless in Papua New Guinea. Winston Churchill had to endure what he called his 'wilderness years' in peacetime. He just happened to be perfect as a wartime leader. The same leader enjoyed different outcomes in different situations.

> the good news is that we do not have to be perfect to be a leader

How to Lead is about becoming an effective leader, not the perfect leader.

In search of the pixie dust of leadership

There has been a long search for the alchemy of leadership: we all want to find the elusive pixie dust that we can sprinkle on ourselves to turn us into glittering leaders.

The research for this book sometimes felt like a search for the pixie dust of leadership. Over 1,000 individuals helped by identifying what they saw as effective leadership at all levels of their organisations. In addition, over 30 CEO-level individuals in the public, private and voluntary sectors in both small and large organisations gave in-depth interviews. If anyone knows about the pixie dust, they should. I also reviewed 30 years' experience of working with over 100 of the world's best, and one or two of the world's worst, organisations to see what patterns of leadership emerged. Over the past seven years I have even worked with some traditional tribal groups from Mali to Mongolia and the Arctic to Australia by way of Papua

New Guinea to see how they are led. Closer to home, I led a study for Oxford University of Anglo-French leadership to discover how far the world of the leader changes when you cross the Channel.

The bad news is that there is no pixie dust. Or if there is, they are hiding it very well.

But there is plenty of good news:

- Everyone can be a leader. The leaders we talked to came in all sorts of flavours and styles and all had different success formulas.

- You can load the dice in your favour. There are some things that all leaders do well. It does not guarantee success, but it does make success more likely.

- You can learn to be a leader. You do not have to be someone else: you do not have to become Napoleon or Mother Teresa. You simply have to be the best of who you are.

This book shows how you can acquire the consistent characteristics of effective leadership and how you can adapt them to your own style.

Unravelling the mysteries of leadership

Leadership is inundated by small words with big meanings like *vision* and *values* and *integrity*. It is a subject which suffers from an extraordinary amount of hype and nonsense. In my exploration of leadership the mysteries began to melt away. The leaders gave reassuringly practical answers for some common questions about leadership:

> it is a subject which suffers from an extraordinary amount of hype and nonsense

- Can you learn to be a leader?
- What is this vision thing?
- Do values have any value in reality?
- How do leaders with apparent weaknesses succeed?
- Why do some great people fail as leaders?
- What do leaders look for in their followers?
- What makes a good leader?
- Is a leader just the person at the top?
- How do you handle conflict and crises?

What follows is not a theory of leadership. It is the collected wisdom of people who are leading at all levels in different types of organisation. The result is a book which can act as your coach to being an effective leader at any level of any organisation.

In search of any leadership

The search for leadership started with an easy question: what is leadership? This promptly lost everyone in a jungle of conflicting views expressed both forcibly and persuasively. Everyone recognises a good leader when they see one, but no one agrees on a common definition.

One dead end was the belief that leadership is related to seniority. Leadership is not about position: it is about what you do and how you behave. So it follows that:

- The person at the top of the organisation may be in a leadership position, but they may not be leading. They may be careful stewards of a legacy organisation.
- Leaders can exist at nearly all levels of the organisation.
- Leaders need followers. You may be smarter than Einstein, but if no one is following you, you cannot be a leader.

At this point it made sense to start looking for the skills and behaviours that effective leaders have. I made a surprising discovery. Many leaders not only lack some basic management skills, they know they lack those skills. Being good at writing memos, having accounting acumen, strategic insight or deep technical expertise is useful, but not essential. Most leaders rated intelligence as a low priority for leadership. Either they were telling the truth or they were demonstrating the humility of great leaders. Think of some familiar political or business leaders; it is clear that they are not necessarily the brightest or the best or the most competent or the most skilled in every area. Many of the world's top entrepreneurs and wealthiest people, like Bill Gates, Mukesh Ambani, Eike Batista, Li Ka-Shing and Roman Abramovich, are MBA-free zones. Between them, they have amassed $140 billion of personal wealth and zero university degrees. You do not need formal qualifications to be a successful leader.

By now I was lost in the leadership jungle. Skills seemed to be a dead end; styles of leadership could take us in nearly any direction.

It was time to look more closely at behaviours of leaders. Suddenly, a way forward opened up. People know what behaviours they expect from the leaders of their organisation. The key behaviours expected of a leader at the top are:

- ability to motivate others
- vision
- honesty and integrity
- decisiveness
- ability to handle crises.

It is worth reflecting for a moment on what is not on the list: management skills, reliability, intelligence, ambition, attention to detail, planning and organisation all failed to register. As this leadership journey unfolds, we will explore what these behaviours really mean and what we can do to demonstrate these behaviours effectively.

It was now tempting to declare victory. But the list did not look right. What we expect of top leaders is not necessarily the same as what we expect of emerging leaders. The 1,000 volunteers who helped in the search for leadership confirmed this suspicion. The behaviours they value in emerging leaders are totally different from the behaviours they expect in senior leaders, as shown in the list below.

Expected behaviours of recent graduates and senior management

Recent graduate	Senior manager
Adaptability	Ability to motivate others
Self-confidence	Vision
Proactivity	Honesty and integrity
Reliability	Decisiveness
Ambition	Ability to handle crises

(Source: Teach First Survey Results, Monitor Group analysis)

There is one glaring omission from the list above. Performance. It does not get a mention. In working with leaders it is clear that they are, normally, performance obsessed. But they do not talk about it as a leadership quality: they assume that if you have the right qualities, then good performance will flow naturally from those qualities.

By now, the leadership search was in danger of becoming lost in a swamp of words and ideas. Life is already complicated enough without drowning in a swamp of leadership ideas. Fortunately, a simple map slowly began to emerge out of the swamp. All the grand words and ideas came down to a few simple principles which apply to leaders at all levels. For the sake of alliteration and simplicity, I have called them the three-and-a-half Ps of leadership.

Three of the Ps dropped out of our research readily. Performance is the odd one out. If I was being intellectually rigorous, it would have no place in the leadership framework because only one of the selected leaders really focused on performance. Most leaders saw performance as a symptom, not a cause, of good leadership. For this reason, performance earns no more than half a P in the leadership framework.

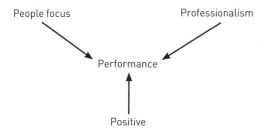

These words can mean more or less anything to anyone. So the next task was to create a more detailed picture of what lay behind these grand words and convert it into something practical that all leaders can use in their daily lives.

Creating the leadership map

Slowly, the map of the leadership journey started to unfold. Expectations of leaders across all types of organisation were clear. But expectations of leaders at different levels of each organisation varied. The rules of success and survival varied. This helps explain why people often find themselves over-promoted. The rules they followed at one level do not work at the next higher level of the organisation. Altitude sickness is a real challenge in leadership terms: you can succeed at one level and then simply find the challenge too great at a higher level where the rules of success have changed out of all recognition.

Too much work on leadership focuses on what happens at the top of an organisation. This is a significant issue. Rules which work at the top of the organisation are not relevant to someone setting out on the leadership journey. An organisation full of Ghengis Khan wannabes is unlikely to be a happy place. It is no good mapping only the destination. We all need a map for the journey to the destination as well.

> an organisation full of Ghengis Khan wannabes is unlikely to be a happy place

Managing the transition from one level of leadership to another is always a challenge. Failure rates are high even at the highest level of the organisation. The career expectancy of a FTSE-100 CEO is now under five years. It pays to know how the rules of success and survival vary by level.

Eventually, a map of what good leadership looks like at each level of the organisation emerged.

Much of what you can read in the effective leadership behaviours map below may seem obvious. But before reading on, try two exercises. In the first exercise, think of some people whom you rate as effective leaders at different levels of your organisation and see how well they display the characteristics listed. There will certainly be some differences: as long as leaders are human there will be variation. But the chances are that, if they are good, they will show many of the characteristics to a greater degree than their peers.

Effective leadership behaviours

Effective leadership	Foundations of leadership: emerging leaders	Practice of leadership: leading from the middle	Mastering leadership: leading from the top
Focusing on people	Decentres self, manages up, supports others.	Builds commitment, good influencer. Builds networks.	Forms, aligns, motivates a leadership team.
Being positive	Has drive, ambition; is self-aware, adaptable. Finds solutions, not problems. Volunteers.	Embraces ambiguity as opportunity, not risk. Manages conflict well.	Communicates a clear vision; handles crises well; focuses on must-win battles. Decisive.
Being professional	Learns the business, learns leadership. Loyal. Reliable.	Masters core skills, sees beyond own silo.	Shows honesty, integrity; role model for core values.

There is one catch in the leadership map. When you make the transition from one level of leadership to another, the rules of the game do not change completely. You cannot substitute one set of rules for another. Instead, the rules of success are additive: you have to do all the things you did at the previous level, and then add the new rules for the new level. The leadership hurdle rises with each level of the organisation.

In practice, this means that the early years of the leadership career are vital. The habits formed then will not go away. Learn the wrong habits early on, and they become very difficult to kick.

Now try looking through the other end of the telescope at some less effective managers in your organisation. Reflect on why they are less effective. There are some consistent traps that leaders fall into at every level of the organisation. These are not problems of gross incompetence, although those problems do exist occasionally; they are traps that decent managers easily fall into. The result is that they stay as managers and never emerge as leaders.

Ineffective leadership behaviours

Ineffective leadership	Foundations of leadership: emerging leaders	Practice of leadership: leading from the middle	Mastering leadership: leading from the top
Focusing on people	Egocentric; lives in rational world, no EQ (emotional quotient) or political awareness.	Expertise focus, not people focus; naïve about networks and politics.	Hires weak clones; threatened by talent. Delegates poorly.
Being positive	Can't do; problem focused; delegates upwards.	Retreats into comfort zone of authority, not responsibility.	Lack of stretch for self or the organisation; manages a legacy.
Being professional	One of the lads or lasses.	Too political, loses trust. Leader in the locker room.	Rides the gravy train of status and entitlement.

These descriptions of effective and ineffective leaders should come as no surprise. But one more step is needed to create a useful map of our leadership journey. It is not helpful to tell people that leaders must be inspirational, or heroic, or charismatic. Most of us do not fill that mould and never will. You cannot teach or learn charisma easily. More to the point, most of the leaders felt that charisma and heroism were exactly the wrong style of leadership. Good leaders do not pretend to know it all and they do not try to do everything themselves. Leadership, for them, is a team sport. They all know they have weaknesses; their teams balance their own strengths and weaknesses.

The nature of leadership

1 **Everyone can learn to lead, and to lead better**

   You do not have to be born to lead. Leadership is based on skills which everyone can and should learn. You can learn from good and bad role models and experience. Never stop learning.

2 **No leader is perfect**

   No leader gets ticks in all the boxes. Do not strive for perfection; strive for improvement and build on your strengths.

3 **You can lead at any level**

   Leadership is about performance, not position. If you take people where they would not have gone by themselves, you are leading.

4 **Build on your strengths**

   All leaders have a unique signature strength which lets them succeed in the right context. Build on your strengths; work around weaknesses.

5 **Leadership is a team sport**

   Do not try to be the lone hero. Work with others who have strengths that are different from yours and will compensate for your gaps.

6 **Make a difference**

   Do not accept the status quo. Leaders push themselves and others to over-achieve, to go beyond their comfort zone and to develop themselves and their organisation.

7 **Find your context**

   Leaders who succeed in one context can fail in another; find out where you can use your signature strengths to best advantage if you want to succeed.

8 **People and political skills become more important with seniority**

   Technical skills are enough to gain promotion at junior levels. The more senior you become, the more you must master the arts of managing people and managing politics.

9 **The rules of leadership change at each level of the organisation**

Success at one level does not lead to success at the next level.

Expectations change – learn those expectations and develop new skills to meet the new expectations.

10 **You are responsible**

You are responsible for your performance, your career and your feelings.

Instead of focusing on heroism and charisma, the leaders focused on the practical skills which a leader needs. They helped to identify over 40 practical skills, which are different from the technical skills of the job (bookkeeping, legal knowledge, cutting code). They are also different in quality from the way the managers learn the same or similar skills. They are skills which the leader has to start acquiring from the start of their career.

There is plenty of good news in this skills-based approach to leadership. It blows away the mysterious guff about heroic leaders and reduces it to things that ordinary people can aspire to learn. Effective leaders do not even need to learn all the skills. All the leaders recognised that they have weaknesses and are still learning. By having the self-confidence and self-awareness to know their own weaknesses, they can build the right leadership team to help them and they could be open about continuing to learn.

All the leaders were clear that they succeeded by building on their strengths. Everyone has weaknesses – building on weakness is not a recipe for success. Not many Olympic athletes win gold by focusing on their weaknesses. Not many leaders succeed by focusing on their weaknesses either. We do not need to try to be someone else. We simply need to be the best of who we are. We need to build on our strengths and work around our weaknesses.

> we do not need to try to be someone else. We simply need to be the best of who we are

This book is your guide to the leadership journey. It focuses on the many practical skills which help distinguish effective from less effective leaders. It does not guarantee success, but it will load the dice in your favour.

this book does not guarantee success, but it will load the dice in your favour

Learning to lead

There is some debate on whether you can learn to lead, and if so, how. The good news is that everyone can learn to lead to some level of proficiency, just as we can all learn to play a musical instrument or play a sport. We may not land up being the greatest musician, sportsperson or leader, but at least we can be a better one.

The alternative theory, that leaders are born not bred, is terrifying. England tried this theory for roughly 900 years when the monarchy and aristocracy ruled by right of birth. The result was that for 900 years the country was led by murderers, rapists, kleptocrats, madmen, drug runners and the occasional genius who was meant to make up for the rest. Applying the same theory to business does not bode well: most family businesses discover that the saying 'Clogs to clogs in three generations' holds true. The first generation makes the money, the second generation spends it and the third is back to where the first generation started.

Believing that leaders are born not bred is fatalistic. You may as well give everyone a DNA test when they start their careers and let that determine their fate. In practice we can help everyone improve their leadership potential. The only question is how. To test this, we asked our leaders how they learned to lead. We let them choose two ways of learning from the following six:

● books
● courses

- peers
- bosses (good and bad lessons)
- role models (in and beyond work)
- experience.

Before looking at the answer, you may want to think which two sources of learning have been most important to you. Having tried the same question with thousands of executives around the world, there is a uniform answer. No one claims to have learned mainly from books or courses. This could be bad news for someone who writes books and leads courses. We all learn either from direct experience, or from the experience of others around us. These are the lessons we value most.

The problem with learning from experience is that experience is a random walk. If we are lucky we bump into good experiences, bosses, peers and role models. If we are unlucky we get poor experiences, bosses, peers and role models. We can hope to get lucky with our random walk. But luck is not a strategy and hope is not a method. We need to manage our journey to leadership. And that is where the books and courses help. You cannot start at page 1 of a book and finish at page 250 as a leader. That is not the point of books or courses. They help you make sense of your experiences, help you remove some of the randomness from the random walk of experience and help you accelerate your path to leadership. *How to Lead* provides you with frameworks to support your learning from experience: it is a structure on which you can build your journey to success.

> luck is not a strategy and hope is not a method

Part 1

The foundations of leadership

Chapter 1

Focusing on people

The research for this book showed that what people most value in their top leaders is an ability to motivate others. But the ability to motivate others does not even register on the radar screen when looking at the qualities of emerging leaders. There is a reason for this. Most people starting out on their leadership journeys do not have anyone to manage or to motivate.

Nevertheless, the ability to focus on people is an essential early indicator of progress on the leadership journey. There are three major elements to focusing on people for emerging leaders:

1 **Decentring**: knowing yourself and how you affect other people.

2 **Persuading people**: selling ideas and the sales process.

3 **Managing upwards**: influencing the boss.

These are core skills which leaders at all levels of the organisation have to master. Even the CEO has a chairperson and a board to manage upwards; the effective CEO does not just order people to do things but also uses powers of persuasion and influence. Strong CEOs know themselves, know their weaknesses and build teams to compensate for their gaps.

Decentring: knowing yourself and how you affect other people

When your boss urges you to get to know yourself, smile politely and run a mile. What may follow is a barrage of psychometric testing, some psycho-babble with long words and group events where you get in touch with your inner self. At a personal level, it may be useful to check in with your inner self once in a while. For a leader, inward navel-gazing is not the high road to success.

Knowing yourself is not just about looking inwards. For leaders, knowing yourself means knowing how you affect other people.

As a leader, you need to understand your own personal style and the style of the person you are working with. If you know those two things, you have a chance of knowing how to influence the other person more effectively. Some leaders seem to do this intuitively: they play people like a piano and instinctively know what tune to play to make them sing. The rest of us, who do not have this innate ability, can do some simple things to improve the odds in our favour.

> knowing yourself means knowing how you affect other people

There are some basic frameworks for thinking about your style and how you affect other people. One of the most popular is the Myers–Briggs Type Indicator (MB/TI). To become an expert at it takes years, which rather defeats the object of the exercise. The goal is to become a leader, not a psychological expert. MB/TI presents the leader with a series of style or type trade-offs. You can be:

- Extrovert or Introvert (E or I)
- Sensing or Intuitive (S or N)
- Thinking or Feeling (T or F)
- Judging or Perceiving (J or P).

There are also sophisticated tests to tell you which style you are: the result is normally a four-letter acronym like ESTJ or INFP. As leaders, we do not have time to make everyone we meet take a sophisticated test. So look at Table 1.1 overleaf and see where you think (or feel) you come out. As you look at the positive impacts of different styles, you would only be human if you hope that you had all of these characteristics. So look at the negative impact column. This will quickly tell you what you are like and what the person you are dealing with is like. It is not sophisticated, but it is usable.

There is no 'right' or 'wrong' answer to what style a leader should have. You are as likely to find two identical leaders as you are to find two identical snowflakes. But you need to be aware of the consequences of some of the different styles of leadership.

Extroverts and introverts: a room full of extroverts will be as noisy as a chimpanzees' tea party, while a room full of introverts will echo to the sound of silence. Extroverts need to give space to introverts to speak: introverts think before they speak, while extroverts use speaking to help them think.

Sensing and intuitive types: the intuitive types can be great friends and irritating colleagues. They are all ideas and no action. The sensing types may be dull friends but invaluable and reliable colleagues who get things done. If both types can learn to respect each other, you have a recipe for great ideas being turned into great action. They often find it hard to respect each other.

Thinking and feeling types: in a crisis, the feeling people will work hard to help the team and the people through tough times. The thinking type will work hard to figure out the right solution. As with other types, this makes for a powerful combination if the two types can learn to live with each other.

Judging and perceiving types: look at their clean or messy desks. These two types find it hard to get on with each other

Type	Description	Positive impact	Negative impact
Extrovert (E)	Gains energy from others; speaks, then thinks	Spreads energy, enthusiasm	Loud mouth, does not include other people
Introvert (I)	Gains energy from within; thinks before speaks	Thoughtful, gives space to others	Nothing worth saying? Uneasy networker
Sensing (S)	Observes outside world; more facts, fewer ideas	Practical, concrete, detailed	Dull, unimaginative
Intuitive (N)	Pays attention to self, inner world, ideas	Creative, imaginative	Flighty, impractical, unrealistic
Thinking (T)	Decides with the head and logic	Logical, rational, intellectual	Cold and heartless
Feeling (F)	Listens to the heart	Empathetic, understanding	Soft-headed, fuzzy thinker, bleeding heart
Judging (J)	Organised, scheduled, tidy	High work ethic, focused and reliable	Compulsive neat freak; uptight, rigid, rule bound
Perceiving (P)	Keeps options open, opportunistic	Work–life balance, enjoys work	Lazy, messy, aimless and unreliable

Table 1.1 Myers–Briggs Type Indicator (MB/TI) outline

because they so obviously have different priorities. It is the challenge of order versus opportunity. The judging type makes sure the trains run on time. The perceiving type will discover that a flight would get there much faster, thank you very much.

Keep on using the table as you meet people, and you will quickly be able to put them in the various categories above. Putting people in boxes works for organisational charts and burying people. But we need to do something with the information.

MB/TI may be good theory. It is not good practice. It takes too long to master. It is hard to tell which box to put people in. As a general rule, people should not be put in boxes until they are dead. Practising managers need a simpler way of decoding their colleagues. So here is a simpler way.

> people should not be put in boxes until they are dead

Start by writing down the top three or four characteristics of how your colleague likes to work. Here are a few trade-offs to help you think about the different possibilities:

- big picture or detail
- morning or afternoon
- words or numbers
- risk tolerant or risk averse
- controlling or empowering
- quick or slow and deliberate
- open or defensive
- positive or cynical
- analysis or action.

Now use this knowledge to adapt to their way of working. For example, I was working with a CEO whom many people found very hard to work with. He was brilliant, demanding and unpredictable. He would come in on Monday morning like a demented toy clockwork soldier which had been wound up too tightly. He would starting shooting out orders left, right and centre: everyone tried to avoid him. By Friday lunchtime, everyone was exhausted and would take advantage of the convention that you could leave early for the weekend. So how would you work with someone like that?

The first step was to map out what his main characteristics were like. In this case, I saw that the CEO:

● focused on outcomes, not on how to get there

● liked ideas and action, hated too much analysis and detail

● preferred dealing with people than with paper

● would only chill out on Friday afternoon, when everyone else had left. The rest of the time he would get very frustrated and would be in fire-fighting mode.

So the solution was simple. I listened hard to what he really wanted to achieve. Then I wandered into his office on a Friday afternoon. He was chilled out. I let him vent his frustration with everything and everyone. Eventually, he relaxed and was ready to listen. All I had to do was to offer to fix one of the problems he had mentioned, and he agreed. He asked a few questions, but he did not want any detail and he certainly did not want any papers. Suddenly, I had the job I had always wanted. More importantly, I had established a working style that gave me regular access to the CEO. This was nothing to do with talent, but everything to do with adapting to the style of the person I wanted to influence. Far better managers could not understand how I had a good relationship with this difficult CEO, and they were frozen out. Style counts.

if you want to influence someone else, start with the other person

Most psychometric and style tests look down the wrong end of the telescope. They attempt to make you look at yourself. This is not helpful. If you want to influence someone else, you do not start with 'Me, me, me, me'. You have to start with the other person. Try to understand how they work. Then adapt your way of working to suit them. To make the point, I had another boss who was the opposite of the CEO above. This boss was a control freak who:

- focused on process, not on outcomes
- was deeply risk averse
- found dealing with paper easier than dealing with people
- became even more irritable in the afternoon.

He was not the easiest boss to work with. But the key to keeping him quiet was predictability. So he and I would invest large amounts of time in mapping out exactly the process we would follow for a project, or in mapping out precisely what all the elements of a report would look like. Once he had a map which I would follow, he was happy. I learned to stick to it even if a better way of doing things emerged. He was so risk averse that any change, even for the better, would take hours of persuasion.

In neither case was my personal style relevant. My bosses had the power, and if I wanted to influence them I had to work out their style and adapt to it.

Style is a powerful tool for influencing in private. If you focus on style, look through the right end of the telescope. Focus on the other person's style, not on your own. Work out what makes them tick, and then adapt your style to theirs. Good leaders learn to be chameleons: they adapt to circumstances.

One to one is where the most effective influencing happens in practice. As soon as meetings become public, your ability to influence people is reduced. In public, people are more reluctant to commit to new ideas. Typically, people want to show that they are smart in front of their peers. The easiest way to show you are smart is to identify all the risks, problems and inconsistencies associated with someone's new idea or presentation. Smart questions are less risky than smart solutions. Once the person you are trying to influence has expressed all these doubts in public, it becomes twice as hard to make them change their mind: they would lose face in front of their peers by doing so. For this reason, any meeting with more than two people becomes a public meeting. The third person creates the potential for any ideas and positions to be reported back into the organisation grapevine in ways you may or may not recognise.

Unfortunately, you cannot rely on getting a private meeting with the person you need to influence. Sometimes, you are stuck with a public forum as the only way of communicating with the person you want to reach. In a public meeting with, say, eight people present, you have two choices.

The first choice is to be yourself. This maximises your chances of looking confident and enthusiastic. Given that people react more strongly to visual clues and to style than they do to substance, this is important. Trying to be all things to all people is a certain recipe for failure. You will not look natural, you will not feel confident and comfortable and you will not be able to adapt to all the different styles in the room.

There is a second, more subtle and more effective choice. In practice, you are probably not trying to influence all eight people equally. If the chief executive is present, it is reasonably likely that this is the person you most need to influence. If this is the case, focus the content and the style of your presentation on this person. If you are wise, you will also have quietly met some of the other people in the room beforehand and secured their support in private. That leaves just the one key decision maker whom you have not met. With the tacit support of the others, and the advice they may have given in private, you should be in a good position to know how to influence the CEO – you should know their hot buttons (what gets them excited), their red flags (what they dislike) and what their preferred style is. You may be in a meeting with eight people, but prepare properly and you can focus on the one person who counts most.

Persuading people

Leadership is about getting other people to do things. As a new leader, this is a particular challenge. You cannot tell people what to do because you have no power. So you have to learn the subtle arts of persuasion. These are skills which last a lifetime. Even CEOs spend a large part of their time selling their vision, selling their plans, selling their values and selling change to people inside and outside their organisation.

> leadership is about getting other people to do things

Effective persuasion is not about the stereotypes. You are not in the position of the gangster who 'makes an offer you cannot refuse'. Nor should you be like the door-to-door salesman who puts his foot in the door and has a patter which wears you down until you agree to some incredibly over-priced double glazing for your house. And you certainly do not want to be like a hapless call centre operative working to a script.

Effective persuasion is about having a structured conversation. Social conversations can meander along in unexpected directions: that is part of their pleasure. A persuasive conversation has a structure which will be clear to you but invisible to the person you are persuading. Once you have mastered the structure, it will become second nature to you. Here is how it works.

1 Prepare

You do not need to prepare for social conversations. You must prepare for persuasive conversations. Here are the questions you need to ask before starting the conversation:

- How will my idea look to the other person? Will it solve a problem or create a problem for them? What will they like and dislike about it? How can I make my idea fit with their needs and their agenda? What are their likely objections and how can I pre-empt those objections?

- How does the other person like working? What is the best time of day to talk with them? How can I adapt my style to fit theirs?

- Have I got the right advice and coaching for this? Who else needs to be involved? Is there anyone who can give me guidance on how to make the most of this opportunity?

- What logistics do I need to have in place? Have I got the right time and place in the diary? Have I got the right contact details? Do I need any written material or samples?

- What is my desired outcome from the meeting? What am I asking for and what is the specific follow-up I expect on both sides? What is my plan B if plan A does not work out?

All of that looks like a mountain to think about. Don't worry. Your preparation should be proportionate. If you know someone well and you have a small favour to ask, you do not need weeks of preparation. If you are pitching a big idea to the CEO whom you have never met before, then spend as much time as you can to prepare. With practice, most of these questions become reflex reactions and you learn to answer them fast.

Think of the times you have tried to persuade someone about something and you have been surprised by their reaction. Surprises are rarely good news. They normally lead to a setback in the persuasive conversation, and they normally reflect lack of preparation. If you do not want an unpleasant surprise, prepare properly.

2 Build rapport and trust

When you meet someone, it is very tempting to pitch in immediately with your great idea. It is tempting, but wrong for two reasons. First, the focus should not be on your idea but on their need or challenge and how you can work together. Second, people will not agree until they are ready to agree. You need to warm them up a little.

If you are persuading a colleague whom you know very well, building rapport may be no more than a couple of moments checking that you are talking to them at a convenient time. If their last meeting has brought out the axe-wielding maniac in them, it may not be the best time to start laying more problems on them.

If you want to persuade someone whom you have not met before, then building trust and rapport is vital. To put it simply: would you buy anything from someone you do not trust?

> would you buy anything from someone you do not trust?

If you are meeting someone for the first time, you need to build trust fast. That means finding common ground. So start using your eyes and ears: look for clues and ask questions. Common ground may include the following:

- Common personal interests: holidays, cars, pastimes. Pictures on the wall are often clues.
- Common professional background: people or firms you have both worked for in the past; conferences you have attended; common challenges which you face.

Don't get into bragging contests: 'My holiday was more exotic than yours, and my professional achievements are bigger.' This is a good way to alienate people fast. Now is the time to flatter. Research shows that there is no point at which flattery becomes counter-productive. You cannot flatter too much. That makes sense. How many people think they are over-promoted, over-rewarded and over-recognised? Most people think the opposite. Then you come along and recognise their innate brilliance and diligence. They will reciprocate by thinking you are a wonderful and insightful human being. Gentle flattery builds rapport.

By the end of this stage, you want your opposite number to be in 'noddy' mode. They will be nodding and agreeing with you. They are now ready to start nodding and agreeing with bigger things.

3 Adapt your style to that of the other person

We have already covered this. This is the magic by which you appear to tune into anyone and gain their support. It is invisible persuasion, which is what makes it so effective.

4 Listen

Good persuaders listen twice as much as they talk. They get the other person to talk themselves into submission. They persuade themselves. So how do you get people to talk? Start by asking smart questions.

> good persuaders listen twice as much as they talk

Smart questions guide them to the answer. Start by asking questions around the challenges they face, especially in relation to your needs; ask them about how important it is and what work they are already doing in that area. Gather intelligence, build their sense of need and opportunity. Keep your questions open. Open questions are ones where it is not possible to answer 'yes' or 'no'. You want rich replies which will usually give you the chance to ask more questions.

Show you are listening by paraphrasing what they say. This helps you remember what they said and reassures the other person that you have understood them. If you have misunderstood them, you quickly avert any continued misunderstanding. Good listening continues to build trust and respect.

Through good listening you should be able to find out:

● what your need or opportunity looks like from their perspective
● what the benefits and risks of the opportunity look like to them

- what work is already being done in the area, and if there are any competing agendas
- what objections and obstacles they will perceive with the idea.

This is the vital ammunition you need to have before you start pitching your idea. If you blurt out your idea too quickly, you have no idea what the reaction will be. You may be lucky, but you may not. Luck is not a method.

5 Agree the challenge from their perspective

The best way to suggest your idea is by paraphrasing what the other person has already said: people rarely argue with their own ideas. Paraphrasing makes it seem like their idea. Recognise what they want and what worries them. Don't pretend everything will be perfect: you have to remain credible. Make it simple, like this:

- 'So you want a new IT system because it will help reduce supply chain costs, but you are worried about how it will work with existing staff and procedures ...'
- 'So you want a new logo, which must build on the existing logo but have more authority and be less populist than the current version ...'
- 'So you want to make these organisational changes, but you are worried about the staff reaction ...'

If you have listened well, the other person will nod in agreement. If they disagree, do more homework and more listening to understand how they see the challenge. If they do not see any need, they are unlikely to be persuaded by you to do anything.

6 Size the prize

Managers are busy. We all have too much to do. When someone comes up with the latest and greatest idea, our instinctive reaction is to duck. We do not need the extra work which any new idea involves. So we have to show that our idea has value. The value of the idea has to outweigh the costs and risks of making it happen. The bigger the value, the more likely we are to persuade people to agree with us. Again, if you have a trivial request, then you do not need to 'size the prize' elaborately. If it is a serious request, there need to be serious benefits.

The prize can be both financial and non-financial, but it should always be relevant and should normally be quantifiable:

- 'The new IT system will reduce work in progress through the supply chain by $12 million, reduce time to market from eight weeks to four weeks and make us more competitive ...'
- 'The new logo will build our brand reputation among key corporate decision makers ...'
- 'These organisational changes will remove $3 million of costs, increase accountability and improve decision making by stripping out unnecessary bureaucracy and layers of management ...'

Of these three prizes, the new logo prize is weakest: it is neither financial nor quantifiable. It is a vague assertion of hope. No wonder that rebranding exercises are often regarded so cynically by staff. The other prizes mix both financial and non-financial benefits and can be quantified. They are more credible.

The best way to size the prize is to validate it with key executives. In the IT example, work with the relevant managers in IT, the supply chain and finance to build up a detailed picture of what is achievable. Ask each executive to identify and confirm what they believe is achievable from their perspective. Your job is to gather and pool their technical expertise. Ask each technical expert just to validate the findings in their technical area. Don't ask financial people to do the work of supply chain experts. When you have a validated prize to chase, this is the rock on which you can base everything. It may be easy to knock down the case for a new logo; it is much harder to knock down the case for saving $12 million.

Even at this stage you have not suggested your idea. You have been quietly drawing the fish into your net through a series of incremental commitments. The first commitment you might have sought was simply agreement that there has been a lot of weather recently: you were building rapport and gaining permission to talk. By the time you reach this stage the incremental commitments have become deep. The other person has agreed with you about the nature of the opportunity, the size of the prize and the potential obstacles you face. You have gathered all the intelligence you need to suggest your idea. As important, the other person is still in noddy mode and is ready to agree.

7 Suggest the idea and show how it works

Make this short and simple. The more you say, the more you may un-persuade someone by introducing new information which surprises them. Stick to dealing with what they have already talked about. You may have other brilliant reasons why your idea is great; but what is brilliant to you may be toxic to the other person. Less is more.

The best way of dealing with an objection is to pre-empt it. And this is your moment. As you show how your idea works, make sure you cover all the concerns which the other person has. They will be delighted that you are taking an interest in their needs. You will have an ally, not an adversary, in dealing with any problems.

> the best way of dealing with an objection is to pre-empt it

8 Give them a story and a win

We all like to think that we are smart. No one wants to be the klutz who agreed to a dumb idea or negotiated a lousy deal. We really, really do not want to look like suckers to our peers and colleagues. That means persuading is not about you winning and them losing.

find a way in which you can both win

Find a way in which you can both win. Make the other person look good. Give them a story which they can tell their colleagues about how they made a great intervention, added huge insight, struck a great bargain or averted disaster. Let them have their glory because it commits them to supporting you in public.

They will not know what the win is, unless you tell them. So you have to listen hard and find an excuse to give them a story to tell. In the course of your conversation, they will probably say things you already knew and agreed with. Leap on such comments as if they are stunning insights: thank them for such wonderful input and show how it has fundamentally shaped your thinking. You have just given the other person their win.

At other times you may need to give a more substantive win. But substance is in the eye of the beholder. For the $5 million IT programme, one department might want laptops instead of desktops: a huge win for them which is a trivial giveaway in terms of the whole programme. Give it. Think of when you buy cars or computers for personal use. We can always construct a story to show how smart we were: we got a good trade-in, an extra year of insurance, special alloy wheels or some fancy software for free. These concessions make us look good and feel good. You can be sure that the sellers were not losing money on the deal overall.

9 Don't fight objections

When someone raises an objection to your great plan, it is natural to feel offended and perhaps a little threatened. You feel obliged to defend your position; they then have to defend their position and soon you find yourself resorting to pistols at dawn. This is a win/lose outcome. There are only two problems with win/lose: the first is that you might lose; the second is that you might win. Even if you win the argument, you lose a friend. As your defeated opponent slinks away, be sure that they will be thinking about revenge.

So how do you deal with an objection to your idea? Agree with it. Agree that the objection is entirely valid. In fact, go further and say that it is something you had also been worrying about. By now, you have not set up an argument. You have set up the chance of a constructive discussion. Having agreed that the objection is valid, you can explain how you solved the problem. Even better, suggest how someone else offered a solution. That takes your idea out of the firing line and the other person now has to disagree with two people: you and the person who helped figure out the solution. And to finish dealing with the objection, ask if the other person can see a better way of dealing with it. Invite them to be part of the solution, not part of the problem. You have transformed conflict into cooperation. For instance, the conversation might go like this:

- Your colleague: 'That is going to cost far too much.'
- You: 'You're right. It is very expensive. I was worried about that. I mentioned this to finance and they said it would only be affordable if we could raise prices by 7% and keep volumes up. I then talked to marketing and they said they are planning a 10% price increase if we can deliver this new product improvement to them. Do you think there is a way we can improve on that?'

If there are more objections, do two things. First, qualify the objections. Ask if that is their only or main remaining objection. If it is there one remaining big objection, you can deal with it as before. If they have a whole series of objections, then do not deal with them at all. Go back to the start again. Ask smart questions to understand the nature of the problem or opportunity. Listen again: you may well have missed some important information. If you have missed something important, be open about it and deal with it.

Second, beware that all objections sound rational but are often emotional. When people talk about the risks of change or of a new idea, they will always find logical risks: costs, reputation, quality, operational risks. These risks are relatively easy to deal with: logical problems have logical solutions. But real risk is not logical, it is emotional. Emotional risks raise questions such as:

- 'Will this cause me extra work?'
- 'Will this squeeze out an idea I have been planning?'
- 'Will I land up doing all the work while you get all the credit?'
- 'If it fails, will I be left to carry the can?'

---

deal with emotional
objections by
pre-empting

On planet Business it is not seen to be business-like to raise these questions. So they get hidden behind apparently logical concerns which are designed to kill your idea. You cannot fight emotion with logic. You have to deal with emotional objections by pre-empting. Recognise that people are driven by three things:

- greed
- fear
- idleness.

Put these drivers to work for you. Here's how:

- **Greed**. Show that they will get recognised for their great contribution. This is good, but it is weak compared to fear.
- **Fear**. Show that the risks of doing nothing are far greater than the risks of doing something. That means you have to minimise the risks of your idea: important risk is personal risk. And if necessary show that the current way of doing things is simply not sustainable. Move the risk–reward trade-off away from the default position of most colleagues, which is to do nothing.
- **Idleness**. Make it easy for them to agree. Don't ask them to fill out a 300-page consent form. Equally, show that there is sufficient momentum behind your proposal that anyone opposing it will have their work cut out and will not look like a team player. Do not make the threat explicit. If you simply talk up your idea and show who is supporting it, most people will get the plot and fall into line.

10 Move to action

Most people are not psychic. They cannot tell what you want them to do, or what happens next. You have to tell them. You should always aim to have two outcomes.

First, you should confirm what you have agreed, and what the consequences of that agreement are. Even if you have only agreed to do some more research, then make that agreement clear. Be specific about what it means: agree the nature of the research, what it will cover, when it will be complete and what will be done with it. If you have complete agreement to your entire proposal, then spell out the consequences. Throughout your conversation you having been building commitment step by step: this is where you have to make the commitment clear and explicit. Do not leave room for them to come back later and say, 'I didn't realise ... I thought you meant ...'

Second, make sure that they really have agreed. Do not take absence of resistance as agreement: it may simply show absence of interest. The simplest way to check for agreement is to summarise and ask for their confirmation. That is relatively weak commitment. The best way to build commitment is to ask for a simple action from them. In some firms this may be a formal sign-off process. Better,

> ask for positive commitment

ask for positive commitment: perhaps there is a meeting they could attend with you, or an email they can send. The idea is to make their commitment as public as possible: once someone has committed in public, they do not want to lose face by changing their position.

From start to end of the persuasion process, you have been building commitment in very small steps. Each step seems natural to both of you, but by taking many small steps you can complete a long journey. Ask someone from the outset to make the journey in one big leap and they will tell you that it is impossible. By having an invisible structure to guide you, your business conversations have power and purpose. Use any of these 10 principles and you will become more effective. Use all 10 of them and you will be persuasive in a mysterious but natural way that no one else will quite understand.

How to persuade

1 Prepare

Know your target: what they want, how they work, who makes decisions. Have a plan A and a plan B for what you want to achieve. Have all the right logistics in place.

2 Build rapport and trust, find common ground

Don't rush in with your pitch. When was the last time you were persuaded by someone you did not trust? Build trust first. Persuasion is incremental: get them into 'noddy' mode, where they are agreeing with you, even on trivia to start with.

3 Adapt your style to the other person

Let the other person relax; don't let different ways of working divide you.

4 Listen

You have two ears and one mouth: use them in that proportion. Listen twice as much as you talk.

5 Agree the challenge from their perspective

They want solutions to their problems, not to yours. Suggest your idea by putting it in their language: make it feel like their idea.

6 Size the prize

The bigger the prize, the more likely they will jump through hurdles to help you. If you let them focus on the hurdles, they will never jump.

7 Suggest the idea and tell a story which shows how it works

Suggest the idea briefly and show them how it works.

8 Give them a story and a win

We all want to look good: so give them a story or a win which they can tell their colleagues about to show that they have made a good decision.

9   **Don't fight objections, you will only have an argument**

Use judo to overcome objections; agree with them, validate them and then jointly overcome them.

10   **Move to action**

People are not psychic: you need to summarise what the next steps are and gain their confirmation.

Managing upwards: influencing the boss

All the leaders who took part in the research for this book recognised the importance of managing upwards. It is a career necessity. It is also a very good way of learning core skills. Because we have no authority over our boss, by definition we have to learn some highly effective influencing skills to succeed. If we can influence our boss, we should be able to influence anyone. Because the boss tends to be around a lot, we also get a lot of practice in trying our influencing skills. It can, naturally, be a very frustrating experience.

Managing the boss is vital. The reality is that our boss is more important to us than we are to the boss. It is an unequal relationship. Because of this, we all tend to spend a lot of time figuring out how to succeed with the boss. In effect, we are actively developing all the influencing and management skills which we need to succeed. The boss makes a very good guinea pig for this exercise. We can see the effects of our efforts nearly every day, and we can try a variety of different tactics and styles.

On the other side of the coin, the boss expects to be managed. Even CEOs want their direct reports to manage the relationship effectively.

In this section we will look at two alternative perspectives on managing upwards:

1   What bosses look for in emerging leaders.

2   How you can influence your boss successfully.

What bosses look for in emerging leaders

The 1,000 leaders who took part in the research for this book showed what they expect, in general, from emerging leaders:

● adaptability
● self-confidence
● proactivity
● reliability
● ambition.

By themselves, these words can mean more or less anything. We will look in more detail at what the words really mean in later chapters.

To make the research interviews more interesting, the leaders were asked if there were any fatal mistakes that emerging leaders could make. Reassuringly, most leaders appeared to be reasonably forgiving and tolerant. Most bosses accept mistakes, because they make mistakes as well.

They all identified one unforgivable sin: disloyalty.

Many sins are forgivable, but disloyalty is not one of them. To be disloyal is to break the fundamental basis of trust on which any team has to operate. The boss has to be able to trust the team and also has to be able to earn their trust in return; loyalty and trust is a two-way street. Disloyalty can be expressed by gossiping negatively about the boss, failing to support fully some unpopular or necessary decision, or following a separate agenda. In the words of one rather defensive boss, 'Don't outshine me, don't outsmart me and don't outflank me.' In other words, disloyalty is not a case of plotting the downfall of the boss. It is a failure to act as a fully committed member of the team.

> many sins are forgivable, but disloyalty is not one of them

Naturally, your organisation will have plenty of formal evaluation criteria around things like teamwork, initiative and problem solving. Whatever the formal criteria are, if you are totally loyal and committed to your boss, you will probably find that the formal evaluation will be made to look good as well. It is difficult for bosses to be hard on people who have tried hard and been totally loyal. Bosses tolerate poor performance for longer than they tolerate disloyalty. Of course, if you have a gold medal in incompetence then nothing will save you.

How you can influence your boss successfully

Influencing the boss has three elements:

1   Finding the right boss.
2   Delivering the right results.
3   Having the right behaviours.

Received wisdom is that bosses manage and staff are managed. This is, potentially, a recipe for hell on earth. If you have a good boss, you are lucky and will enjoy the relationship. If you have a bad boss, you are in trouble. Most of the leaders I interviewed said that they could identify emerging leaders at an early stage in their careers. They could see individuals with leadership potential: the real indicator of likely future success was the boss they worked for. If they worked for a good boss, they were likely to learn effective skills and behaviours. If they worked for a bad boss, they picked up all the wrong skills and behaviours. Picking the right boss is essential from a very early stage.

Depending on the luck of the assignment process is not a good way to manage the leadership journey. It becomes less of a climb to the top and more of a random walk through the foothills and swamps of management.

Finding the right boss

Emerging leaders need to manage their careers, and they need to manage their bosses.

You may get lucky and stumble across the right boss for you. But you might also get unlucky. You will not just have an unpleasant time with the wrong boss. You will also pick up all the wrong leadership behaviours from the wrong boss. Many people are happy to play the lottery on the vital assignment process. When you enter a company for the first time, you do not have much choice. In practice, there are a couple of things you can do to load the dice in your favour:

- **Find a sponsor, or sponsors**, in your organisation who are senior to your immediate boss. Make yourself useful to them. They are likely to return the compliment when it comes to assignment time and can help guide you to the better assignments and bosses.

- **Work the assignment process**. People tend to know which are the death-wish jobs and bosses. When those jobs and bosses are looking for staff, it makes sense to assume the cloak of invisibility or extreme work overload – either way, you are mysteriously unavailable. Volunteering to do some work for your delighted sponsor is a good avoidance strategy. Conversely, when a good boss is looking for staff it does no harm at all to let them know how excited you would be about working with them on that assignment.

If this looks unduly political, then welcome to the world of work. Political skills count.

This assumes that you are managing your career within one organisation. However, there will come a time when you want to look beyond your current workplace. If you are thinking of moving, take care. Other organisations always look better from the outside than they do from the inside. You may simply be swapping life in the frying pan for life in the fire. The reality is that bosses come and go, just as your assignments come and go. So even if you have a lousy boss, you need to think how permanent that situation is likely to be.

You are in a better position to judge opportunities and bosses within your current organisation than you will be in a new organisation. When you move organisations, you inevitably find that you have to start all over again in building networks of support and trust, finding out how things work and finding the right boss and the right assignment. Even if you think you have found the ideal boss in another organisation, you need to think how long that person is likely to stay your boss.

Delivering the right results

Influencing the boss is a matter of both style and substance. Style has been dealt with at some length above.

Style without substance may be good for C-list celebrities, and even for some B- and A-list celebrities. It is not a good recipe for leadership success. You need to be able to deliver the right results. The question is: 'What are the right results?'

Sometimes the right results are pretty obvious. If you are a bond dealer or any sort of salesperson, you will have clear and explicit targets. More often, there is a degree of ambiguity about what you are really meant to achieve. The vagueness of the formal evaluation criteria (teamwork? judgement?) does not help.

The formally correct answer is to sit down with your boss and have an expectations exchange. Discuss openly and candidly what is really expected on both sides. You may get a partial answer at best. If you do not yet know each other, it is difficult to know what both sides can and should expect. Moreover, not all bosses are comfortable being open and honest about expectations.

In practice, you have to work out for yourself what is really expected. You have to become an expert at reading the smoke signals from the office of your boss. You have to figure out what the boss's agenda looks like. There are probably a couple of big things that your boss needs to achieve in the year, and then there is an awful lot of other stuff that has to be dealt with. You can help either by taking away some of the 'other stuff' so that your boss can focus more attention on the must-win battles. Or you can help directly by removing road blocks and accelerating progress towards the must-win battles. The recipe for failure is dragging your boss into spending too much effort on the 'other stuff' or failing to recognise the importance of the must-win battles.

How to manage your boss

1 **Find the right boss**

   Do not rely on random HR assignments. Manage your career. Load the dice in your favour: make yourself known to bosses you admire; become invisible and unavailable when the death star boss is around; work with HR to spot the right slot for you.

2 **Always deliver**

   Reliability is essential on small things as well as big.

3 **Offer solutions, not problems**

   Your boss has enough problems without you adding to the list. If you have a problem, offer a potential solution.

4 **Stay positive**

   If you are not enthusiastic, no one else will be for you. You will be judged on how you behave as well as what you do.

5 **No surprises**

   Over-communicate. Do not hide information or problems. Bosses forgive mistakes because they make mistakes as well. But you must be open about them and bring a solution.

6 **Ditch the excuses**

   The 'I said, she said, they said, anyway I meant and he didn't . . .' discussion gets you nowhere. Accept responsibility and move to action.

7 **Be loyal**

   Bosses forgive most sins, but disloyalty is not one of them. If you are disloyal, your boss will no longer trust you and the game is over.

8 **Adapt your style**

Your boss will not adapt to your way of working; you have to adapt. If that means working early or late, or being detail or big picture focused, do what it takes.

9 **Have an alternative**

If you depend 100% on your boss, you become a slave. Find a sponsor who can guide you to other opportunities; keep your eyes and ears open for other opportunities; develop skills which you can use elsewhere.

10 **Learn**

Even the boss from hell has some strengths, otherwise they would not have become a boss. Learn from the strengths and weaknesses of your boss. Be ready to step up based on what you see.

Having the right behaviours

Different bosses have different styles. You have to adapt to their behaviour because they will not adapt to yours.

Ideally, the relationship with the boss is a partnership. It may be an unequal partnership but you still have to play your part. At the heart of the successful relationship are clear expectations. Your boss should delegate to you not just the 'administrivia' and messy tasks. Effective delegation also gives you projects which play to your strengths. You need to help your boss know what to delegate and how much. You need to make sure your boss understands three things at all times:

> ideally, the relationship with the boss is a partnership

- **What you are good at**. The boss cannot play to your strengths if you do not know them yourself. Some people are good at analysis, or dealing with people, or selling, or organisation; different projects suit each type of strength.

- **What your capacity is**. In the professional world, it is very hard to estimate workloads accurately. There is too much ambiguity about the size of the job. Bosses have a simple way of dealing with this: they keep loading work on you until you scream. If you work at home all night, that is your problem. Manage expectations. Let them know when you have spare capacity (volunteer for work) and when you are at full capacity. The easy way of doing this is to ask your boss what the priorities are for your assignments. This is a diplomatic way of saying you cannot do everything.

● **What your progress is**. Bosses hate surprises. If you are ill, they need to know enough so that they can arrange cover. If you cannot complete a task, say so early. Let your boss find a solution before a drama becomes a crisis.

These are all simple disciplines which are routinely ignored. The result is that people get the wrong assignments, work too hard, have crises and underperform. They then complain about their boss, showing they are disloyal, and soon find themselves on the leadership exit ramp over the cliff edge.

Emerging leaders do not blame their bosses. They take control and influence the boss as far as they reasonably can.

Chapter 2

Being positive

L ook at what the surveyed 1,000 leaders said they looked for in emerging leaders:

- adaptability
- self-confidence
- proactivity
- reliability
- ambition.

Much of what they are looking for can be summarised in one idea: being positive. We live in a cynical age. The media daily bring news of wars, disasters, corruption and crises. In any organisation it is easy to see many things that are wrong: unreasonable and demanding bosses and customers, shoddy service, confusing organisation and endless petty and not so petty demands. These failings are often discussed at length, around the coffee machine. It is sometimes hard to rise above such cynicism.

The surveyed CEOs were all fundamentally positive. They believed they could change and improve things. Where other people saw problems, they could see opportunities. Even conflicts would be accepted as an opportunity to learn and grow. None of the CEOs were cynical about what they were doing or about their organisation. Perhaps cynical leaders do exist in some organisations. Whether you would want to work for them is another matter.

being positive is a fundamental requirement for leadership

Cynicism is something that can be indulged in among junior staff who intend to stay that way: cynical and junior. Being positive is a fundamental requirement for leadership. Before progressing further it is worth thinking about what being positive is and is not about.

Being positive is about:

- seeing opportunities, not problems
- learning to be lucky consistently
- moving from analysis to action
- living better.

Being positive is not about:

- happy-clappy happiness and saying 'Have a nice day' through gritted teeth
- false optimism
- false praise and 'one-minute-managing' people
- ignoring problems, risks and realities
- hoping for the best and gambling.

Being positive can be learned. To accelerate the process of discovering the positive world we will look at six aspects of being positive:

1 Shrinks and the art of being positive in everyday life.

2 Leaders and the art of being positive in business life.

3 Leaders and the art of being consistently lucky.

4 Being smart versus being positive.

5 Problem solving positively.

6 Making the most of your time.

Shrinks and the art of being positive in everyday life

If economics is the dismal art, then psychology is perhaps the dismal science. It spends most of its time looking at why we are all messed up.

But not all psychology is dismal. Martin Seligman, a professor at the University of Pennsylvania, was elected President of the American Psychological Association in 1996. He proceeded to stun his membership by pointing out that focusing on illness all the time was missing an important point. If we could focus on wellness and help people stay well, then many psychological problems would either not occur or disappear: prevention is better than cure. He realised that shrinks needed to pay more attention to people who were well and find out why.

Seligman's message is important for leaders. The journey to leadership is a marathon, not a sprint. Many people drop out not because they lack the skills or aptitude, but because they burn out. The initial enthusiasm of the career – the pizza-fuelled late nights working to meet deadlines – begins to wear off. Sustaining the career takes stamina. Even now, the research on how to achieve these goals is incomplete. Perhaps it never will be complete. But there are some core lessons about how to sustain being positive:

- **Focus on strengths, not weaknesses**. This is essential for all leaders; you cannot succeed by dealing with weaknesses. Successful leaders play to their strengths: they focus on tasks where they can make a positive difference. They also find tasks for staff that allow people to shine and compensate for their own weaknesses.

- **Manage your feelings**. If you feel upset or angry, that is your problem, not that of the person who has caused you to feel that way. At all times you have a choice: you can feel angry, upset or bored; or you can feel engaged and interested. If you want rain showers in your soul, that is your decision; if you want sunshine in your soul, that is your decision too. Leaders learn to wear the mask of leadership: whatever they may feel inside, they are able to project the face that they want to project.

- **Visualise**. Sportspeople always try to visualise success. When they focus and concentrate enough on this, they shut out the outside world. Focus on the goal, and then on how to get there. Our surveyed leaders could all articulate in simple words what they wanted their organisations to achieve.

- **Do something worthwhile**. This may or may not be in work. It could be family, friends or philanthropy. If you are not doing something worthwhile, it may be time to look elsewhere. Not everyone can or wants to become a leader. If you prefer to go fishing, leadership will not help you.

- **Move to action**. Do not pick over the past. Look to the future and take control of it. Most of the leaders we met had experienced crises or failures. Most of them did not see it quite that way – they saw each experience as a chance to learn, grow and become stronger. There was no victim mentality of looking at the past and blaming others for misfortune; they looked to the future and took responsibility for themselves.

- **Wear the mask of leadership**. If you are feeling aggrieved, upset or annoyed, you help no one by spreading your little cloud of gloom. Being negative provokes negative reactions. You will be seen as a negative person. Learn to wear a professional mask that drives to action and avoids getting sucked into personal and interpersonal squabbles.

- **Take control**. Often, we suffer because of events or people beyond our control. We cannot change the world for our benefit. But even in the darkest hour there are one or two things which we can control, where we can help ourselves. Focus on those things you can do, rather than worry about the many things which you cannot control.

All of this is mind-numbingly obvious stuff, but is very hard to see when in the heat of battle or depths of depression. Successful leaders use a mixture of the strategies above to remain positive. By remaining positive, they encourage people around themselves to be positive as well. This means that dramas rarely become crises. It also marks out the role model as a potential future leader. Being positive is good for the organisation and good for the individual.

Leaders and the art of being positive in business life

Leaders always seem to be able to be positive. At the heroic level, the words of Churchill still echo down the ages: 'We will fight them on the beaches …', 'their finest hour …'. No one remembers him saying, 'We're all doomed, I give up.' He could find the positive and focus on action. He could also express it very well.

At a slightly less heroic level, business leaders see opportunities where others see problems. Akio Morita, the founder of Sony, visited New York. He saw gangs of youths with boom boxes on their shoulders blasting out music. Most people saw and heard pure nuisance. He saw that young people wanted music which they could take with them. The idea of the Sony Walkman was born in his head, and a few billion dollars later the problem had become a landmark success.

The leaders interviewed also had the same positive outlook on more or less everything. They even viewed conflict as being positive – it is a way of sorting out priorities within the organisation, and it is a way of learning more about yourself and the other person.

There are some consistent ways in which the emerging leader can demonstrate a positive outlook:

● Bring solutions and opportunities to the table, not problems.

● Respond to new ideas by looking for the positives, not the negatives, of the ideas. Most junior executives try to prove they are smart by finding all the risks and problems, not by exploring the opportunities.

● Volunteer for special projects. Smart emerging leaders volunteer early so that they get a project which suits their strengths rather than waiting and then finding they are assigned the project from hell.

● Take measured risks. You will always be forgiven for doing your best and going the extra yard, even if you fall over in the process. You learn more and earn more respect from trying to go the extra yard than by playing it safe.

There are also some 'don'ts' when it comes to looking positive:

● Don't whine about the menial work you have to do. It's a rite of passage. Get over it. It's in the menial work that you often learn the most valuable lessons about how the organisation really works.

● Don't gossip about your boss and colleagues. Word gets round and it damages the reputation of the gossiper.

● Don't duck responsibility. It is very obvious to bosses who goes the extra yard and who does not.

Being positive pays for a leader. One CEO has a unique reputation in the fierce and aggressive world of investment banking – no one has ever heard him say an ill word about any colleague or competitor. The result is that he is universally trusted and liked. Anyone who has a conversation with him knows that they are not at risk of being bad-mouthed behind their backs. Because he is so positive, he is a leader who easily acquires followers. Nor does he duck the tough decisions that have to be made, especially in investment banking. If a unit is not succeeding, he will cut it back, not because the people are failing but because the market is weak. If an executive is failing, it is because the executive is in the wrong position, not because the executive is lousy.

being positive pays
for a leader

Being positive is a discipline that can be learned. Learn not to complain or gossip or point out negatives; volunteer for stuff; bring solutions not problems to the table. Occasionally, try smiling. These are all disciplines that can be acquired and eventually they become second nature.

Being cynical and negative, pointing out problems and risks, is an easy way to show that you are smart. Being positive involves more risk, but in the longer term people who are positive command greater respect than people who are negative.

Leaders and the art of being consistently lucky

When the surveyed leaders were asked if they had been lucky, they all said that they had enjoyed lucky breaks. Then they would quickly add, 'but you have to make your own luck'. They were somewhat like Napoleon, who liked lucky generals until he met Wellington and Blucher. In other words, there is more to luck than the spin of the roulette wheel. You can be consistently lucky or unlucky – it is up to you.

At the risk of drowning in a deluge of alliterative *P*s, luck normally boils down to three principal *P*s:

1 Practice.

2 Persistence.

3 Perspective.

Practice

'The harder I practice, the luckier I get' has been attributed to both Gary Player and Arnold Palmer. Both of them lived the quotation. With practice, the 20% chance of a holed putt becomes 30%, the 30% chance becomes a 40% chance and so on. The lucky putt is in effect the skilled putt.

All the CEOs surveyed had considerable experience of their sector, be it in law, consulting, investment banking, voluntary service, education, retail, consumer goods or politics.

Experience is to the leader what practice is to the sportsperson. Experience enables the leader to identify patterns, spot opportunities, make the connections between new technology and existing customers, and see trends early enough to act on them. The leader who hops from sector to sector has none of these advantages. Sector-hopping leaders are as successful as sports-hopping athletes: they fail because they lack the relevant expertise.

The CEOs emphasised the importance of experience. They do not expect emerging leaders to change the world early in their careers. What they expect is that emerging leaders will develop a keen understanding of the organisation and the sector, and perhaps bring a fresh perspective to challenge established norms.

Persistence

The difference between success and failure is often no more than a matter of giving up or carrying on. In the film industry, stars often become an overnight success after 10 or 20 years of trying.

Richard Wiseman, a professor at Hertfordshire University, has made a study of luck. In his book *The Luck Factor* he describes a housewife who is always winning competitions, on average three or more a week. This is astounding good luck which has brought her free cars, free holidays and free money. Her luck is perhaps more understandable if you know that she enters about 60 competitions a week. This is serious effort. Naturally, the more competitions she enters, the better she gets at competing. Practice and persistence often go hand in hand.

In the United States it is more or less a badge of honour for an entrepreneur to have had at least one bankruptcy in the past. The leaders interviewed could all recount crises in their careers when everything went wrong. Failure is a natural part of leadership: if you have never failed, you have probably never tried hard enough. An emerging leader will need to take measured risks and push to the limits. Without doing this it is difficult to learn what you can and cannot do.

The test of a leader is how they react to failure. Giving up, getting depressed and feeling cheated or let down by other people are not good reactions. Learning positively from the mistakes made and moving forward to the next challenge are better reactions. In Chapter 6 we will look in more detail at how leaders deal with conflict and crises.

Perspective

'The harder I look, the more I find' could be the summary of perspective. Lucky people often find themselves in the right place at the right time. Lucky people know that they are in the right place at the right time because they have been looking for it. Unlucky people probably do not even know that they are in the right place at the right time. One leader talked of being offered a very exciting position by the chairman of HSBC. The first time it was offered, she did not realise it was being offered to her. She had prepared herself for a different conversation in which she had to defend her organisation against loss of sponsorship. She was the right person in the right place at the right time but she could not see it. She was working on the wrong agenda. Only when someone else pointed out what was happening did she realise her mistake. She was able to get a second chance and made no mistake.

Leaders have to be able to see the opportunities that are in front of them. Virgin Atlantic started out as a successor to the low-cost and ill-fated Laker Airlines. It had a tiny upper-class area which could take about 12 people in the upstairs section of the old 747s. The service in upper class was far better than anything else its rivals provided, if only because it was small and it existed to satisfy the whims of Virgin's owner Richard Branson and his music industry friends. Soon enough, the popularity of upper class spread. Branson had the wit to realise that success would not come from cheap economy tickets, but from great service to attract the premium-fare customers. So he changed the business model from cheap and cheerful to a premium price and service model. He succeeded; Laker failed.

At the other end of the scale, Michael O'Leary found himself CEO of a one-aircraft Irish airline which was going bankrupt. Twenty years later the airline, Ryanair, is larger than British Airways in market capitalisation. O'Leary simply imported the no-frills, low-cost, deep discount airline model from North America. The model had been succeeding in full view of everyone. O'Leary was the first to see it and import it.

This perspective does not come from a random process of looking around the world. All the leaders interviewed have a deep knowledge of both their own organisation and the industry in which it operates. They are always looking and learning more about themselves and their peer group. The harder they look, the more they find.

Around us there are endless examples of people who have created businesses which now seem so obvious that we could have done it. The internet has spawned online bookselling (Amazon), betting (betfair.com), travel (lastminute.com) and computers direct to the public (Dell). These are obvious now; at the time they were not obvious to most people. Least of all were they obvious to the traditional booksellers, bookies, travel agencies and computer makers. They were all looking in the wrong direction – at their traditional way of doing business and at their traditional rivals. It is one thing to see an opportunity, it is another to act on it. There is no such thing as a good idea which has not happened. With perspective, you need courage to start, as much as you need courage to persist when things go wrong.

Being smart versus being positive

Smart people often fall into the trap of being clever. This is not a good idea for leaders. Unfortunately, smart people are very good at seeing what is wrong, seeing problems, seeing risks. They see how the dumb boss is always messing up. They ooze superiority and cynicism.

As a simple rule, emerging leaders respond to challenges with one of the four *A*s:

1   Apathy.

2   Analysis.

3   Answers.

4   Action.

The apathetic are never going to become leaders and are unlikely to remain employees for long. The problem for smart people starts with the analysis response. A typical staff response to a proposal is to identify risks, challenge data, question assumptions and highlight problems. It shows that the staff member is diligent, thorough and clever. But it simply gives everyone else more problems to deal with.

The potential leader will not just bring a problem to the table, but also suggest a solution. This involves the risk of being wrong. That is a risk that all leaders have to learn to deal with. And most leaders are very forgiving of people who try to bring solutions, not just problems, into their office. At least you are trying to make their life easier.

The most courageous response is to move to action. There is an informal rule in most organisations that 'it is easier to ask forgiveness than it is to ask for permission'. Leaders are prepared to take calculated risks and move to action when working through the formal machinery of the organisation would take too long. Whatever the outcome of the action you take, you should benefit.

If you succeed, you should gain recognition. If at first you fail, you probably have enough initiative and drive to get help, try again and find a way of succeeding. Most bosses are delighted to back and help anyone who is trying to take a problem off their plate. Failure in its own right can be a very useful, if painful, learning experience. Those who sit quietly on the sidelines taking no risks learn nothing.

Smart people often try to find the perfect answer through analysis. Leaders will find an answer that works through a combination of experience and experiment: they move to action fast and recognise that the perfect answer is often the enemy of the practical answer.

Problem solving positively

Problem solving is at the heart of both management and leadership. Problem solving is not just an intellectual exercise. Effective problem solving drives to action. This makes it a political and practical exercise as well. Decisiveness came high in the leaders' list of expected characteristics of an effective leader. In many ways, decisiveness is a better word than problem solving. In the academic world, it is possible to do great problem solving which results in zero action. In the business world, problem solving has to lead to decisions and to action. Unlike the academic world, the business world never waits for the perfect solution. The perfect solution takes too long to find. The perfect solution is the enemy of the practical solution.

> the perfect solution is the enemy of the practical solution

The standard requirement for business problem solving is to have too little time and too much ambiguous data to solve the problem. This makes problem solving more interesting.

Most problem-solving approaches are solid. They recommend a thorough, structured approach which ensures that you will not fail. At best, you might get B+. To get an A* grade, you need more than a thorough, structured analysis. You need some insight.

Telling people to be insightful is like telling them to be intelligent. It does not really help them. So we will look not only at how to be structured and thorough. We will also look at how you can raise your chances of at least appearing to be insightful.

The structured and mechanical approach to problem solving looks like this:

1   Find the problem.

2   Create a hypothesis.

3   Create a data structure.

4   Find the data.

5   Review and analyse the data.

6   Make a recommendation.

The more insightful approach looks like this:

1   **Find the problem** and the owner of the problem. Challenge the stated problem: is it a cause or a symptom? Why is it a problem?

2   **Create a hypothesis**. Find an alternative perspective and approach; talk to people.

3   **Create a data structure**. Challenge the data and the definitions. Find alternatives.

4   **Find the data**. Look widely for insights and killer facts, then quickly narrow the search. Do not boil the ocean.

5   **Review and analyse the data**. Build a story based on the hypothesis; do not be neutral. If the story does not work, create another hypothesis which works better.

6   **Make a recommendation**. Pre-sell the solution and recommendation to all the interested parties. Identify and resolve concerns before the recommendation becomes public.

Most problem-solving guides focus on solving the problem. This is rational and unhelpful. In practice, the time spent on problem solving often looks more like this:

- Defining the problem and the approach: 25% of the time.
- Finding data, researching and analysing: 50% of the time.
- Pre-selling and refining the solution: 25% of the time.

Solving the problem is half the effort, at most. Investing time in defining the problem or selling the solution is rarely wasted. They are as important as solving the problem itself.

Below, we will look at the different approaches to problem solving.

Find the problem

If you can find the problem, the solution is often quite easy. Even CEOs find it easy to latch on to the wrong problem, and hence the wrong solution, very quickly. The right answer to the wrong problem is still going to be wrong in the end. Invest time at the start to make sure you are heading in the right direction.

Three traps await the unwary:

1 Problem-free solutions.

2 Problem-free analysis.

3 Symptoms versus causes.

Problem-free solutions

This is the most common trap for leaders. In its simplest form the snake oil seller calls on the leader with the latest version of corporate snake oil: supply chain management, core competences, acquisitions, re-engineering, whatever. And there are the testimonials to show that the snake oil genuinely transforms businesses. No leader dares be left behind: if everyone else transforms their business, doing nothing is not an option. The snake oil seller makes another sale.

> selling umbrellas is fine if it is raining, not if your customer is going scuba diving

The snake oil seller is a solution in search of a problem. Selling umbrellas is fine if it is raining, not if your customer is going scuba diving. When you hear a solution, your first reactions should be:

● What is the problem this solves?

● Is this our most important problem?

You will soon find out if the solution is relevant or not. As in exams, it pays to know what the exam question is.

Problem-free analysis

I once did (what I thought was) a brilliant analysis on a company. I presented (I thought) brilliantly to the board. At the end the CEO coughed quietly. He thanked me. He then paused and said: 'I only have one question. What, exactly, was the problem you were analysing?'

I promptly evaporated in a mist of vanity and confusion. Always know what the problem is you are analysing. Most importantly, know *whose* problem it is. If it is your problem, keep it to yourself. If it belongs to someone else, make sure that you are analysing the problem they want you to solve.

> always know what the problem is you are analysing

Symptoms versus causes

Challenge the stated problem. Treating the spots on a child's face won't help if the child has measles. Get to the cause of the problem. A common business problem is to complain that costs are too high; the solution is to cut costs.

Case Study

Identifying the problem

I was asked to help the back office of an investment bank in Japan to cut costs. This seemed odd, because the business was growing fast. Cutting people, property and infrastructure is an interesting way to grow. After many discussions their problem became clear: unit costs (productivity) were poor. This meant that growth was unprofitable. They wanted to grow in total, but they wanted to keep costs and headcount down. They needed to raise the capacity of the existing infrastructure, not cut it. The two problems are totally different. The cost-cutting approach would have led to firing people (expensive for a Tokyo-based client); the capacity-raising approach retained the people but with better systems and processes.

Create a hypothesis

If you know what the problem is, you can probably create some hypotheses about the solution. The hypothesis is vital so that you keep focused on the outcomes and so that you can focus the analysis. There is not time to boil the ocean of facts in the hope of finding every last drop of information. Good hypotheses help achieve focus.

There are two ways of creating a hypothesis. The easiest way is to talk to people. Ask lots of people in different areas for their views. People are rarely short of opinions and are normally flattered to be asked for them. Inevitably, each opinion is biased. As you hear the people speak, you will probably hear the sound of axes being ground.

The second way is to structure the problem so that it can be split up into bite-sized chunks of analysis and potential insight. This is outlined below.

Create a data structure

This is the staple of problem solving. There are two principles at work here:

1　The 80/20 rule.

2　The issue tree.

Pareto's 80/20 rule

Pareto's 80/20 rule is a non-scientific assumption that 80% of the results can be achieved with 20% of the effort. This may be an under-estimate. Whatever the ratio really is, it implies that you should prioritise your efforts. Focus the data search on those areas which are most likely to yield results. Once you have seen what those results look like, then you can decide if and where to focus further effort. Do not try to do everything; there is never enough time.

You can turn the 80/20 rule around. In terms of time management, 80% of your effort is spent achieving 20% of the results. Leaders need to time manage ruthlessly: delegate away the time sinks and focus on the few things that make the biggest difference. You will also find that 20% of your staff consume 80% of your time, 20% of your customers produce 80% of your profit and 20% of this book produces 80% of the value to you. The trick is to know which is the 20% that counts.

Here are some issues which often help decide which is the 80% and which is the 20% in problem solving:

● impact on organisation

● importance to owner of the problem

● feasibility of potential solution

● ease of analysis

● cost of analysis and potential solution.

How to make decisions

1 **Do what you think is right**

The chances are, you are right. Have confidence in yourself.

2 **Size the prize**

Identify the potential benefits of each choice. A big prize is worth big effort. If you start with the risks and problems of each choice, you may well miss the big prize.

3 **Understand the costs and risks of each choice**

Rational costs are obvious. The bigger risks are political opposition, back tracking and sabotage. Work every constituency: get advice, build support.

4 **Follow the strategy**

Which choice fits most closely with the mission and strategy of the firm and department?

5 **Follow the values**

Does one choice fit with the values of the firm better than another? In marginal decisions, values count. If one choice is completely against the values of the firm, count it out.

6 **What would the boss do?**

You do not have to second guess your boss all the time. But it pays to understand their perspectives and priorities. A choice which fits their priorities will be much easier to implement.

7 **What does your team want to do?**

If your team firmly backs one choice, then they will be committed to delivering it. If you impose a decision they dislike, they will sabotage it. Trust your team.

8 **Build consensus**

There is no such thing as a good decision which was never implemented. You have to make your idea happen. Build support, remove opposition. Sell your decision: do not assume that it will just happen once you have issued an email.

9 **Flip a coin**

Ultimately, any decision is better than no decision. If the decision is that evenly balanced, then it should not matter if the coin lands heads or tails.

10 **Don't hide; decide**

Good leaders are expected to be decisive, and you are paid to make decisions. Make your mind up.

The issue tree

They say that the best way to eat an elephant is one mouthful at a time. It is perhaps better not to eat elephants at all. However, if you are faced with a complex problem, the same principles apply. If you have to do it, break it down into manageable, bite-sized chunks. Once you have identified the bite-sized chunks, you can apply the 80/20 rule to decide which parts of the analysis are most worthwhile to attack first.

A simplified example of an issue tree is shown in Figure 2.1. It looks at how an organisation might increase profitability. If only life were as simple as this issue tree, but at least it gives a structure and a focus to the problem-solving effort.

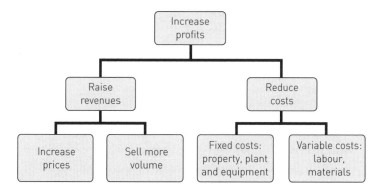

Figure 2.1 Simplified issue tree

Find the data

Information is rapidly becoming a commodity, but insight remains as precious as ever. The process of finding good data is relatively straightforward for anyone who is familiar with the sources and the industry. Use market research on a product or service. Even better, film it in use to show how it is really experienced. Find the killer facts and data. Often the drama and emotional impact of a film or a killer fact far outweigh reams of turgid market research tables. Once you have the right answer, use information like a lawyer, not a detective – to support a case rather than find the truth. Examples of killer facts I have found and used include the following:

- A utility thought it already had a highly demanding performance culture. But it emerged that staff were 72 times more likely to die in service than to suffer performance sanctions: top companies like GE and IBM annually cull the bottom 10% of performers.

- An insurance company believed it was becoming flatter and more empowering: we identified 12 layers of management in an organisation of 1,500 people. There were three levels of executive dining room. We argued, slightly provocatively, that one billion Catholics make do with just five levels of management (on Earth) from pope to people: pope, cardinals, bishops, priests and people.

Case Study

B+ versus A* grade problem solving in action: the conglomerate

This was an assignment I took on as a newly minted MBA: the mechanical analysis I did produced a textbook answer which was very precisely wrong. Luckily, I had a partner who had a brain and insight instead of an MBA and a textbook. He got to the right answer.

Problem

Which of its portfolio of businesses should the client build up, sell or close?

B+ approach

I did a thorough portfolio analysis. I used standard business school grids: BCG grid; cash use/generation and competitive position/market attractiveness grids. These gave the standard answers: milk the cash-generating but low-growth businesses. Invest in some of the strong, high-growth businesses. Good theory, bad practice.

A* approach

The senior partner looked at the analysis and ignored the results. I thought he was insane. He focused on where the company added value and had expertise relative to other companies. It was strong in the boring but cash-generating low-growth businesses: it could buy up rival businesses on the cheap and turn them around. It could fund the acquisitions by selling some of the high-growth businesses. Because all the competitors were doing the same B+ analysis, they were selling the low-growth businesses on the cheap and were prepared to buy the high-growth businesses for a fortune.

Summary

The A* approach recommendation is the opposite of the B+:

A*: buy low-growth businesses at low cost; sell high-growth at high price.

B+: sell low-growth businesses at low cost; buy high-growth at high cost.

The A* approach succeeded because it built on the company's strengths, not on abstract business theory. The company bought up many orphan brands at low cost from large companies and used its expertise to maintain and build the intrinsic value of the brands.

Killer facts are not a substitute for the hard grind of analysis. They bring drama and conviction to analysis, which another 100 pages of research are unlikely to achieve.

Case Study

B+ versus A* grade problem solving in action: the electronics retailer

By the time I did this case, I had learned that mechanical answers get mechanical results; you need to look a little harder to get insight.

Problem

The electronics retailer wanted to know what its customers really wanted: low prices, convenience, service, expertise, product range, etc.

B+ approach

The client had truckloads of consumer research: attitude studies and tracking studies and benchmarking. Customers, not surprisingly, told researchers they preferred low prices to high prices. Duh. So the client built up a low-price strategy.

A* approach

We challenged the data. Attitudes are biased. After the event people will rationalise their choice and give you the answer they think they ought to give. No one likes to think they paid over the odds. So we researched what people did, not what they thought. We caught shoppers as they left shops and asked them how much they had spent (if anything), how many shops they had been to and what they were looking for. It became clear that shoppers were totally confused by the choice: they could not make meaningful comparisons across all the features, brands, warranty and financing options. After getting confused, they would buy from anyone who was helpful and gave them a reason to buy: they wanted a story to tell their neighbours to show they had been smart ('I got free delivery/double memory/a larger screen/a 10% discount' – any story would do).

Summary

The B+ approach led to cost cutting, price wars and no profit. The A* approach led to price reassurance (advertising special deals) but to a higher overall price/service/profit offering. We looked for an alternative perspective on the data by looking at behaviour, not attitudes.

Review and analyse the data

The intellectually pure way to review data is to search it for anything which might disprove the initial hypothesis. Then you revise the theory in the light of the new information until you have a hypothesis which stands up to the highest levels of intellectual scrutiny. This may well succeed in a university. It does not succeed in a business.

There is an easier way: tell a story.

We are all natural storytellers, and we all tend to remember stories. Try to remember a few stories, and then try to remember a few business documents. Stories, for most people, tend to be more memorable. If you have created a good hypothesis, you should be able to construct a simple story to make your point. Here are two stories I have told:

> if you have created a good hypothesis, you should be able to construct a simple story to make your point

1 **To an over-centralised retailer**. They did everything in-house: their own printing, design, advertising, label manufacture, research. They were so self-contained, war could have broken out and they would not have noticed. We had mountains of value analysis to show how inefficient this was. They were not impressed. So we took the board on a walk round the medieval centre of their home city. We had a professor from the local university talk about how the city only started to prosper when it focused on one or two major activities for which it became famous across the land. It stopped trying to do everything within the city walls; it started to trade instead. When we got back to the boardroom they recognised they had become like the medieval walled city. They needed to start to focus, and they decided to start outsourcing non-core functions for the first time.

2 **To an internally focused utility company**. We filmed an elderly lady whose home had been flooded with sewage. The water company had responded slowly and ineffectively; the film of the lady in distress brought reams of dry market research to life. Similarly, we filmed the experience of checking in for an airline, and the customer experience of trying to set up a computer. These visual stories are not substitutes for research, but they provide drama and emotional engagement which a PowerPoint presentation will not achieve.

Telling a story needs a little creativity. But the result is that all the dry analysis has to be focused around a simple, memorable message. Once this happens, it becomes easy to sort out all the verbiage and excess analysis. The effort of doing analysis makes many people want to present it all: it is their way of showing that they have done a good job. Ultimately, leaders are not rewarded for working long and hard – they are rewarded for working well. So put the excess analysis into an impressive appendix and focus the recommendation on the story.

Make a recommendation

By the time you make a recommendation, there should be no surprises. To anyone. If you are surprised by someone objecting to your recommendation, you have failed. The process of pre-selling an idea to all the interested parties helps improve both the quality of the analysis and the quality of the outcome.

The quality of analysis is helped by talking to all the interested parties from an early stage. If they disagree with the way that your hypotheses or analyses are going, you can get early feedback. You can then amend your hypothesis, do further analysis, or find a way of incorporating their ideas into your recommendation. Politically, it makes sense to pre-sell the recommendation. It is far better to have disagreements in private. People tend to be more honest in private. Once they have taken a public position, it becomes difficult for them to back down without looking weak; they tend to reinforce their initial position, and a disagreement can quickly escalate into full-scale warfare.

The process of consensus building is time consuming and frustrating. But ultimately, you are not meant just to solve a problem: you have to make something happen. You need consensus to ensure action. If one constituency is very threatened by what you recommend and resists, despite your pre-selling, at least you will know the nature of the opposition and you will have built up enough support to help the organisation move forward.

Remember that leaders tend to evaluate the quality of information and recommendations in two ways. They will look closely at the logic of what is before them. If they are good, they will know the core statistics for the organisation by heart; if there is a doubtful number they will challenge it. One bad number destroys the credibility of the entire presentation. Check and double-check all data. Validate each piece of data with a relevant stakeholder.

> one bad number destroys the credibility of the entire presentation

If there are financial data, make sure that the financial people will stand up for the data if they are challenged; make sure marketing will stand up for any marketing data you present.

The second way that leaders evaluate recommendations is on the reputation of the person presenting. Each person is like a brand who has differing levels of trust and quality. If you are unknown, or not trusted, expect some scepticism. Enlist the support of people who are trusted either to present or to validate the recommendation.

Making the most of your time

Ultimately, time is our most precious resource. We should use our allotted time wisely. We are unlikely to remember happily time spent working late in the office. Hopefully, we all have lives beyond work as well.

It is possible to spend a very long time learning about time management. Spending too long learning time management is self-defeating. We need to learn good time management fast. This is the quick guide to time management.

Most time management techniques focus on using time efficiently. They help you minimise the amount of time you spend on each activity. This is of no use if you are doing the wrong things. Saving time efficiently is as wasteful as saving money in the January sales: if you are spending time or money on the wrong things then no amount of savings will help you.

> the one big question you should be able to answer is: 'Am I doing the right things?'

Instead of efficiency, time management starts by focusing on effectiveness. The one big question you should be able to answer is: 'Am I doing the right things?' This question is easy to ask, but often harder to answer. To help you answer this deceptively simple question, you need to ask and answer four more questions:

- Where do I want to be in 12–18 months' time, and how do I get there?
- What are the three most important things I need to achieve over the next three months?
- What are the most important things my boss needs to achieve, and am I helping achieve those goals?
- What is it that I can do that no one else among my team and colleagues can do?

If you can answer these questions well, you should find that you can prioritise much of your work and delegate or distribute much of the rest. Some people will work less as a result. Leaders will still work as hard, but they will work better and more effectively and be more focused on the right things. Because the four time effectiveness questions are so important, they merit further examination.

Where do I want to be in 12–18 months' time, and how do I get there?

This question helps you focus on doing the right thing for your career. Make sure you are working on the right projects, gaining the right experiences, building the right skills and developing your track record. If you are not doing these things, then you will waste the next 12–18 months of your life. Life is too short to waste away.

What are the three most important things I need to achieve over the next three months?

A good starting point is, once again, Pareto's 80/20 rule. Applied to time management it implies that 80% of your results depend on 20% of your effort. Salespeople recognise this: normally few clients will account for most of their sales. Even managers living in the ambiguity of a matrix organisation will recognise that there are a few projects which make a big difference by the end of the year. This does not mean that you can ignore all the administrivia: ignore administrivia and it will come back to haunt you. But the good time manager will dispense with administrative tasks as fast as possible to create time for working on important matters.

What are the most important things my boss needs to achieve, and am I helping achieve those goals?

This is a good test of whether you are doing something worthwhile with your time. If you are diligently clearing up all the dross which your boss does not like working on, you will finish the year having achieved little and learned less. Take time to learn what is important for your boss. Then work hard to make sure that you are delegated meaningful work, rather than letting all the rubbish flow downhill to you.

What is it that I can do that no one else among my team and colleagues can do?

The greatest time saving of all is to find someone else to do the work for you. Many people find delegating hard; failing to delegate is even harder because you land up having to do all the work. A good boss will not only delegate the routine rubbish, but also delegate some meaningful tasks which stretch and develop the team. Far from feeling exploited, most team members appreciate this: it shows that you trust them and it gives them a chance to shine, to learn and to grow.

Manage your time

1 **Have clear goals**

   Know what you want to achieve this year, this quarter, this month, this week and today. Get on with it.

2 **Delegate**

   Only do those tasks which you alone can do; know where you add value. Delegate everything else to your team, your colleagues or your bosses.

3 **Avoid rework**

   Do it right first time. Deal with each email, report or piece of paper once. You can either ditch it, delegate it or do it.

4 **Avoid distractions**

   Email, internet and phone calls disrupt work patterns and kill time. If a task is important, carve out time to work on it without interruption.

5 **Use dead time well**

   Queues, delays and commuting were invented to help managers deal with the noise of work: emails, catch-up phone calls, reviewing reports and memos, writing notes.

6 **Don't procrastinate**

   Work will not happen by itself; fix a problem now before it grows out of control and takes twice as much effort to fix.

7 **Schedule assertively**

Fix meetings to suit your times; minimise dead time between meetings and travel time; only go to meetings which matter to you and your agenda.

8 **Learn to say 'no'**

Only take on tasks which are important and relevant to you, and which you cannot delegate to others.

9 **Break big tasks down into short and simple steps**

Avoid being overwhelmed by a task. Make it simple. Take many small steps instead of trying to make one huge leap.

10 **Reward yourself**

Give yourself regular breaks to rest and recover, each day, week, month and year. But set yourself a clear goal to achieve before each break, even if the break is only 20 minutes away.

Managing time efficiently

Whole industries are based on using time efficiently. To go into a car plant is to see motion as poetry: every movement of every worker has been reduced to the absolute bare minimum. This is less to help the line worker, and more to help the car company make the worker be as productive as possible. Car factories and burger bars are the apotheosis of Scientific Management, first espoused by Frederick Taylor in 1911 (*The Principles of Scientific Management*).

Time efficiency is less obvious in the office. The presence of the coffee machine suggests that office workers have a slightly more relaxed approach to time management than car workers. If the EU 35-hour working week were strictly enforced, some workers would have to be in the office for 100 hours a week before they accomplished 35 hours of actual work. This is probably not what the legislators intended. The legislators themselves would probably need several years in an office before they accomplished 35 hours of worthwhile work.

Using time well in the ambiguous world of the manager requires playing the office equivalent of an old parlour game: 'Just a Minute'. The object of 'Just a Minute' is to speak for 60 seconds on a given topic without hesitation, deviation or repetition. The objective of the time-efficient leader is to work for a day without hesitation, deviation or repetition. Both goals are very hard to achieve.

Hesitation

Delaying work creates more work, and reduces its quality. For example, meeting minutes are best done on the same day as the meeting. It is then easy to remember exactly what was said and intended, to understand what was behind all the notes in the meeting. It makes it easy to follow up with the participants when the meeting is fresh in their minds. Write the minutes and follow up a week later and you will find that the intellectual and emotional trails have gone cold: the commitment and urgency will have gone and you will now have to work twice as hard to make up for lost time.

Deviation

At a simple level, deviation is about getting distracted from the task in hand: by easy but trivial administration, by the coffee machine, by other more glamorous initiatives. Staying focused and on task is an essential discipline which most of us find hard to maintain. Deviation also happens when you think you are working on the right issue, but fail to check and confirm expectations both before and during the work. Working hard to deliver a great, but unexpected and unwanted, result is frustrating to all concerned. Manage expectations of your clients and stakeholders carefully.

> staying focused and on task is an essential discipline

Repetition

This is a favourite of the time management experts, and rightly so. The easiest way to achieve this with each task, email, piece of paper or request is to work on the three Ds:

● **Ditch it**. If it is not necessary, file it in the 'Delete' file. Do not get dragged down by the spam of corporate life: pointless meetings, memos and administrivia.

● **Delegate it**. If someone else can do it, let them do it. Focus only on what is important for you.

● **Do it**. And if you are going to do it, do it now. If you cannot accomplish the whole task immediately, identify the essential next steps that you can take which will allow progress to be made.

Chapter 3

Being professional

Professionalism encompasses the core skills and values that define the character and potential of your organisation and you as an individual. It is central to the success of leadership. It means different things at different levels of leadership.

For the leaders at the top of an organisation, professionalism is fundamentally about the values that they display. Some leaders fail this basic test. They get to the top of the organisation and promptly put their snouts in the trough of perks, privilege and pay. The worst ones go to jail, the others simply serve to undermine morale within their organisation and undermine respect for business in the wider community. Other leaders set an example and live the values of the organisation. Professionalism can never be taken for granted.

For the emerging leaders, professionalism has four elements:

1　Learning to learn leadership.
2　Learning the local rules of the game: understanding professionalism in the context of your organisation.
3　Learning some universal lessons of professionalism.
4　Learning business survival etiquette.

These professional capabilities are cumulative: the lessons you learn as an emerging leader have to be carried forward and added to the professional skills which you build by leading in the middle. As the leader at the top, you have to add a final set of professional values to the values and skills that you have picked up on the way to the top.

Learning to learn leadership

if you know how to learn leadership, you are well on the way to success

Let's start with the good news: it is possible to learn leadership. If you know how to learn leadership, you are well on the way to success.

The bad news is that neither the education system nor corporate training systems will help you. The formal education system teaches people exactly the wrong lessons about leadership, which may help explain why so many successful leaders, like Richard Branson and Bill Gates, dropped out of education prematurely.

The education system teaches you to work in a highly structured environment, where you work largely alone to find a logical answer. Any potential leader who hopes for a structured, predictable environment where there is a logical answer and in which they can work alone is likely to be deeply disappointed.

Corporate training sessions do not help much either. They can, like business schools, do a fine job of transferring a body of knowledge about accounting or operations or finance. But leadership is not about technical knowledge alone. Leadership requires enabling people to achieve things.

Corporate training tends to focus on explicit knowledge: technical skills which can be embodied in books, e-learning and courses. This is the knowledge that the West has focused on with great success. Tacit knowledge is more about know-how than about know-what – it is the elusive knowledge about how to do things well. Much of the Japanese tradition, which has served them well in manufacturing and quality, has been about tacit knowledge. Corporate training which tries to focus on tacit knowledge often subsides into tree hugging, raft building and abseiling. Some people like it, but few leaders develop from it. No leaders we talked to pointed to any training courses as the essence of their success.

In practice, leadership is not about explicit knowledge that goes into books and courses. It is about tacit knowledge; books only help the process of structured observation and discovery that helps leaders find the leadership style which works best for them.

Leaders typically develop their capabilities in three ways:

1 Learning from role models: learning from leaders.

2 Learning from experience: career as a noun and a verb.

3 Learning from structured observation and discovery (sometimes).

Learning from role models: learning from leaders

Everyone learns from role models. Within an organisation, your role models are successful peers and, for better or worse, your boss. This learning process can be quite unconscious. David Begg, the head of Tanaka Business School, recalls hearing someone give his own lecture, with his own mannerisms and his own phrases. It was like looking in a mirror. He was, in fact, watching his very first mentor from whom he had unconsciously copied much of his own successful style of lecturing. It is important to find the right role models and to learn the right lessons from them: pick up the wrong habits from the wrong role model early in a career, and it becomes very hard to change course.

As individuals we all create our own leadership DNA; we steal a bit from one leader and a bit more from another leader we admire. Equally, we use a little leadership gene therapy to get rid of unhelpful DNA; seeing a colleague mess up is a very valuable lesson about what not to do. By stealing lots of DNA from lots of sources we land up becoming unique. In turn, other people steal bits of our DNA. Thankfully, we never clone each other completely. In one consulting firm we had a water cooler game of 'spot the mannerism': we could identify certain mannerisms that different partners had and we could trace it back to one or two people whom they all admired. Leadership skills are infectious.

As with all infections, we do not realise either that we are infecting anyone or that we are being infected in turn.

For the most part, the process of learning starts out unconsciously. Emerging leaders see some people blow up and do their best to avoid the same fate. They see some bosses do really smart things and will try to incorporate that into how they operate. At an early stage, emerging leaders quickly absorb the rules of success and failure in their chosen organisation. Many find that the rules of the game are not to their liking and will venture off to another organisation in search of a game where they can do better.

Copying role models is particularly useful in conflict, crises and difficult situations. Asking the question, 'What would X (whom I admire greatly) do in this situation?' often creates clarity where there was fog and fear. Try it next time you face a challenge.

For many people, learning leadership in this way is a random walk; you bump into good role models and bad ones alike. This puts the emerging leader at the mercy of luck. Get a good boss and role model and you learn all the right habits. Get a poor boss and you get lousy learning which takes a long time to unlearn. There are obvious career management implications here: get the right boss. There are also implications for making learning leadership a more structured and productive exercise. These implications are spelled out below.

Learning from experience: career as a noun and a verb

The second way that leaders learn is from personal experiences, triumphs and disasters. They gain this experience in two different ways.

Leaders who have had a *career* (noun) build up a deep knowledge of their industry and organisation. Some corporate organisations, like Unilever and GE, actively move their younger talent around the world and around businesses and functions so that they can build the breadth of experience to become effective leaders.

For other leaders, *career* is a verb which describes how they have moved from one experience to another in different sorts of organisation. In a less structured way than the large corporate organisation, they too have built a breadth of experience which enables them to become leaders.

Whether *career* is a verb or a noun, existing leaders emphasise the importance of getting the right experience and the right role models early. Taking risks at the start of a career is easier than taking risks later on – a 26-year-old can start over again more easily than a 46-year-old. Many 26-year-olds recover from a false career start by the simple expedient of doing an MBA.

Smart people often fail as leaders because they chose the wrong experience at the start of their careers. The bags of gold being offered by banks and professional services firms are attractive to anyone with student debts. But sitting in front of a screen for three years trading bonds or preparing presentations prepares no one for leadership. Less glamorous careers where you learn to deal with people, not computers, are often a better grounding for future leadership.

Learning from structured observation and discovery

Learning from experience and role models is not hugely attractive to a generation which wants it all and wants it now. Listening to the older generation advising them to settle down for the long haul and wait their turn which may, or may not, come along in 25 years is not inspiring to a 25-year-old.

You have two ways of accelerating your path to leadership.

The first is to go out and set up your own organisation. The learning will happen very fast. Even if the enterprise fails, you will have learned a lot. It can be an expensive way to learn. You will also find it very hard to go back to being an employee with a boss: once you have tasted freedom, the security of a large organisation will feel more like a prison.

The alternative way of accelerating leadership learning is by structured observation and discovery. Do not leave the learning to a random process of osmosis, which depends on getting some good role model bosses and good experiences. You might land up with some lousy role models and have some lousy experiences.

Instead, structure your learning from experience and from role models by using this book. Actively look, listen and learn. Use this book to understand what others do and what you do, then decide what works best for you. Use this book to accelerate your discovery process by knowing what to look for. There is no universal leadership formula: there is only what works for you and the people you work with.

> use this book to accelerate your discovery process by knowing what to look for

Experience suggests that people largely ignore worksheets in books such as this. So we will save your time and the planet's trees by not printing lots of structured observation worksheets. Instead, you can create your own customised worksheets to help you reflect on how peers and bosses do things either well or less well. If you force yourself to observe and reflect on what is working and what is not working, you will quickly build up your own preferred operating style, which will be far better than some theoretically perfect technique described in a book.

To help you on your way, the list on the next page gives you 30 headings to start thinking about and observing. In each case, the goal is to find an example of someone who you thought did something well or poorly and figure out why you thought they did it well or poorly.

Do not be constrained by the headings in the list. Many of the things you observe will not fit into any obvious category. As we talked to leaders about the role models they admired, we picked up things which are often too subtle to be placed in any one category. For instance:

- 'Our chairman never said a bad word about anyone, ever. As a result, we all trusted him. We knew we would not be bad-mouthed behind our backs.'

- 'The head of products was decisive because he was focused. If you asked him for a decision on a marginal issue, he would decide instantly. If it was not part of his central agenda and the decision was finely balanced anyway, he figured that you might as well toss a coin.'

- 'My boss helped when I was struggling. He did not tell me I was failing. He said he thought I was potentially great and could not understand what was holding me back. He asked for my ideas. I talked, he listened and by the end I left with total confidence that I and he knew what we needed to do to succeed.'

- 'I used to get angry and would lose my temper. Then I realised, like road rage, it achieved nothing. I still get angry, but I cannot remember when I last lost my temper. I just assume the mask of leadership and ask myself, "How would a good leader act now?" I then calm down and act much better with the mask on.'

Over time, you will assemble a list of insights that work for you. In the course of this book you will discover some of the things that have worked for other leaders in the areas listed below. What works for others is not an answer for you, but it is a starting point on the journey to discovering how to make the best of who you are.

Interpersonal skills

Setting goals and expectations

Giving informal performance feedback (good and bad)

Giving a formal assessment

Motivating

Managing and resolving conflict

Giving praise and recognition

Personal behaviours

Courtesy and etiquette

Empathy

Enthusiasm

Stamina

Risk taking and management

Management skills

Meeting management

Problem solving

Negotiation

Networking

Upwards management

Vision

Time management

Decision making

Team management

Project management

Delegation

Crisis management

Communication skills

Presentations

Listening

Effective emails

Effective reports

Handling bad news

Interviewing skills

Learning the local rules of the game

Every organisation has a set of rules which are not written down but are ignored at your peril. In some cases, the rules are plain confusing. When it comes to dress codes, an increasing number of organisations are totally schizophrenic. A large IT services company wants to look professional to its customers, so the dress code is fairly conservative suits and ties in the client marketplace. But it wants to appear funky, high-tech and youthful in the recruiting marketplace, so internally the dress code is very much dress down. In advertising agencies the client side and the creative side dress totally differently. Senior staff dress differently from junior staff. Dress codes are an elaborate way of declaring tribal loyalty and caste status.

Dress codes are a trivial but highly visible sign of the need to understand the local rules of the game. Understanding the rules becomes more important when it comes to matters such as taking risks and taking initiative. In the dealing room of an investment bank, risk taking is the life blood of the organisation. In the Civil Service it would be a nightmare for all the staff to be taking risks with the policies and procedures of the government.

The challenge is to learn the rules of the game fast. Even experienced leaders trip up on this. They hear the siren calls of the headhunter who lures them away to apparently greener pastures to work for a competitor. In theory, it should be easy. They know the industry and they know the job. But they do not know the culture of the new organisation; they do not have a network of support and alliances; they have no internal track record; and they do not know which levers to pull to make things happen. When the headhunter promises greener pastures elsewhere, remember that it is greenest where it rains most.

> when the headhunter promises greener pastures elsewhere, remember that it is greenest where it rains most

In theory, it should be possible to ask about the rules of the game. In practice, no one will tell you. It is a bit like asking people how they breathe; even if they knew the answer, they would still think it a pretty weird question. You have to pick up some clues and hints. At minimum, sit down with your boss early on and ask what their expectations are and what a good outcome in six months' time looks like. You might also ask how you can really mess up. One boss who had hired me to be a salesman said the worst thing I could do would be to sell anything. This was, to put it mildly, surprising. I asked what I should do. 'Make yourself useful,' he said, unhelpfully. So I did: I left and set up a bank instead. It helps to get misunderstandings and bad bosses out of the way early.

The simplest way to find out the rules of the game is to look at people who are seen to be successful in the organisation – people who get promotions and bonuses. See how they dress, act, talk and work.

Learning some universal lessons of professionalism

The view from the top

The top leaders interviewed in the course of writing this book were very clear about what they expected from emerging leaders:

1 Loyalty.

2 Honesty.

3 Reliability.

4 Solutions.

5 Energy.

These five characteristics are closely linked. As you read through the characteristics, they may strike you as obvious and simple – who on earth would be disloyal, dishonest, unreliable, problem focused and slothful? Viewed from the top of the organisation, the answer is: too many people. These are very common traps. This is great news for the emerging leader. It means that you do not have heroically to change the world single-handedly before you get noticed. You just have to do some very basic things thoroughly and well.

> this is great news for the emerging leader – you just have to do some very basic things thoroughly and well

Loyalty

By far the most important of these characteristics is loyalty. Most leaders are forgiving of most things. As noted earlier, disloyalty is the one unforgivable sin; some leaders allow a second chance, but many will not.

In theory, loyalty should be a two-way street: it should be mutual. If you perform, your boss will help you succeed. In practice, the relationship is very uneven. You can hurt their career; they can kill yours. In its worst form, the loyalty pledge is used by control freak managers to keep followers tightly in line. If the control freak delivers on commitments to help you gain the right experience, the right assignments and the right promotion, you are lucky. Sometimes they simply block your career by controlling you and not developing you. At that point either you have to escape the boss and look for another organisation or you have to break the loyalty rule and find another boss in the same organisation.

Honesty

For leaders, honesty is closely connected to loyalty. Honesty does not mean 'politician's honesty' where you are honest as long as you are not caught red-handed, lying through your teeth. Honesty means being open with the facts, especially when they are awkward facts about setbacks. Bosses hate surprises; it makes them look like they are not in control and not competent. If they know the awkward facts, at least you give them a chance to help you find a solution.

Reliability

If honesty is about having the courage to be open with awkward facts, reliability is about avoiding the need to deal with the awkward facts in the first place. As one leader put it: 'Never bullshit me. Don't over-promise. If you can do something, say so. If you say you can do it, do it. If you must, under-promise and over-deliver. Never over-promise and under-deliver.' A critical part of reliability is learning to say 'no' to unreasonable requests and setting expectations right from the start. It is better to have one tough conversation about expectations before a project starts than to have three months of trying and failing to deliver the impossible. This is a lesson that effective leaders at all levels of the organisation understand intimately, especially when it is time to set and agree budgets.

Solutions

Some people bring problems; other people bring solutions. The curse of smart people is that they can see all the problems, they can see all the risks of any course of action and they can see how the boss is messing up. They ooze superiority and cynicism. Then they fail. Leaders do not succeed by proving they are smart. They succeed at least in part by seeing solutions, driving to action and getting results. This takes more courage than analysing and finding problems. It often means messing up, falling flat on your face and enduring the snide remarks of smarter people who predicted your fall. The difference is that you will learn more, achieve more and go further than the people who are smarter and less courageous.

Energy

Energy incorporates a lot of values that leaders look for: stamina, commitment, resilience, optimism, adaptability and a can-do spirit. These are positive words. In practice it means that the emerging leader is given a lot of rubbish to deal with and is expected to get on with it without complaining.

It is common for the newly minted MBA in a bank or consulting firm to figure out that despite their high salary, they are being paid less per hour than the partner's secretary. This is a fair reflection of their relative value to the firm. It also reflects the reality that the marginal cost of a consultant or banker is close to zero – for a few free pizzas they can be kept working all night for no extra salary.

The 10 skills all leaders must master

1 **Motivate others**

Show you care; recognise, reward and praise; build a sense of purpose, worth and community.

2 **Set a direction**

Be clear about where you are going, how you will get there and how each person on your team has a role to play in getting there.

3 **Delegate**

Stretch your team with challenging tasks; be rigid about the goals, flexible about the means; trust your team; delegate power; never delegate your responsibility or the blame.

4 **Deal with crises**

Use crises to show your potential; drive to action; be positive; take the lead, don't hide; avoid blame.

5 **Make decisions**

6 **Communicate well**

Listen more than you talk; put yourself in the shoes of the person you are persuading; be clear and consistent; understand.

7 **Fight the right battles**

Only fight when there is a prize worth fighting for, when you know you will win and when there is no other way of achieving your goal. It is better to win a friend than to win an argument.

8 Manage performance

Set clear expectations and stick with them; be consistent; provide support; give feedback early; accept no excuses.

9 Manage change

Address a worthwhile challenge; find the right team; start at the end and focus on the outcome you want; make it simple; break the big task down into short and simple steps.

10 Focus on the right things

Have clear goals for the year, quarter, month, week and today. Get on with it. Do not mistake the noise of management, such as emails, with the purpose of leadership.

The sweatshop approach to learning the business is not pretty. But all the leaders we talked to had an intimate knowledge of their business. The owner of a chain of 650 shops not only knew all the area managers; he also knew by name and face most of the shop managers and their staff. He had driven several hundred thousand miles around the country over 40 years building his knowledge of the business.

The view from the bottom

Professionalism is not just about impressing the boss. It also means acquiring a set of behaviours which make it easy for peers and teams to work with you. These are behaviours that become more important the more senior a leader becomes. From doing 360-degree reviews with emerging leaders, there are a few consistent complaints that people make about their colleagues. As I do these reviews, I find that everyone tends to share the same view, with the one exception of the person who is irritating all their colleagues. They are damaging themselves and their reputations without realising it. The following complaints come from an exceptionally good organisation. In other organisations, similar comments are typical but the intensity with which they are voiced is much greater. In rough order of priority, the comments are:

- **Not communicating**. Staff like to know what the boss is doing and why. Equally, the boss likes to know what staff are doing. It is very hard in a professional organisation to manage capacity: are people overworked or not? Work is often open ended and ambiguous. Regularly letting the boss know where you are helps with capacity planning; it helps as an early warning system for problems; it helps with disaster recovery. If you fall ill with stress, at least it should be clear how to pick up the pieces.
- **Public, not private, arguments**. This can be as simple as one off-guard comment, something like 'this group is the best we have', which then is sure to demotivate all the other groups. In its worst form, it involves public abuse.

- **Game playing and politicking**. Everyone knows who the politicians are. They play one side off against another and use half-truths to confuse things and get their way. They succeed in the short term but kill their credibility in the long term.

- **Bullying**. This is as simple as delegating badly and late. The 'hospital pass' delegation is to receive a project too late and when it fails, you get the blame. A near variation is to delegate all the rubbish and convert staff into administrative assistants. Effective delegation means delegating projects, as well as some rubbish, which will allow emerging leaders to learn and grow.

- **Bad habits**. This can be anything from turning up late to poor dress. Everyone else knows it. Make yourself approachable so that you are not left in the dark about how your habits affect other people.

- **Personalising feedback and conflicts**. The ensuing sulks help no one and achieve nothing.

So how do you deal with dysfunctional behaviour from peers, colleagues and bosses? Inevitably, every situation is both messy and unique. But here are five principles for you to follow. You should use each technique in turn. If the first technique does not work, escalate to the second and beyond:

1 **Control your feelings**. If someone irritates you, that is your problem and not theirs. Sometimes the hardest thing to control is our own feelings. But we always have a choice about how we feel: happy, angry, frustrated, relaxed. If you can master your emotions, then you will find that dysfunctional behaviour has little effect on you. You may observe it, but you will not be affected by it. Problem solved. But it is not always that easy.

2 **Remain as a role model**. You will be judged as much by how you behave as by what you do. So it pays to remain positive and professional. If you mirror the dysfunctional behaviour of others, you will find that things get worse, not better.

3 **Give feedback**. If you are genuinely affected by someone's behaviour, then you have to deal with it. Do not pretend that you are helping them: be clear that you want their help in making your life easier. Ask them to help you by stopping or changing what they do.

4 **Protect your interests**. If none of the above works and your performance is being disrupted by politicking or interference, then you need to protect your interests. Do not be passive and roll over. Do not be aggressive and fight. The middle way is to be assertive: be clear about what your interests, needs and obligations are. Marshal support from peers and colleagues to protect your interests. Do not personalise the problem: stay professional and focus on the issues. This is always a messy process, so remember that you have to remain the role model. Let others mess up by behaving the wrong way.

> stay professional and focus on the issues

5 **Get help**. No boss likes intervening in disputes. It only lands up in a 'he said, she said, but they didn't and I meant ...' discussion. But you can ask for coaching and advice. You will still appear weak for not having sorted out the problem yourself, but this is better than letting the problem get out of hand. Talk to people you trust.

Learning business survival etiquette

Leaders do not have to have great etiquette, but it helps. With some notable exceptions, etiquette tends to improve the further up the organisation people go. At the bottom, there is often low awareness of what is acceptable and what is not. In the middle, people are jostling so hard for position that courtesy gets shoved to one side. At the top, people have the time and space for grace.

So why bother until you get to the top?

Etiquette is fundamentally about putting the other person at ease and making them feel valued, respected and important. Poor etiquette fails on all these counts. Think about it. Who would

> etiquette is about making them feel valued, respected and important

you rather deal with: someone who feels at ease, valued and respected or someone who is feeling uncomfortable, defensive and devalued? Many people, sadly, would answer the latter. Powerful buyers have been known to make suppliers dance for their amusement; job applicants are often put under great stress. Little power makes little people into little tyrants. They may enjoy abusing interviewees and suppliers, but it does little to help the business.

Emerging leaders need a network of support and trust. They need followers, peers and bosses who value and respect them. Poor etiquette simply makes it harder to gain respect; good etiquette helps gain respect.

Clearly, etiquette varies from country to country and from company to company. Japan, for example, has very formal rituals for meeting people for the first time:

- offer *meishi* (name card) with both hands and bow
- read *meishi*: the name card really gives guidance to who should have bowed first, longest and deepest depending on level, location, company, etc.

If this seems difficult for a non-Japanese businessperson to do, think how hard British etiquette is. One senior Japanese businessman finally plucked up the courage to ask me how to shake hands. Duh. It's so obvious, isn't it? Until you try to explain it: how and on what occasions, how do you signal that you want to shake hands, how do you know when the other person wants to shake, how hard do you press and for how long? Bowing is simple by comparison.

So let's look at some fairly basic etiquette which is routinely missed.

Promptness

This is not just about respecting the other person's time, although that is important. It is also about using time well.

Case Study

Being on time

The best salesperson I know routinely prepares and leaves for important meetings early; if the plane or train is delayed or the travel instructions are ambiguous, he will still be early. As a result, when he travels he is always focused on his final meeting preparations; he is never late or stressed or unfocused on arrival. He gets through fewer meetings, but he is very good at them. Another salesperson I know is charming but routinely late. She spends the first 15 minutes apologising and catching up on the meeting's progress. Sometimes her charm seduces clients. Other times, although the client smiles when she leaves, we are later told never to send her back again.

You do not lose clients or friends being early, but you can lose them being late.

Focus

Good leaders, even at the top, have the habit of making you feel that you are the most important thing in their lives at that moment. They focus completely on you. This can be unnerving but is also effective leadership. They really are focused and they really do make the other person feel important. Good leaders assure focus in some simple ways:

- no interruptions from calls
- mobile phone off
- no playing with PDAs in the meeting.

A good way to show that you think other people are really unimportant is to check your PDA often to see if there are any interesting blogs by yodelling accordion players or to answer your phone on the off chance that someone might be able to teach your hamster yoga.

Courtesy

'Thank you' is not a difficult phrase. Try it.

Case Study

Good manners cost nothing

After I joined a new partnership, I unexpectedly found that the secretarial group was being very helpful to me at all times. I asked what was going on. They told me that at the annual partners' conference, I had been the only one of a thousand partners who had gone to their lair to thank them for all the thankless work they had been putting in behind the scenes.

People like to be praised, and it costs very little to do.

Responsiveness

Answering the phone inside three rings, replying to emails quickly and following up on commitments promptly makes it look like you are in control and it also minimises effort. Slow response often leads to confusion and rework: do it once, do it right. Of course, if there are people you really do not want to be harassed by, then not answering is the best way forward.

The personal touch

In the high-tech world, it pays to be high touch. There are many ways of adding the personal touch. A few examples:

- Try walking with your guest back to the lobby or lift when they depart, instead of having them escorted by a secretary. This can be a 'Columbo moment' (after the TV detective in a dirty mac). As he was leaving, Columbo would turn and ask one innocent but devastating question; the suspect, who would have relaxed, would blurt out the truth unintentionally. In the same way, after a formal meeting or interview, you often get to the truth as your guest relaxes on the way out. In any event, they will feel appreciated.

- Email is just another of the hundred irritations every day; a handwritten note in an old-fashioned envelope commands attention.

- Learn names and use them back. The sweetest word in the language is someone's own name. They not only respond; they are grateful you took the trouble to remember. If you are stuck for conversation, remember that few people can resist talking about their favourite subject: themselves. Ask them, look interested and you will win a friend.

> few people can resist talking about their favourite subject: themselves

Etiquette can get to be very painful if the focus is only on rules – everything from how invitations should be prepared to how to make small talk at dinner. The rules change from place to place and from time to time. The rules of etiquette are not important from a leadership perspective. The purpose of etiquette is important:

- Make the other person feel at ease.
- Make the other person feel valued, respected and important.

These are useful skills for a leader to have. Ultimately, good etiquette involves decentring: focus on seeing the world through the eyes of the other person. If you can do this, then you will not need rules of behaviour – you will naturally work out the right thing to do in each situation.

Part 2

The practice
of leadership

Chapter 4

Leading from the middle

The leadership journey can be simplified down to three major steps:

1 **Foundations of leadership**. The challenge for the emerging leader is to learn the basics of leadership. You need to understand yourself; learn the trade of your industry; understand the culture and local rules of the game; perform against known targets.

2 **The practice of leadership**. In the middle of an organisation, in the typical matrix, leaders need to learn new skills. You have to learn to manage others; manage networks, ambiguity and complexity; master core leadership skills; negotiate targets and deliver against them.

3 **Mastering leadership**. At the top of the organisation, the skills of leadership change again. You have to develop an inclusive vision; be a role model for values; build the top team; create the conditions for success; acquire and direct resources to achieve the vision.

Pitfalls of survival

Part 2 focuses on leaders in the middle of the organisation, who often find themselves in the dangerous world of the matrix. In the middle of the matrix, the rules of success are different from the rules of survival. Many potential leaders never emerge from the matrix because they have learned how to survive within it, rather than how to escape from it. The five most common 'pitfalls of survival', which are also barriers to success, are listed below.

1 The boffin in the box

Many people get promoted into the matrix on the basis of technical competence. This becomes their comfort zone. But they confuse technical expertise with management and leadership. They use their expertise to handle all the most difficult challenges in their department. A leader would figure out how to make the team rise to the challenge instead. Experts lose sight of the leadership skill of helping others achieve things, of delegation, trust and empowerment. They cannot get promoted any further because their deep technical skills are not useful in a wider context. The great IT expert can survive leading part of the IT function but is useless when faced with the challenge of managing a team of marketers, accountants and operational staff.

2 The politician

Politicians are too enthusiastic about learning the dark arts of the matrix. They work assiduously to cultivate a power network. They constantly look out for new initiatives: they make sure they are associated closely enough with all of them to share some of the limelight if it works, but far enough away that they share none of the blame if it goes wrong. Being associated with success and achieving success are different. Ultimately, many politicians are undone because they are seen to be like a can with a pea in it: they are empty vessels making a lot of noise. They achieve nothing. Worse, the politicking eventually backfires; it gains enemies who are only too happy to come out of the woodwork at the worst possible time for the politician.

3 The boy scout

The boy scout is the opposite of the politician. The boy scout thinks that by working hard and delivering results they will automatically be recognised and promoted. In practice, they simply get lost in the matrix, where it is often difficult to see who has really achieved what. They are naïve. They need a claim to fame, but they also need to stake their claim; they need to show that they are really leading and delivering.

4 The cave dweller

Large organisations often have silos which divide groups vertically, by region, product or function. They are also layered like pancakes. Many 'flat' organisations are towering layers of pancakes. Corporately, if you cross a silo with a pancake, you get a cave. This is where some people decide to hide: they can survive the matrix, but they cannot escape from it. They can control and dominate their little cave and recreate the certainty that served them so well at junior management levels. These territorial types guard their caves jealously. When the reorganisation comes along and the matrix changes shape, they are like fish out of water. They are very easy to rationalise out of the organisation.

5 The autocrat

The autocrat acts as if they are already a senior leader. They often talk about the importance of being a team player. By this they mean:

'If you do exactly what I tell you to, you are a good team player. If you show less than 100% personal loyalty to me, you are not a team player.' For these people, performance is essential. If they deliver exceptional results, they may well progress. If they deliver less than excellent results, they will just be seen as a dysfunctional pain in the backside by those above, below and beside them.

The path through the matrix

One way or the other, there are many roads to ruin within the matrix. Picking the right path for the leadership journey through the matrix is seriously difficult. At the risk of stretching the bounds of intellectual integrity, we will return to the three-and-a-half Ps framework to find the path through the matrix.

The success route through the matrix is as follows.

Focusing on people

Matrix leaders learn how to achieve results through other people. They may have formal authority over some people. More importantly, leaders achieve results through people over whom they have no formal authority. They learn the subtle arts of motivating and coaching people they are responsible for, and they learn the arts of networking and influencing people over whom they have no formal control.

Being professional

Matrix leaders start to model the values that they will need as senior leaders. They also master some core skills of management and leadership, which are as simple as running: reading, writing, talking and listening skills. Most of us can run; few can win an Olympic gold for running. The leader can do at least some of the basics, like chairing meetings, very well.

Being positive

In the middle of the matrix, the art of being positive is particularly important. Here, it means treating ambiguity and change as an opportunity, not a risk. Matrix leaders learn how to deal with conflict, which is endemic in the matrix, and how to deal with crises, which are inevitable. The positive outlook of the successful matrix leader is what distinguishes them from the survivalist matrix manager. The survivalist will avoid risk and ambiguity. The successful leader will take on risk, change and ambiguity. The survivalist is on the slow road to nowhere. Leaders enjoy significant career acceleration: they succeed fast or they fail fast.

> the successful leader will take on risk, change and ambiguity

Finally, we dare not forget the half *P*: performance. To emerge from the matrix, you need a claim to fame. You need to show that you can deliver exceptional results out of exceptional ambiguity and complexity. It is only through taking on challenges and delivering results that you can learn the subtle arts of people focus, being positive and professionalism. Achieving results and achieving learning go hand in hand.

In the next three chapters, we will plot a path through the matrix using the three-and-a-half *P*s as a map. Here, more than ever, a guide is essential.

Chapter 5

Focusing on people

Churchill described Russia as a 'riddle, wrapped in a mystery, inside an enigma'. He may as well have been describing human nature. The collective efforts of tens of thousands of shrinks over the last hundred years have not made people happier or more motivated. They have shown that we are all more messed up than we ever thought. Stress, low self-esteem, depression and other mental dysfunctions are at epidemic levels.

All the leader must do is to solve the riddle wrapped in the mystery inside the enigma. The leader has to succeed where all the shrinks have failed; your riddle is to find a way of motivating all your people.

To solve this we will look at three approaches:

1   Three practical theories of motivation.
2   How leaders apply the theory in practice.
3   Motivation and moments of truth.

Before we embark on the journey in search of motivation, it is worth being clear about what motivation is and is not. It helps if we are searching for the right thing.

Motivation is not inspiration. There is too much talk about inspirational leaders. There *are* some inspirational leaders out there, but most of us are not natural inspirers. We can do many basic things well which will motivate people. We may even inspire people if we do the basics well enough. But if we set off in search of inspiration we are likely to find ourselves in the land of men in white suits waving their arms on stages, whipping massed audiences into a frenzy of excitement. They can sell inspiration, insurance or religion with equal vigour. Sustaining motivation for the weeks, months and years that follow the speech is a different art form.

Practical theories of motivation: part one

Let's start with a simple choice.

Let us assume that you are a budding leader who likes work, is committed to it, lives to work and to lead and is deeply involved in your business. Look around you, not just at your peers, but also at people at all levels of your organisation. If they are all like you in their attitude to your organisation, pick Y.

If you think people fundamentally dislike work, are lazy, work to live and feel alienated from work, pick X.

Obviously, how you motivate people will depend on whether you think they are X-types or Y-types. It is possible that you are surrounded by a mixture of the two.

Let's start with the **X-types**. In a perfect world, you would be able to convert them into happy, zealous Y-types. We may land up in a perfect world when we die. In the meantime, we have to deal with the X-types. The traditional response to the X-types is to have tight control, close monitoring, minimal delegation and clear rewards and punishments for success and failure. There are still plenty of bosses who will assume that everyone who works for them is an X-type. They are highly controlling and demanding. They may not be fun to work for, but they can work their way up the career ladder.

Y-types can be managed differently. They can be trusted to do their best as committed colleagues. Trust, empowerment and delegation take the place of control.

This exploration of the X and Y worlds is based on McGregor's *Human Side of Enterprise* (1960), which remains a classic description of different types of motivation at work. Increasingly, much of the world is moving from X to Y. The cynical, untrusting world of the X-type is perhaps typical of the nineteenth-century sweatshop where uneducated masses were hired for their hands, not their brains. The bosses bossed and the workers worked. In some cases the workers revolted and got exploited by tyrannical governments instead of tyrannical capitalists. In the West, the workers got educated. So now we see more of theory Y world, where workers work in offices and with their brains. We need more than compliance – we need commitment. We need employees' talent to work through the increasing complexity and confusion of modern work.

McGregor focused on the worker. But what works for the worker should also work for the leader. Although the world may be moving from X to Y, many managers feel much more comfortable in X mode. Look at the two types of management in Table 5.1 and decide which you are. Also, decide which type of boss you would prefer to work for.

Management criteria	X-type manager	Y-type leader
Basis of power	Formal authority	Authority and respect
Focus of control	Process compliance	Outcomes, achievement
Communication style	One-way: tell and do	Two-way: tell and listen
Success criteria	Make no mistakes	Beat targets
Attention to detail	High	Moderate
Ambiguity tolerance	Minimal	Moderate
Political ability	Moderate	High
Preferred structure	Hierarchy	Network

Table 5.1 Types of management

Many people instinctively prefer the more inspirational Y-type leader. I have worked for both. The Y-type leader was much more demanding. They may forgive the occasional mistake, but overall their expectations are much higher. The X-type was a mean and nasty apology for a manager. But working for him was a simple matter of keeping your nose clean, doing what you were told and no more, and being blindly loyal and obedient. He expected compliance, not commitment. The Y-type expected commitment and would tolerate occasional non-compliance if that helped achieve a goal.

The catch is that both types of leader can succeed, in the right context. The X-type manager succeeds in a classic machine bureaucracy where the emphasis is on avoiding mistakes and achieving predictability and control. Systems integration houses, insurance companies and large parts of the public sector fit this style.

The Y-type leader fits where there is a need to change and to adapt to different and uncertain customer and competitive pressures. This better describes creative agencies, entrepreneurial organisations and professional service firms. The Y-type leader explodes in the X-type environment and vice versa. You have to find the environment where your style will work.

Practical theories of motivation: part two

McGregor's X- and Y-types find an echo in Herzberg's two-factor theory of motivation. As a leader, he argued, you can motivate people in one of two ways. Pick the option below which you think works in your organisation.

Option One

Make sure individuals have the status and title and terms and conditions which they deserve. Pay for performance, and pay a bonus for over-performance. Use hours, holidays, flexitime and family-friendly work policies to get the right balance of staff. This is classic rational management. It is the sort of thing that public sector unions like to discuss with public sector employers.

The problem with Option One is that this is a never-ending treadmill. Once someone has got the pay rise and the bonus, then they want the shorter working hours. Herzberg called these 'hygiene factors'. In practice, not only do they do little to motivate but they can be demotivators too. Bad pay and conditions demotivate; good pay and conditions are never sufficient to produce stellar performance.

Despite this, many organisations still use pay and bonuses as a substitute for management or motivation. Pay discussions sound very managerial: senior executives sit round a table discussing people (like managers should) and performance (like managers should) and make decisions (like managers should) about money (very managerial). And at the end of several hours in a sweaty room and locked in mortal combat over the bonus scheme, they successfully irritate everyone. Pay a successful trader or fund manager a £100,000 bonus and they may promptly resign (after the money is in their bank account) when they find that one of their peers has received a £120,000 bonus.

> no one likes being told that they are worth less than someone else

From the company's perspective, the bonus, in theory if not in practice, measures the worth of an individual's contribution. From the individual's perspective, it measures their worth against their peers. No one likes being told that they are worth less than someone else, especially if they have the city-sized ego of a trader or fund manager.

Option Two

Focus on the intrinsic rewards, recognition and value of the job, creating a sense of community and belonging. This can achieve exceptional results at exceptionally low cost. Many vocational careers, like the army, teaching and academia, pay poorly but can attract exceptional talent and achieve exceptional results. Some of the best and brightest graduates go off to work as underpaid researchers for politicians or work for peanuts in the glamorous world of the international auction houses.

The choice between these two options goes to the heart of current discussions about stress, employee protection and regulation. The received wisdom is that employees need to be protected by regulation from the harsh winds of the marketplace. Flexitime, family-friendly policies and shorter working weeks are all part of this trend. There are few people who would want to reverse this. The public sector sets the best practice example in terms of working hours, flexitime and being family friendly. It also suffers by far the highest rates of absenteeism, sickness and stress-related complaints. Focusing on Option One may be important, but in the case of the public sector, it is clearly not enough to motivate staff.

Conversely, it is clear that many people are quite happy to seek out what appear to be stressful careers. The modern professions, from accounting to law, consulting and finance all put new graduates through sweat-it-out apprenticeships. And they are overwhelmed with demand for positions. These are classic Option Two-type careers: the hours may be antisocial and the demands may be extreme, but the opportunities are great. If people see that they are doing something worthwhile in an organisation that has prospects and they have some control over their future, that goes a long way to making up for the lack of an on-site crèche. Conversely, put someone in an organisation under siege (much of the public sector), with limited career prospects and limited autonomy, and the only sources of motivation are essentially Option One-type bribes: more money, easier conditions. This is fertile ground for strikes and conflict.

For the leader, this contrast between Option One and Option Two is critical. The easy way out for all leaders is to go down Option One routes: more money, easy terms. The motivation lasts as long as it takes for the bonus to hit the bank account. The harder route, but which sustains motivation longer, is Option Two: give people meaningful work, create a sense of belonging, opportunity and recognition, and you are more likely to motivate. The cynics will argue that you will be able to exploit people better – more work for modest pay.

As a leader in the middle of the organisation, there is not much you can do to change Option One. You have to make the most of the hand you have been dealt by the organisation. You have to deploy some of the motivational skills in Option Two.

Case Study

Teach First: making a motivational offering

At first sight, Teach First had perhaps the least attractive recruiting proposition ever devised for top graduates. It asked them to do two years' teaching in the most challenging schools in London with some of the most disadvantaged children. They received six weeks' training, which meant giving up any chance of a holiday after graduation. They would be paid about half what they would receive if they joined a top-flight consulting firm. Teach First lacked the prestige of the big recruiters. It was a start-up – no one had heard of it. It was a charity. It had a tiny budget.

In its first year, over 5% of Oxbridge and Imperial final-year undergraduates with good degrees had applied. At the time, no graduates from these universities were teaching in the target schools. It is now one of the top five graduate recruiters in the UK. Dropout rates were low and enthusiasm of the new teachers was high, despite the huge stress and challenges they faced on a daily basis.

Why should high-flying graduates be motivated to join such an unlikely scheme, against better-paid offerings, and why did they feel motivated to stay in the scheme even after the reality of working in the challenging schools became clear?

The good news is that there are graduates out there who have good social values. Teach First gave them a chance to make a worthwhile contribution. But that was never going to be enough. They may have hearts, but they also have heads. Teach First is designed to develop graduates into leaders of the future. It gives them far more practical experience of core leadership skills such as motivating, influencing, dealing with conflict and surviving adversity than any amount of staring into computer screens will do. Trading bonds or writing reports may make money, but at the end of two years it will be the Teach First participants who are prepared for leadership, not the highly paid galley slaves chained to their computers.

To make this promise credible, many top recruiters in consulting, investment banking and law supported Teach First. The participants do not get huge pay and they do not get huge holidays. They do very poorly on Herzberg's Option One route: good money and easy hours. They do very well on Option Two: they have a meaningful job, they have real prospects, they are highly recognised and they are given high autonomy and responsibility. Option Two is very hard work for the employer and the employed. It can have dramatic results.

Practical theories of motivation: part three

Life is a little more subtle than flipping a coin and choosing between X and Y. Different people have different needs at different times.

I learned about how needs differ at an early stage. I set out for India in search of enlightenment. I got to Afghanistan and ran out of money. This was in the days before there were mobile phones for the emotionally incontinent and credit cards for the financially feckless. My interest in enlightenment plummeted and my interest in money soared. So I sold my blood, but not my soul, to the locals. I got money, not enlightenment, and was grateful for it.

For the rich and successful, survival is taken for granted. Many seek immortality by buying up art collections, endowing charities and naming universities, buildings and departments after themselves. Most of us are in between those two extremes most of the time. We want to be paid, we want to feel a sense of belonging to something worthwhile and we would like to be recognised for what we do.

Perhaps all this is obvious. So it is refreshing to find that this is a case of practical theory from Maslow's hierarchy of needs (see Figure 5.1).

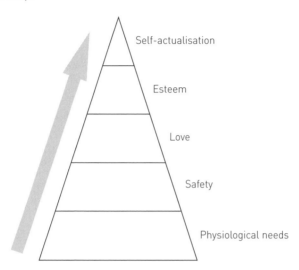

Figure 5.1 Maslow's hierarchy of needs

Maslow argued that we are all needs junkies. We want to climb the ladder of needs from survival to immortality. Let us climb the ladder with him, converting his language into the language of leaders.

- **Physiological needs** for Maslow are items like food and water: without them we become hungry and thirsty. Pay and conditions are the food and water of the employment world.

- **Safety** is a sense of security which comes in part from the employer and also from knowing that you have the skills to do the job. If the worst comes to the worst, they are skills which you can use elsewhere.

- **Love** can be dangerous at work. So instead of loving your staff, it is enough to make sure that they have a sense of belonging and community. They are trusted and respected for who they are. At its most basic, this is about leaders taking a positive interest in the careers and lives of those they are responsible for.

- **Esteem** is about recognising and rewarding individuals.
  The old saying holds true: 'Praise in public, criticise in private.'
  One leader makes sure that he praises 10 times as often as he
  criticises. Sometimes he finds it difficult. But once you start
  looking, there is usually much to praise and be thankful for.
- **Self-actualisation** is about achievement – creating a legacy
  which is meaningful and recognised.

If you asked a leader what each rung of Maslow's hierarchy of
needs was about, they would not know. But effective leaders
understand this model intuitively, and they play to it.

An unauthorised version of the model converted into the reality of
the workplace is shown in Figure 5.2.

Figure 5.2 Maslow's hierarchy of needs (the unauthorised, revisionist,
leadership version)

Everyone has something more they want. Everyone has something they fear. We fear a project going wrong, or a supplier or staff member failing us. We fear losing our jobs sometimes. We fear being left behind in the leadership marathon by our peers. There is always something we fear.

There is also always something we want. Perhaps many of us would really like to become billionaires, Oscar winners, sports stars or astronauts. All at the same time. But these things are not easy. We are always making a trade-off between what we want and the risk and effort involved in getting there. We are risk averse (we fear failure) and we prefer things to be made easier, not more difficult.

Some leaders use the fear part of the equation most. Fear-based leaders stress the negative: 'If you don't . . .' or 'You can't afford to get this wrong . . .'. In the short term, this can be highly effective. Eventually, however, people burn out, stress out and walk out. Meanwhile, the fear-based leader has achieved results and may well have moved onwards and upwards to greater things. They climb to the top over the career corpses of those they have killed.

> the fear-based leader climbs to the top over the career corpses of those they have killed

Other leaders use the greed element most. Greed is not just about money: it is about ego, recognition and immortality. Having a professorial chair or a museum named after you is greed fulfilled, for a while. Even at the top of a career, there is hunger for something more: most CEOs are not content to be mere custodians of a legacy they have inherited. They want to create their own legacy. They crave more recognition. This way, disaster can lie. The lure of greatness is a distraction from the obligation to deliver.

Finally, good leaders use idleness to their advantage in two ways.

First, good leaders do not make life difficult for their followers. They are clear about what they want, where they are going and how to get there. They give structure and guidance to their teams to minimise wasted effort. They help clear the way forward with the rest of the organisation by removing political obstacles and aligning other parts of the organisation with what they are trying to achieve. They set their followers up for success.

Second, good leaders do not interfere with their teams. They do not over-manage. They give teams discretion within a structure. The leader risks looking idle, because they let go. This is a very hard lesson for many leaders to learn.

One popular form of good leadership is 'MBWA', or Management By Walking Around. MBWA can create the 'leader in the locker room' problem. Arguably, the opposite of MBWA is required: Management By Walking Away. For a leader, this is nerve-racking; you direct a team to do something, and you want to see how it is doing. You want to pull the seed up every few moments to see how it is progressing. Leave it alone. Be available for help, but do not interfere. The end result may not be exactly what you predicted; it may be better. By not interfering, you show you trust the team, they feel motivated, they do their best and they learn more by trying to do things themselves than by blindly following your exact orders.

Maslow can be complicated. In practice leaders cannot go round calculating if each person is at the love stage or the self-actualisation stage, let alone know what to do about it. Going into a boardroom and asking which board members are at the love level would be original, if not totally advisable or actionable. The simpler way is to remember three things: fear, greed and idleness.

Work on people's hopes. Work on people's fears – humane leaders seek to remove risk and remove fear. Inhumane leaders happily stoke up fear. Finally, put idleness to work. Make things easy for others: give a clear structure and direction. Make it easy for yourself: do not over-manage. Fear, greed and idleness work as much for selling ideas as they do for motivating people. If your idea appeals to someone's hopes and removes a fear, and you make it easy for them to say 'yes', they are likely to say 'yes'.

Leaders may not understand or care for the theory. They just put it into practice.

How to motivate your team

1 **Show you care for each member of the team, and for their career**

Invest time to understand their hopes, fears and dreams. Casual time by the coffee machine, not a formal meeting in an office, is the best way to get to know your team members.

2 **Say thank you**

We all crave recognition: we want to know that we are doing something worthwhile and we are doing it well. Make your praise real, for real achievement. And make it specific. Avoid the synthetic one-minute manager praise ('gee, you typed that email really well …').

3 **Never demean a team member**

If you have any criticism, keep it private and make it constructive. Don't scold your team members like schoolchildren: treat them as partners and work together to find a way forward.

4 **Delegate well**

Delegate meaningful work which will stretch and develop your team member. Yes, there is routine rubbish to be delegated, but delegate some of the interesting stuff as well. Be clear and consistent about your expectations.

5 **Have a clear vision**

Show where your team is going and how each team member can help you all get there. Have a clear vision for each team member: know where they are going and how they can develop their careers.

6 **Trust your team**

Do not micro manage them. Have courage to implement MBWA: Management By Walking Away.

7   **Be honest**

That means having difficult, but constructive, conversations with struggling team members. Don't hide or shade the truth. Honesty builds trust and respect.

8   **Set clear expectations**

Be very clear about promotion prospects, bonuses and the required outcome of each piece of work. Assume you will be misunderstood: people hear what they want to hear. So make it simple and repeat it often and be consistent.

9   **Over-communicate**

You have two ears and one mouth: use them in that proportion. Listen twice as much as you speak. Then you will find out what is really going on and what drives your team members, and you can act accordingly.

10 **Don't try to be friends**

It is more important to be respected than liked: trust endures where popularity is fickle and leads to weak compromises. If your team trusts and respects you, they will want to work for you.

How leaders apply the theory in practice

We have looked at what the theory of leadership says. Now let's hear what leaders say about human nature.

First, in our survey of over 1,000 current and emerging leaders, the most important quality valued in a leader was the ability to motivate others. When we asked our participants how satisfied they were with the motivational capabilities of their leaders, we found a huge motivation gap. Although motivation was seen as the most important attribute of a leader, only 37% were satisfied with the performance of their leaders in this respect. Clearly, there was a problem.

We looked further to find out more about what people expected in terms of motivation, and then we looked at specific situations to see how well or poorly they were handled.

We asked people about leaders who had motivated them and leaders who had not motivated them. This is what they expected:

1   My boss shows an interest in my career.
2   I trust my boss: (s)he is honest with me.
3   I know where we are going and how to get there.
4   I am doing a worthwhile job.
5   I am recognised for my contribution.

We will look at each briefly. But first let's look at what is not there:

- **Money**. When it was mentioned, it was seen as a demotivator, not a motivator. Get the money wrong and you send a signal either that you cannot be trusted to deliver on a promise or that you do not value the person highly enough relative to their peers. Either way, you have broken trust, and your credibility as a leader of that person is lost.

- **Family-friendly hours, shorter hours, flexitime, facilities**. These simply did not appear on the radar screen. People who have signed up for the leadership journey have signed up for some self-sacrifice and are also good at compartmentalising their lives. They do not share personal concerns in a professional environment. If they have doubts, they conceal them until they have decided to leave.

Look again at the list of expectations that followers have of leaders when it comes to motivation. It is very simple. There are no dark arts to be learned in leading people. Treat them and care for them as humans, and the chances are that they will respond. We will look at each expectation in turn.

My boss shows an interest in my career

Hierarchical relationships are unequal. You are more important to your followers than they are to you. Their jobs and livelihoods depend on you: the reverse is only partially and indirectly true. It also means that you probably focus intently on managing your boss, but less intently on managing downwards. Most people know more about their bosses than they do about their followers.

As a follower, if your boss is clearly not interested in your career, it is unnerving.

Normally, there is an implicit psychological contract between leader and follower, which is far more important than any job description. The contract says that the follower will do what it takes to support the leader, and the leader will look after the pay, promotion and assignment prospects of the follower. If the leader is either unwilling or unable to deliver on the leader's half of the contract, there is little incentive for the follower to feel good about following.

Some leaders make this contract highly explicit. In return they demand absolute loyalty. They create a personal fiefdom. At promotion and bonus councils they will play very hard to deliver the promises they made to their teams. The result can be dysfunctional: a power baron with their own team emerges, playing to their own rules, with their own team. The team will tend to show great loyalty to a leader who looks after them so well. The team becomes a cult: inward looking, demanding, and divisive with the rest of the organisation.

I trust my boss: (s)he is honest with me

'Honesty' and 'business' are not words that are often heard together in the media. But all the leaders I interviewed, even in industries such as investment banking, stressed honesty. This is not about honour and ethics and being nice to the planet. This is much more hard-faced and practical.

Followers want to know where they stand. If they have been working hard for a year and think they are doing fine, it is devastating if the boss turns up at the annual review and gives an unsatisfactory ranking. The boss has been dishonest.

Dishonesty is not about lying; it is about failing to tell the whole truth, even the uncomfortable truth, promptly. This is an honesty test that would cause panic for some politicians.

Honesty is ultimately about trust. If you do not trust someone, it becomes very hard to work for them as a leader.

dishonesty is not about lying; it is about failing to tell the whole truth, even the uncomfortable truth, promptly

I know where we are going and how to get there

Sometimes this is called 'vision'. But vision is too grand: it sounds like Moses, Martin Luther King and Gandhi all rolled together. Provide a simple description of where your team has to get to on the next three-month project. Let your people know what they need to develop personally over the next six months and the practical actions they can take to develop those skills. Show where your business is going over the next one to three years. Do these things and you start to give people the clarity, structure and direction they need. Put it the other way: if your people do not know where they are going or how they are going to get there, they are soon going to become very frustrated.

I am doing a worthwhile job

Not everyone gets to do exciting, high-powered jobs all the time. Some jobs are plain dull, tedious, stressful or unglamorous. But they need to be done.

The world of repairing shoes is perhaps not the most exciting. Go to a shoe repair shop and the conditions are hardly brilliant. Some of them are little more than holes in the wall. Staff tend to be on wages which are modest by any standards and would be small change for a banker. And yet John Timpson manages to create a loyal workforce in his shoe repair shops and he is widely regarded as a very good leader. One of the many things he does is to focus on customer satisfaction and constantly recognise and reward great service: he always has a supply of prizes available in his car. His staff focus on the positive impact they are having on customers; each happy customer is evidence that they are doing a worthwhile job.

In investment banking there are plenty of dull jobs to be done in checking documents: the dullness is offset by knowing that a billion-pound deal may fail if you get it wrong. Even dull stuff can be made worthwhile in the right context.

I am recognised for my contribution

Let's make this simple. If you never get any recognition for all your efforts, you get upset. You probably do not feel very motivated to put in more effort. So recognise the efforts of your team. Some leaders feel the need to grab all the glory if their teams do well: they are also the leaders who are the first to walk away and delegate blame if things go wrong. Strong leaders have the self-confidence to recognise the success of their teams. Recognising success is effective because:

- it shows the leader has built a strong and effective team
- it motivates the team.

Recognition takes multiple forms: it can be as simple as a few well-chosen words in front of the CEO. Take time to say thank you, and to mean it, to the individual or team directly. Recognition can also be prizes, newsletter mentions or celebrations at a night out. Pay rises are often the least effective form of recognition because in most organisations they are not public knowledge.

Motivation and moments of truth

In any relationship there are moments of truth. This is when you discover the real nature of the other person. The moment of truth can come at any time. Both our leaders and followers identified three classic moments of truth in the leader–follower relationship:

1 **Payback time**.

2 **Feedback time**: formal and informal.

3 **Problem time**: the screaming monkeys.

Payback time

As a leader you are making an implicit, sometimes explicit, promise to look after the interests of your followers. Fail to deliver for them, and you are a failure, not a leader, to them.

We have already seen how some leaders play hardball for their followers at promotion and bonus time. One budding power baron played this game to perfection. Essentially, he rigged the process. He worked out all the evaluation criteria and wrote evaluations which were designed to score maximum points for his followers. Anyone who had been disloyal got lousy evaluations, even if they were very good. He then backed his evaluations all the way. It was impossible to argue with him; his followers had only worked for him so there was no other point of view. The only benchmarks were the lousy reviews he had written for disloyal people who had gone on to succeed elsewhere: this was evidence, he claimed, that his evaluation criteria were tougher than anyone else's. He delivered results to his teams, who wisely remained loyal to him.

Other promises are just as important.

Case Study

Developing trust

Once, I found myself earning real sweat equity in Riyadh, Saudi Arabia. The project went well. The client wanted to go to a second stage. The partner came in at the end of the first project expecting to agree the second stage with the client. I dreaded the meeting: I had planned a great holiday as an escape from all the hard work. The partner knew this, but I could see economic ▶

necessity would outweigh personal need. The moment of truth came. The client agreed to the second stage, and my heart sank.

Then the partner turned to the client and said, 'Of course, you don't mind starting phase two later so that Jo can have his holiday, do you?'

The client was delighted: suddenly he saw me as a human (you can fool some of the people…) not just a work drudge. My relationship with the client improved further. More importantly, I realised I had discovered a partner I could trust. We worked together on and off for the next 10 years.

Always deliver on expectations. This means you must be careful what you say, because your team will hear what they want to hear. When you say, 'I hope/intend/will try to get you your promotion/bonus/improved budget …', your team will hear you say, 'I will …' Your vague promise of help will be taken as a firm committment to deliver. If you don't deliver, your excuses will fall on deaf ears. Delivering on expectations means you must manage expectations well.

Feedback time

Formal feedback

Giving positive feedback is easy. People like receiving it. People like giving it. The test of the leader is not praising followers, rather it is helping them through some of their professional challenges. Giving negative feedback is deeply uncomfortable for most people; there are few leaders who seem to relish such opportunities. We are not even meant to talk about negative feedback. We retreat into the comfort of obscurity and jargon. We talk about development opportunities. If someone has really messed up, we might talk about development challenges. When we are close to firing them, we concede they have performance challenges.

> the test of the leader is not praising followers, rather helping them through professional challenges

Most feedback and most assessments are fundamentally dishonest. In one consulting firm 95% of staff are routinely rated as 'above average' or better. This is mathematically impossible, but politically inevitable. No one thinks of themselves as average. Do a quick test. Think of your peer group. Compared to them, do you really think that you are a below-average worker, lover, driver, thinker or human being? How many of your peers will think they are below average?

Most people land up being dishonest in giving reviews. It is emotionally necessary for the reviewee and the reviewer, and it is politically necessary given the way the system works if you are to fulfil your pay and promotion promises to your staff. Administratively it is necessary, because nearly all assessment systems are run like school reports – they grade people on some sort of good/bad continuum.

In practice, we have found only one effective alternative to the school report system – use a development grid. At each level of an organisation people develop, going through stages like this:

- new
- developing
- maturing
- mature.

This development happens across the whole range of skills and competences required in the role, such as problem solving, team-work and team management. If you rank someone who has been one year in the role as a mixture of 'new' or 'developing', there is likely to be little argument. There will be constructive discussion about how to progress on all the development criteria. On a traditional assessment, if you ranked the same person as 1 or 2 out of a 4-point scale on the same criteria, it would be toys out of pram time. The arguing, shouting and demands for an appeal and impartial assessment would be deafening. Of course, the two assessments are essentially the same. However, the development assessment is positive and constructive while the traditional assessment is negative and confrontational. In an organisation which is stuck with the traditional system, it is possible to run an informal development system alongside the formal system. Just be sure not to tell HR what you are doing.

The development assessment is more challenging to staff than the traditional system. But it provides a non-confrontational way of giving constructive criticism to them. It helps you to be honest with them. If you are honest, you will build trust. Staff will be in danger of thinking that you are a good leader.

Informal feedback

If a formal assessment is a surprise, it is a failure. By the time someone arrives at the formal review, they should be roughly aware of where they stand. If they do not know where they stand, then the formal review is likely to degenerate into argument rather than constructive discussion about the way forward. The employee is likely to lose trust in you; they will feel that you have not been honest with them during the review period in highlighting concerns and issues as they arose.

The art of informal feedback is essential for a leader. Regular feedback sets expectations and helps the individual keep on the performance track. But once again we are left with the problem that giving and receiving negative feedback is unpleasant. So we avoid it. The closest some leaders get to giving negative feedback is by showing frustration or anger when things go wrong. This helps no one, as no one knows what to do differently besides working harder and not upsetting the boss. So how can you do it? Negative feedback can cover anything from being irritated that a colleague slurps soup at their desk during lunch to helping someone see that the presentation they think is brilliant might need to be rewritten.

> the art of informal feedback is essential for a leader

In moments of stress – and negative feedback is stressful – it helps to have a system to fall back on. You can create your own version of it. I tend to use a simple acronym for mine – **SPIN**:

- **S**ituation specifics.
- **P**ersonal impact.
- **I**nsight and interpretation.
- **N**ext steps.

Situation

First, make sure the situation is right. If the other person is shouting and screaming, it is not a good time to throw fuel on the fire with a little negative feedback. Talk when the other person is calm. But try to do so as close to the event as possible. Feedback, like milk, goes off fairly quickly.

Second, be specific about exactly what happened. Telling someone they are 'unprofessional' is unhelpful and provocative. If you note that they have turned up more than 10 minutes late for the last five meetings, you have something specific to talk about.

Personal impact

Having established that the person is habitually late, it is tempting to say that they are unprofessional. This leads straight back to the shouting match. Instead, focus on how it makes you feel: you can argue with judgements, not with feelings. If you say, 'It makes me feel that you do not think client or management meetings are important', the worst you risk is a 'So what?' in return. You can follow up and ask if that is the impression they meant to create. If there is still no appropriate reaction, stop. Try again at a time and a place where they will be more responsive.

Insight and interpretation

It is now tempting to tell people what to do: don't. Instead, ask the individual if that is the impact they intend to make or whether they want to make another impact. Do not tell them what to do; let them figure it out. They will value their solutions much more than they value your solutions. If they want your help, they will ask for it.

Next steps

By this point, you should be ready for a relatively calm way of agreeing next steps. Land up on a future-focused, positive and constructive agenda, rather than a backwards-looking blame game.

Take time in applying this model. Do not move from one step to the next until the other person is ready to move on. If the situation is wrong and they disagree with the basic facts, then find a better time and go back and confirm the facts. It is possible that they are right and you are wrong.

Problem time: the screaming monkeys

This is the final test of the leader, and it is very easy to fail. It happens when staff come to you with a problem. Like any good leader, you make sure that you are available for advice. So you are pleased to see someone come through your open door with a problem. You are even more pleased when they walk back out of the door again with the problem lifted from their shoulders. Congratulations. You have just failed the test. Failed? When I did everything right? Are you nuts?

Let's call up the slow motion replay and see why the referee awarded the penalty against you.

A member of staff comes into your office. She has a monkey on her back. It is a screaming monkey and behaving badly. She needs help. So you take the monkey off her back. You now have the monkey and she leaves happy. Hearing that you are in a good mood, another staffer comes in. He has two screaming monkeys: one on each shoulder. You lift the burden from his shoulders. You now have three screaming monkeys in your office. By the end of the day, you have a vast troupe of monkeys in your office. Your staff are very happy, and you are very unhappy.

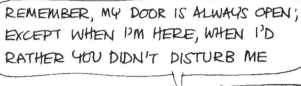

The leader is not there to solve every problem. You have assembled a team to solve the problems for you. You may have the most expertise, but avoid the temptation to become the leader in the locker room. You need to raise your game and focus on the wider issues facing the team – making sure they

only if you force them to solve the problem themselves will they develop the skills and confidence to become effective

are working on the right problem, making sure you have the right team, making sure they have the right support and development. Only if you force them to solve the problem themselves will they develop the skills and confidence to become effective.

When the staff member comes into the office with a monkey, give them advice and coaching on how to deal with the monkey. This is neither quick nor easy. It will take careful questioning to understand their problem and to help them understand it properly as well. It is probably easier in the short term to deal with the problem yourself: to take the monkey off their backs. But make sure they deal with the monkey themselves. If you are really smart, invite them to take one of your own monkeys away as well. It could be a good development opportunity for them. By the end of the day, you will have succeeded if there are no more screaming monkeys in your room.

The essence of this approach is to help people through their problems, not to solve their problems even if you think you know the answer. If you solve all their problems for them, they never learn or develop as individuals. Neither will they have any ownership over your solution; they will lack commitment and belief. Coaching them through their problem helps them learn and develop and it ensures that they have ownership of whatever solution they eventually discover. As they become more adept at solving problems themselves, so they will rely less on coming to you for help. In the short term coaching is high effort, but it pays big long-term dividends.

Coaching for success

Successful coaching sessions

Coaching is different from informal feedback. Informal feedback is a classic boss to team member interaction: a judgement is being made and support is offered. Coaching is a longer-term journey aimed at longer-term improvement.

Coaching is not just for coaches. Every good leader needs to bring out the best in their team, and that requires a mixture of formal and informal feedback, mentoring and coaching. The essence of coaching is to enable someone to work through a challenge, find a solution and act on it: coaching is not about giving solutions or feedback. When someone discovers their own solution, they are more committed to it, more likely to act on it and more likely to learn from it. For a leader who wants to avoid the monkey problem (above), coaching is a vital performance skill.

> the essence of coaching is to enable someone to work through a challenge, find a solution and act on it

Coaching can be thought of as an event and a journey. A coaching event is where a team member comes and asks for help. The coaching journey is about helping that same individual grow and progress over a year or more. A coaching event is part of the coaching journey.

A coaching event can be reduced to the five Os:

1 Objectives.

2 Overview.

3 Options.

4 Obstacles.

5 Outcomes.

These five Os give a simple and natural structure to an effective coaching conversation. Let's look at each in turn:

- **Objectives**. Be clear about what you want to achieve. If you want someone to do something in a certain way, do not try to coach them into reading your mind: tell them. It pays to be clear about what the problem is that you are trying to solve. When you are presented with some symptoms of a problem, dig to find out the root causes of the problem rather than dealing with the symptoms alone. Dealing with symptoms not causes is as pointless as using spot remover to help a child with measles.

- **Overview**. Let your coachee lay out the situation as they see it. Even if it is a flawed perspective, they will want their voice to be heard and respected. Then encourage them to look at the same situation from the perspective of other players. If they are complaining about the behaviour of another department or individual, get them to explore what the situation looks like from their perspective. As you consider different perspectives, you will understand the problem better and you may well be encouraging them to feel their way towards some solutions.

- **Options**. Encourage the coachee to explore a range of options: you want to avoid the 'my way or no way' syndrome which often leads to conflict, not progress. Avoid discussions about who is right or wrong: that is to look to the past, not the future. Help them look to the future. Even if the future looks bleak, there are normally one or two things that anyone can do to make some progress and achieve some stability in an unstable position. Exploring options is about the art of the possible, not about what cannot be done. As the coachee explores different options, you will normally find that one emerges as the most sensible way forward. You may already have thought of the solution, but let the coachee discover it so that they own it.

- **Obstacles**. This is the reality check. Before agreeing to the course of action, ask a simple question: 'What might stop this happening?' You want to avoid having someone run off with great enthusiasm which is dashed by the first obstacle they encounter. Help them identify, prepare for and deal with these challenges in advance.

- **Outcomes**. Ask the coachee to summarise what the outcomes of the session are. They should summarise both what they have learned and what action they are going to take. The purpose of the summary is to check for understanding and to help fix the key points in the mind of both coachee and coach.

None of this is rocket science. You do not need to go on a five-day course and be certified by some self-important institution in order to have a coaching conversation. All you need to do is to know how to have a sensible, structured conversation with the person you are coaching. The five Os model gives a simple framework for your coaching conversation. As you have the conversation, remember one more O: open questions. As a coach,

> know how to have a sensible, structured conversation with the person you are coaching

your goal is not to give the answer, but to help the other person hit upon the answer. They may even hit upon a better answer than the one you were thinking of in the first place.

An open question is one to which there is no 'yes/no' answer: it forces the other person to give a fuller and more thoughtful response. A closed question invites a 'yes/no' answer and can quickly kill the conversation.

Open questions	Closed questions
What was their reaction?	Did they disagree?
What were they expecting?	Is that what they expected?
How did the sales meeting go?	Has the client agreed to our proposal yet?
How's the project going?	Have you finished the project yet?

The final secret of a good coach is shared with great leaders and great salespeople: they all have two ears and one mouth, and they all use them in that proportion. The more you listen, the better you are likely to be doing.

Case Study

Coaching for failure

David was a promising young batsman for his county. There was talk of him becoming an England player one day. To improve his chances, he decided to get some help from the senior batsmen in his county. They were all more than happy to help. Each one advised him on how to hold the bat, how to stand, how to move, how to deal with different types of ball, how to read what the bowler was about to do.

The more advice he got, the worse his performance became. Far from getting into the England side, he was struggling to hold his place in the county team. His career was heading towards extinction.

Ed, one of the county bowlers, noticed what was happening. Ed was pretty much useless as a batsman, but decided to help David anyway. David's heart sank: things could only get worse from here.

The first thing Ed did was to tell David to ignore all the advice from the senior batsmen. 'They are not telling you how to bat well: they are telling you how they bat. They all bat different ways, so they are all going to be giving you conflicting advice. No wonder you look like a confused circus contortionist when you come out to bat.'

The lights went on in David's mind. The senior batsmen had not been coaching him at all: they had assumed that how they batted was the only way to bat. They did not realise that different batsmen could succeed in different ways. Over the coming weeks, Ed helped David rediscover his natural strengths and build on those. Because Ed was a useless batsman, he did not try to give any technical advice: he let David discover what worked for him.

Over the rest of the season, David got steadily better and once again the dreams of an England place became more realistic.

As leaders, we need to recognise that our formula for successful leadership is not universal. There are many ways to succeed, and we need to let our team members discover what works for them, rather than imposing our methods on them.

The coaching journey

Most coaching models fail because they go no further than creating a structure for an individual coaching session. This may help you coach someone through a specific challenge, but this is not enough. If, as a leader, you spend your time simply helping people resolve problems, you run into several problems:

● Your coaching becomes a random walk through random problems.

● Your coachee makes no systemic improvement to the way they think, perform or behave.

● Your coachee learns to be dependent on you, rather than learning to deal with challenges themselves.

● You work reactively to situations, rather than having a proactive agenda.

A successful coaching relationship is based on a structured journey with a beginning, middle and end. Before starting to coach any of your team, you need to agree with them what they want and need to achieve from the coaching relationship. You can only agree this if you both know: where they start (what their needs and opportunities are) and where they are going (how they want to improve over the next year).

Once you have set clear objectives, you have purpose and direction to your coaching. You may also decide someone else might be a better coach for the goals you have agreed: if the goal is to help someone understand and manage organisation politics better and you are not a great politician yourself, find someone else to be the coach.

Once you have agreed goals for the coaching journey, the goals for each coaching session become simpler. Typically, you will have three goals for each coaching session:

1 **Address immediate challenges** for the coachee. Even though you have an overall goal set for the year, you should let

the coachee raise issues of immediate concern even if they are not directly relevant to the longer-term goal. Long-term goals may be important, but the short-term challenges are urgent: deal with them both.

2 **Review progress** against the overall goal for the year. Encourage the coachee to reflect on situations where they have needed the skills that you are trying to help them build: let them learn from what they are doing successfully or less successfully in such situations.

3 **Review what went well**, and what went less well, since you last met them. In each case, find out why it went well or otherwise. The purpose of this third discussion is to help the coachee coach themselves. Most flawed coaching models are deficit models: they focus on what is broken. As a leader, you want your team to discover what they are doing well, what they are good at and how they can focus on their strengths. You also want them to build enough self-awareness of what they are doing and how they are doing it so that they can coach themselves.

Most coaching models focus only on the first of the three discussions above. The second and third elements differentiate a leader's coaching model from that of the professional coach. It gives you a much more positive and proactive approach to helping and building the strengths of your team than traditional coaching models.

At this point, the ever-growing ranks of professional coaches will howl in anger and protest. They will insist that only an impartial and independent person can be an effective coach. This is self-serving nonsense. A good leader has to be a good coach. Good coaching will help each team member achieve their best performance. It will also build the trust and confidence each team member has in you. By demonstrating that you care enough to help them, you build ties of loyalty and commitment that can be worth their weight in gold.

a good leader has to be a good coach

Dealing with the awkward squad

To lead is to discover the full range of human nature. Some people make leadership a pleasure; others make it a challenge. Either way, leaders have to deal with it. As leaders, we should ensure we have the right team working for us. But we cannot guarantee that our peers will be a pleasure to work with: we still have to work with them, knowing that we cannot change them. Ineffective leaders complain about awkward peer groups; effective leaders find ways of working with even the most awkward peer group.

Peer group dysfunction comes in a cornucopia of different flavours. Everyone has their own horror stories of colleagues from hell. To simplify things, most of the awkward types typically have one or more of the following five characteristics:

Victims: 'Poor me' people who believe the world treats them unfairly and that they are powerless to control a cruel universe.

Villains: competitive politicians who always seek to undermine peers, spread blame when things go wrong and claim credit when things go well.

Control freaks: who believe in 'my way or no way'. Often found in staff departments using policies and procedure as a substitute for judgement, teamwork or sanity. For them, teamwork means doing what you are told, or you are not a team player.

Indecisive types: who wait in vain for the perfect, risk-free answer and then panic, and make a decision which they then change, adapt or reverse. They are also often evasive and go missing when you most need them.

Incompetents: who may talk a good talk, but cannot actually do anything. When thing go wrong they confuse matters with the 'I said/he said/she said/they said/I said . . .' discussion.

Each horror story unfolds in its own unique and messy way and needs a unique response. However, there are a few principles to help you decide how to respond and how to help the awkward type spread their poison elsewhere. The principles are based on a range of rational, emotional and political responses which can be applied to all members of the awkward squad.

Rational response: stay action focused

Awkward squad members often enjoy discussing the past (what went wrong, why the world is unfair) and what is not possible (because of all our rules and procedures). These are unhelpful discussions: do not indulge them. Be clear about why you are having the discussion with them and what actions need to happen. Awkward types may push back by arguing that your idea should not happen or does not have priority. Be prepared for this. Initially, explain why you need to move forward. Then push the problem back on to the awkward squad member: ask them what options and alternatives they see. Try to create options rather than a take it or leave it choice which becomes a win/lose discussion. All the time you should be focusing on:

- the future, not the past
- actions, not analysis or behaviour
- win/win, not lose/lose
- options and discussion, not argument.

Emotional response: be positive with them and with yourself

One way to make the awkward squad happy is to indulge their behaviour, either by condoning it or by challenging it. If you condone it by sympathising with it, you reinforce their view that they can behave that way with you. If you challenge them, you open up a battle which, even if you are right rationally, you will lose politically and emotionally because you will have created an enemy. Simply ignore their behaviour: stay positive with your language and action focused with your discussion. Focus on the task, not on the behaviour. You are a leader, not a personal psychologist.

focus on the task, not on the behaviour

The awkward squad are often happiest when they are spreading their misery to everyone else. It is tempting to take their affronts personally, especially when they are meant personally. To do that is to hand them victory. Detach yourself and your emotions from their behaviour: observe their behaviour but do not become caught up in it. Remain focused on the task and remain positive. Although it is sometimes hard to believe, we are responsible for our own emotions: we can choose to feel happy, bored, angry or frustrated. We do not have to have our feelings dictated to us by the behaviour of others. If you ever want revenge on the awkward types, remember that happiness is the greatest revenge: if you have that, you have everything and they have nothing.

As you frame your emotional response, think about how a role model you admire would handle the situation. If your role model is a combination of Rambo, Darth Vader and Attila the Hun, you may want to choose a more positive role model for the office: perhaps a peer or senior executive who seems to handle people well. Ultimately, you should aim to be a role model as well: behave as you would have others behave to you and behave in a way that commands respect in the organisation. In most workplaces, you will not advance by role modelling the behaviour of the awkward squad. The principles to follow are:

- remain positive and professional personally
- focus on the task, not behaviour: do not condone or challenge it.

Eventually, the awkward squad will find easier targets for them to be awkward with. The problem may remain, but it will no longer be your problem.

How to stay cool when the heat is on

1 **Visualise the end of the event**

   Where do you want to be? Focus on that. Do not get caught up in the heat of battle. Stay calm and focused on where you want to get to.

2 **Win a friend, not an argument**

   Arguing the moral righteousness of your position gets you nowhere. Fighting emotion with logic is like fighting fire with fuel: spectacular but not advisable.

3 **Let the other side vent**

   Let them dump their emotion, let them be heard. No one can sustain fury for long. They cannot listen when angry. Having dumped, most people feel embarrassed. At least they can then talk sensibly.

4 **Stay positive and constructive**

   You will be remembered more for how you behaved than for what you did. Leave the right impression; your behaviour may also persuade the other party to start being constructive.

5 **Imagine what your favourite role model would do in this situation, and then do the same thing**

   If your role model is a mix of Darth Vader and Vlad the Impaler, do not use this technique.

6 **Become a fly on the wall and watch the event**

   As you detach, you will be able to think more clearly and objectively, without getting emotionally involved.

7 **Imagine Mr Nasty in a pink tutu**

   It is hard to get angry with a fat 50-year-old in a pink tutu. Not laughing (or being sick) may be a greater challenge than staying calm.

8 **Pull out your imaginary Uzi and splatter their brains over the wall**

   As Mr Nasty does not even know what you have done, he cannot retaliate.

9   **Count to 10, just like your gran told you to**

Let the immediate flush of anger pass and regain control of your feelings.

10   **Breathe deeply, as taught in Buddhist meditation lessons**

Like counting to 10, this allows you to regain control and lets you respond professionally.

Political response: engage your network

The awkward squad are not just awkward personally. They can also be awkward for your career: they may take pleasure in delaying or obstructing your plans, and may be happy quietly to spread poison about you. You have to deal with this: you need to deal with it carefully so that you are not contaminated by the poison. There are private and public ways of working the politics.

Ideally, you should be able to resolve matters directly with whoever is the cause of trouble. If dealing with them rationally, and with good emotional intelligence, does not work, you will need to move to a second line of defence: take advice in private from a trusted coach or mentor, but preferably not your boss. Your boss wants you to handle this sort of challenge yourself and does not want to get involved or pull rank unless absolutely necessary. As you take advice, take care: do not be negative about the awkward squad member. Focus on what needs to happen and what is stopping progress. Assume that anything you say will be repeated to the awkward squad member. The chances are that your coach will know what the individual is like anyway and will not need further briefing about their dysfunctional behaviour.

The final line of defence is to find someone who can exert influence over the individual. The most obvious route is to escalate the matter to their boss. This may work in the short term but at the cost of creating a career enemy: no one likes finding that they have been short-circuited. Use this approach only if absolutely necessary.

Avoid letting your dispute go public. Even if you win, you will be damaged in the process. Keeping the email trail to 'prove' that you are right will not help. No boss wants to turn sleuth and figure out who wrote what when. The boss will want to end the dispute rather than apportion blame.

Chapter 6
Being positive

Leading in the middle of an organisation can be gruelling. It is like the middle of a chess game. The start is clear, and there are well-known openings which you can pick. As a pawn, you advance steadily up the board. If you have picked the wrong opening or are in the wrong place at the wrong time, you get taken out. You have to start a new game. The end game is also clearer. Hopefully, you will be the king or queen of the board. Success or failure revolves entirely around you, and you can control your destiny.

In the middle, you are like a knight going out to do battle for your organisation. But everything is complicated. The board is crowded with other players. You are meant to achieve much with little power. Your career is a zigzag. You no longer advance in a straight line. Like the chess knight, sometimes you take two steps to the side and one forward. Sometimes you even take one step back and two to the side to get round a blockage and find another opportunity to advance.

The knight's life is one of crises, conflicts, risks and ambiguity. And the knight is meant to perform, have influence and use power. Delivering against this requires a combination of positive behaviours and skills, which are the focus of this chapter. We will explore four major themes:

1 Handling conflicts, crises and risks.
2 Managing projects.

3 Managing change.

4 Acquiring power: the 10 laws of power.

These are all core skills that leaders need to develop. The battle-hardened veteran leader will tell you that the only way to build these skills is through experience. The veteran will be right. But it makes sense to prepare for the inevitable crises and conflicts. Going into treacherous waters without a map is a recipe for career shipwreck.

Handling conflicts, crises and risks

Conflicts

There are conflicts in the best-run organisations. The leader should be highly suspicious if there is no conflict, because organisations are set up for conflict.

Let's emphasise the point: organisations are set up for conflict.

In any organisation there is a limited pot of money, management time, skills and resources. Different products, functions and regions will inevitably have different perspectives and priorities. They are all bidding for the same limited resource pot. The ensuing bidding war between departments may be civilised or it may be underhand, political and nasty. In any event, there is a contest and a conflict going on. For many leaders in the middle, the competition is not some abstract organisation in the marketplace. Your real competition is sitting at a desk nearby, competing for the same resources and the same promotion.

> your real competition is sitting at a desk nearby

If we recognise that conflict is a natural fact of life in any organisation, we can take the first step towards dealing with it. Conflict is not about people or personalities: it is about positions and priorities.

I asked all our leaders how they dealt with conflict. They all homed in on the same set of principles:

- **Never avoid conflict**. Embrace it. Conflict is how priorities are set and decisions are made. It develops the leadership and interpersonal skills of the emerging leader.

- **Depersonalise the conflict**. Never take conflict personally, even if it is meant that way. Focus on the issues and interests at stake, not the personalities.

- **Detach yourself**. Observe what is happening and do not get emotionally involved. Lose your temper, lose the argument. Think how a leader or role model you admire would handle the situation. One leader called this 'putting on the mask of leadership'. You may have boiling emotions inside, but present the mask of your ideal leader and use that to guide your actions.

Occasionally, some conflicts do get emotional and unpleasant. (Humans, unlike computers, do have emotions.) These events are rare but dangerous. If they are mishandled, even the innocent party gets tainted by the event. At times like this, a simple model helps as a guide. Try to remember this:

> conflict develops the leadership and interpersonal skills of the emerging leader

FEAR TO EAR

FEAR stands for the natural reaction to outright hostility. It also stands for how we feel before seeing the CEO for the first time. It was a helpful emotion when our ancestors faced a sabre-toothed tiger: it would alert them to fight or flight. Fighting or fleeing at the first sight of the CEO is not helpful.

The wrong response is to let FEAR take over, as follows:

- **F**ight furiously.
- **E**ngage enemy emotionally.
- **A**rgue against anyone.
- **R**etaliate, refute, repudiate reason.

If it is your last day at work, the preceding is a good way to go down. However, take the F out of FEAR and you are left with EAR, which is what you should use to start listening. EAR stands for:

- **E**mpathise.
- **A**gree the problem.
- **R**esolve the way forward.

The temptation is to go straight to resolving the way forward. This simply invites more argument; the other side will knock down anything you say. You need to calm them down. Empathise with them. This does not mean hugging them. It means using active listening skills, which will be covered in the next chapter. As you listen, you will find out more about the real nature of their difficulty and why they feel so threatened. Do not try to argue: try to understand. Win a friend, not an argument. Once you have won a friend, you have a chance of winning the argument if there is any substantive disagreement beneath the emotional froth. You cannot begin to find a solution until you have found the problem which you both can agree on. Once you have agreed the root cause of the problem together, you have a chance of finding a way forward.

Crises

Some people are lucky: they never encounter a real career or business crisis. Most people find that they do have a crisis at some point in their careers. It can feel very lonely. The only person who can get you out of the crisis is yourself. The middle of the organisation is where many emerging leaders find themselves bailing out to set up their organic pig farm in North Wales. This is natural. The first flush of career enthusiasm has disappeared. The long haul to the top still looks long. Then something happens: the final straw is added to the camel's back.

The difference between success and failure sometimes comes down to persistence. Successful leaders work through their crises and find that Nietzsche was right: 'That which does not break you, makes you stronger.' Others are mucking out the organic waste on their pig farms.

How to deal with crises

1 **Recognise the problem early**

   Don't go into denial; don't avoid the crisis which will not resolve itself.

2 **Take control**

   Step up to the mark; offer solutions, not problems; have a plan.

3 **Act fast**

   Avoid analysis paralysis; drive to action; focus on outcomes.

4 **Focus on what you can do and do it**

   Build momentum and confidence, even through small initial actions. Don't worry about what you cannot control: you cannot control it.

5 **Find plenty of support**

   Don't be the lone hero; find the people, money, skills and power barons and supporters who can collectively deliver the solution.

6 **Over-communicate**

   Dispel fear, uncertainty, doubt and confusion: be clear and consistent in your messaging. Have a simple story to tell about where you are going and how you will get there.

7 **Be positive**

   You will be remembered as much for how you behaved as for what you did: be the role model whom others follow. Set the standard for those around you.

8 **Avoid blame**

   Give praise to those who help; don't look back and analyse problems or point the finger of blame; create a positive, action-focused culture, not a culture of fear and inaction.

9 **Show empathy**

Recognise the concerns of others; manage your own feelings and fears; wear the mask of leadership and project confidence and empathy.

10 **Make the most of crises**

Crises are opportunities to make your mark, stand out from your peers and make a difference. The more you encounter crises, the better you become at dealing with them.

The best way to prepare for crises is to develop resilience early on. Having crises and flirting with failure is not easy for a 20-something person. But if the worst comes to the worst, they can start again a little older and much wiser. Doing an MBA is a safe and prestigious way for a 20-something person to start over again. In contrast, the 40-year-old who has never had a crisis has what one CEO called 'brittle' confidence – they look good, sound good and seem confident. But when they face a real challenge or crisis, they crumble. They have no reserves to call on. They make a sad sight as they justify why they are happy to be leaving the rat race and how they had always dreamed of pig farming.

Many graduate training programmes do not develop resilience. They test the graduate's appetite for hard work, but that is not the same as resilience. Teach First is an exception. Top graduates spend two years teaching in some of the most challenging schools in the UK. This is, potentially, a brutal experience. But these graduates develop a depth of confidence, resilience and people skills that can never be acquired by their better-paid peers who spend their first two years staring into computer screens trading bonds or doing research. Leaders of the future need to take risks and learn about adversity and resilience early in their careers. Trying to learn these things when you are 40-something is tough.

The leaders who talked about responding to crises talked about the importance of knowing yourself. Some people let their identity become swamped by their job. When the crisis hits, or when they retire, they have nothing to fall back on. They have become dependent on their job – they live to work. Nearly all the leaders I interviewed had active lives outside work. This gives them a level of independence that makes them better able to deal with challenges.

Ultimately, individuals need to know themselves. Leadership is not for everyone, nor is it necessary for everyone. If you prefer fishing, then focus on that.

Risks

Attitudes to risk and ambiguity are the acid test for differentiating leaders, managers and entrepreneurs.

Risk and ambiguity are kryptonite to managers. They want to create an orderly environment in which predetermined goals can be achieved by the organisation. Orderliness and goal achievement are extremely valuable skills to have in an organisation. If everyone were a risk and ambiguity junkie, you would have either an extremely dysfunctional organisation or an investment bank. In some cases, you would have an extremely dysfunctional investment bank. But if an organisation takes no risk and avoids all ambiguity, it will eventually go nowhere fast.

I learned the value of risk when I learned to ski. We were all stuck on the nursery slopes being told to 'bend zee knees'. After we had mastered a cautious snowplough turn, we were encouraged to try for more ambitious and professional turns. After falling over six or seven times, most of us stuck to the safety of the snowplough turn. One maniac persisted with trying the fancy turns. He became the group joker; he was always falling over to the amusement of everyone else. Towards the end of the week, we all stopped laughing. He had slowly mastered the fancy turns and proceeded to start doing all the more adventurous runs we could only dream of. He left us far behind in ability. Most of us were acting like managers. We were avoiding risk. The embryonic leader was taking risks, learning and developing far faster than we were. We had learned survival. He had learned success.

Leaders will take risks, will persist and will achieve mastery through experience. As they build experience, they build skill and confidence. There is, inevitably, a risk/reward trade-off that we all think about. Most people are risk averse. The fear of failure outweighs the uncertain possibilities of success. Leaders tend to think more positively about the risk/return trade-off, and enjoy accelerated careers as a result: they succeed fast or they fail fast.

Although leaders take risks, most try to minimise ambiguity and uncertainty. Oil exploration, pharmaceutical R&D and insurance are all risk-based industries. Billions of dollars may be at risk. Although the leaders must make billion-dollar bets, they will seek to create as much clarity and certainty around those choices as possible. Good risk-taking is gambling where the dice are as loaded as far as possible in your favour.

Rewards for the leader in the middle of the matrix are not just about completing the project, getting a promotion or bonus. Those are short-term rewards that are soon forgotten. Long-term rewards are more important. Typically, there are four questions to address:

1　Does this opportunity help me build skills which will be useful in future?

2　Am I set up for success or failure?

3　Is there sufficient recognition and reward for taking this risk?

4　Are the consequences of failure manageable?

In other words, the leader in the middle has to make a calculated gamble on the career consequences of taking any risk. In any organisation there are CLMs (Career Limiting Moves) which everyone informally recognises. These include working for the wrong boss or working on the wrong assignment or working in the wrong part of the organisation.

For the emerging leader, the greatest risk of all is to take no risk. Avoiding risk is a career survival decision. But survival and success are not the same thing. To succeed, you need to take risks.

The entrepreneur is also a leader. Aspiring leaders in established organisations can learn from entrepreneurs' attitudes to risk and ambiguity. They are the opposite of what the institutional leader would do. Most entrepreneurs see ambiguity as opportunity. Where the rules of the game are unclear, the entrepreneur will create the rules of the game, even if this means making them up as they go along. Charlie Dunstone (mobile telephones), Michael O'Leary (discount airlines) and Richard Branson (everything else) did not wait for the rules of their industries to be written before attacking them. They entered, created their own rules and won. It is easier to win a game when you write the rules for it.

Managing projects

Project management versus change management

Change management and project management are the bread and butter of leaders in the middle of the matrix. Change and project management are often talked of as if they are the same thing. They are not. Project management is the technical, task-focused subset of change management. Projects focus on who does what where, when and how. For the sake of focus here, we will assume that change management includes project management but looks much more at the human, political and emotional aspects of change. Change is not simply about setting goals and drawing up a plan in an office. It is about creating the alliances, support and power networks to enable the plan to happen. This is a skill which all leaders acquire and use. Most CEOs do not rely on command and control to get their way. They spend much of their time working

> change is about creating the alliances, support and power networks to enable the plan to happen

the levers of the organisation to make things happen. They use influence and persuasion as much as formal power.

Good project management is the hallmark of a good manager. The manager delivers against preordained goals with preordained resources. Good change management is the hallmark of the good leader. The leader goes beyond formal authority, using influencing and political skills effectively, to make things happen.

Case Study

Project management or change management?

The contrast between change and project management became clear in a merger. The two sides of the merger brought in some consultants to help, which is always a dangerous idea. The partner did what the board needed: he acted as a leader. Although he had no formal authority, he convened the executive committee on a daily basis and helped them work through the daily crises that happen in any merger. Behind the scenes, he worked the politics of the individuals involved. The consultants then put in a team to project manage the merger integration. After 10 days, they had established a war room with risk logs and issue logs (spot the difference, if you can), meeting logs, attendance logs, telephone logs and master logs. Everything was being logged, and nothing was being done. The client went crazy. Logs and paper do not change things; people do. They tried to manage change: you have to lead change.

However, leaders also have to deliver the basics of project management. We will look at effective project and change management below.

The basics of project management

Good project management is a real skill and it is in short supply. Projects have a nasty habit of taking twice as long and costing twice as much as the original bid. Anyone who has had building work done knows this, to their cost. Some projects go completely out of control. Building the Scottish Parliament escalated in price from an initial £10–20 million bid to

> good project management is a real skill and it is in short supply

over £400 million. The London Olympics will cost three times the original estimate. Politicians may be great leaders. They are rarely good managers.

Here we will not focus on the vagaries of contract management. One reason contractors cost more than you thought is that they underbid in the first place. Either they were too optimistic, or they hoped to make up their loss on all the changes and additions that are inevitably requested in the course of any project, from building a new kitchen to delivering the London Olympics.

There are exhaustive manuals on how to run tight projects. We will focus on the few items which make the big difference. Most projects, like most battles, are decided before they really start. In the middle of the matrix, it pays to make sure that your projects are set up for success, not failure.

Project management hell is brought about by the four horsemen of project apocalypse:

1 The wrong problem.
2 The wrong sponsor.
3 The wrong team.
4 The wrong process.

Get these wrong and your project is doomed. Get them right and it takes a stroke of evil genius to make it go wrong. Figure 6.1 overleaf illustrates where leaders focus their efforts on projects: at the start, before the heavy lifting begins.

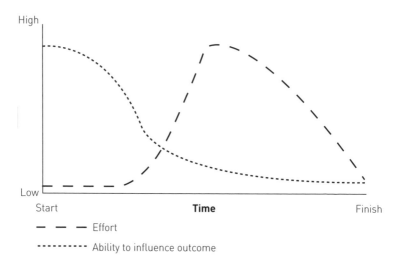

Figure 6.1 Projects: effort and potential to influence the outcome

We will take a look at each of the four horsemen of project apocalypse.

The wrong problem

There is a story of a drunk who loses his car keys in a dark alley. He can't see anything there, so he goes into the main street where there is plenty of street lighting and looks for his car keys there. He figures that at least there he can see what he is looking for. Too many managers look where it is easy, not where it is useful. To be useful, we must look in the right area and solve the right problem, even when it is difficult.

There are many experts who know the answer. They are like solutions drifting across the business world in search of a problem to which they can attach themselves. Their pitch is as beguiling as that of the quack doctors in the Wild West selling their miracle cure-all medicines. Because they offer an easy answer, often management leaps aboard the bandwagon. A good answer is useless if it answers the wrong problem. '42' is a good answer to: 'What is six times seven?' It is also, for some people, a good answer to: 'What is the meaning of life?' It is not such a good answer to: 'What is the capital of Croatia?'

Finding the right problem is not easy. We are offered cost cutting, re-engineering, supply chain management, service excellence and all manner of initiatives. In all cases, repeatedly asking 'why' helps.

Case Study

Finding the real problem

A hotel manager wanted to raise room rates. We started to ask why. We took a couple of weeks of digging around to find the data which produced this logic flow:

We must raise room rates	Why?
Because we must improve profits	Why?
Because profits are down	Why?
Because our costs per customer are up	Why?
Because we are getting fewer customers	Why?
Because competitors charge less than us	So…

We should reduce room rates

Naturally, the logic flow does not drop out quite as simply as that. It might take anything from a few minutes to a few months to tease out the logic flow. In this case, the logic flow encouraged the hotel manager to take exactly the opposite action from his first intention: he cut room rates instead of raising them.

The wrong sponsor

There is an easy way of finding the right problem – find the right sponsor. Consultants love working for chief executives, for several reasons:

- You always get paid.
- The CEO has the power and authority to make things happen and can cut through political log-jams.

● A CEO project always succeeds. Even if it fails, it will still be made to look like a success in public.

It is possible that the CEO is solving the wrong problem. In practice, there is often a conspiracy of silence that lets the CEO plough on in the wrong direction. Challenging the CEO is a dangerous sport. You may land up becoming highly trusted and valued for your insight and honesty. You may land up doing the corporate equivalent of cleaning toilets in Siberia.

Not all projects are CEO projects, but the same characteristics are required of a good sponsor:

● The project should be a 'must-win' battle for the future personal success of the sponsor. You want a sponsor who is totally committed to success. Otherwise, you suffer asymmetric risk: you take the risk of failure while the sponsor walks away, or the sponsor claims the credit if you succeed.

● The sponsor must have the power and influence to be able to overcome all the political log-jams that occur on any project.

● The sponsor has to have enough authority and resources to enable the project to happen.

The wrong team

Inevitably, the people you want on a project team are not available. If people are good, then they are fully committed elsewhere. The only people who are available are the people sitting on the beach, waiting to become fully utilised. They are typically a mix of the untried and untested, together with a few who have been tried and tested and have not covered themselves in glory. Even if some good people are available, they may well not have the particular technical skills that are important for the success of your project.

At this point, the successful project manager should play hardball. Accepting the B team is a recipe for B-grade results, long nights, crises and frustration.

A good way of testing how important a project is, is to see who is placed on to the project team. If the sponsor and CEO are happy to see a B team on the project, they clearly regard it as a B-type priority. This is a good time to walk away from the project. If they are prepared to make sacrifices and release the A-team players from their other commitments, then clearly they regard the project as having A-grade priority.

The wrong process

Of the four horsemen of project apocalypse, this is the least dangerous. It is also where project management manuals focus all their attention. But if you have the right problem, sponsor and team, then the odds are heavily stacked in your favour. The chances are that you will already have the right process. Even if it turns out to be the wrong process, you have enough fire-power in the team to correct your course.

Beyond the elaborate world of GANTT charts and PERT charts, there are three basics to the right process:

1 Start at the end, and work backwards.
2 Figure out the minimum number of steps required to get there.
3 Create an effective governance process.

Starting at the start is never a good idea. Define the end outcome as clearly as possible before the start so that everyone knows where they are heading. Knowing the destination minimises the risks of deviations *en route* and cost escalations from contractors.

> define the end outcome as clearly as possible before the start so that everyone knows where they are heading

If you know the end point, then figure out the minimum number of steps required to get there. There are always staffers who can discover bottomless pits of detail to fall into. The challenge for the leader is to make it simple so that everyone stays focused on what is really important. By looking for the minimum number of steps, the project manager should also be defining the critical path (what events need to happen before others can be started), which will also make it much easier to control and monitor progress.

Effective governance is essential. A good way to escalate costs and time is to change your mind frequently and make decisions slowly. This often happens where there is a political environment and not all the constituencies are truly aligned. Clear goals and clear decision-making processes are vital. The other governance trap is to have no governance: many projects are started but have no effective follow-through from top management. A strong leader in the middle of the matrix will insist on continued oversight from top management. This helps when it comes to keeping the project on track and overcoming obstacles. It also helps maintain the visibility of the project. A successful project which is invisible to top management does not help its leader much.

Managing change

Many people think that projects exist in the rational world of GANTT charts, progress meetings and task groups. Anyone who has breathed air in an organisation will know that they are highly political. Organisations are also full of people. Unlike computers, most people have emotions. So projects do not live on a purely rational planet all of their own. They live in a world which is:

- rational
- political
- emotional.

The assiduous project manager will work in the rational world of the project. As a change leader you have to work with the political and emotional agendas of colleagues to effect change and to assure the success of diverse projects.

'Working the political and emotional agendas' sounds very vague and slightly undoable. Much of it does come down to experience, which does not help much if you don't have the experience. Even if you do have the experience, it pays to have something more structured than your innate genius and intuition to rely on when it comes to making change. What worked last time may not work in different circumstances this time.

In practice, there are three tools that can help you maximise the chances of success in dealing with change:

1 Setting up change to succeed.

2 Managing the change process.

3 Managing the change network.

Setting up change to succeed

Most sane people do not enjoy change. Change implies uncertainty and risk. Even if I can succeed currently, how do I know that I can succeed in a new environment with a new boss doing new things? The less control over the change I have, the more I am likely to fear it. So change is dominated by the **FUD** factor:

- **F**ear.
- **U**ncertainty.
- **D**oubt.

The only people who do not suffer from the FUD factor are CEOs, senior leaders and consultants. They are able to control the change, and they know how they intend to benefit from it.

Over the years, one simple formula has been a constant predictor of change success or failure. Here it is, in all its spurious mathematical accuracy:

$$V + N + C + F \geq R$$

V = Vision. This is not a 'save the planet' type vision. Create a worthwhile goal which convinces people that the destination is a good one, and that they have a role to play in it. The vision has to mean something to the organisation, to the team and to each individual. Increasing Earnings Per Share is pretty meaningless to a shop-floor worker.

N = Need. There has to be a perceived need to change, both for the institution and for the individual. Show that the risks of doing nothing must outweigh the risks of doing something. Fear is often a powerful motivator for change. You will find yourself spending much of your time selling both your vision and the need to change the organisation.

C = Capacity to change. It is no use having both the vision and the need if the organisation lacks the skills or resources to change. Your team wants to know that they can make the journey from today to tomorrow successfully. They also need to trust you. If you announce a new five-year plan every six months, then the next five-year plan is likely to be greeted with some cynicism.

F = First steps. We live in a world of instant gratification. We want to know that we are backing a winner. Use this to your advantage. Seek out some early wins – some early signs of success that will bring all the doubters and fence-sitters on board.

R = Risks and costs of change. The risks and costs to the organisation can normally be dealt with fairly rationally. The killer risks are the emotional and political risks to individuals and departments, who all suffer the FUD factor in change. You have to de-risk the perceived risk of the change. The rational risks can be mitigated rationally: phasing investments to minimise exposure, testing ideas, prototyping and so forth. The FUD factor will often be hidden behind rational reasons. When people don't want to do something, they become very creative and articulate in discovering rational reasons why they should not do it. Look past this rational veil to spot the political and emotional concerns involved. Working in private, you can reduce the FUD factor, typically in three ways:

- **Try to align the vision** of the change with the personal vision and expectations of the other person or department. Find common ground.

- **Try to alter the perceived risk** of doing nothing versus changing. Increasing the fear of inaction is effective although unkind.

- **Give the other people a sense of involvement** or control over the change. Simply asking for their advice helps allay their concerns and makes them feel less threatened.

As a leader, it pays to work the whole agenda. Constantly remind people of the vision and relate it to their needs. Build up the need to change and the risks of doing nothing. Find some early successes to keep people encouraged, and make sure that there is enough capacity to support the change. All of this needs to be balanced against risk reduction: few people truly enjoy risk. The greater the perceived risk, the greater the resistance to change. Make the change very low risk, and no one will get in your way.

Managing the change process

Project managers can manage the technical and rational aspects of change. As a change leader you must manage the political and emotional consequences of change. Most significant change programmes go through a predictable emotional and political cycle, outlined in Figure 6.2 overleaf.

If you have used the change equation successfully, then there will be some early enthusiasm for change. Some early wins bring more of the doubters on board, and everything starts to look good. It is at this point that things start to go wrong. After the initial flush of enthusiasm dies away, slowly people start to understand the scale of the change required. They start to see the logical consequences of change; the exciting vision of the change which you painted becomes obscured by the reality of the effort and risks involved.

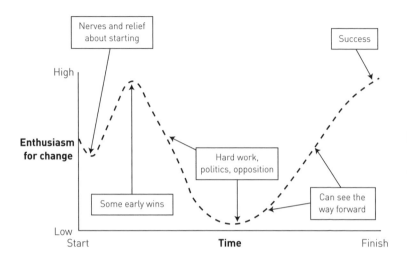

Figure 6.2 Change and the valley of death

There is rarely one event that triggers collapse. Usually the change slowly meanders into a swamp of despair.

The fair-weather friends who hopped on board at the first sign of success are hopping off at the first sign of trouble. They now create distance between themselves and your change. They may offer advice, but it is poisoned advice. Take the advice and then they will claim they turned the programme around. Refuse the advice and they will have the ammunition to show that you failed because you refused the advice. Suddenly, you can start to feel very lonely and very beleaguered.

Inevitably, prevention is better than cure for the mid-life crises of change. If you have put in the right preconditions for success, both in terms of project management and in terms of the change agenda, you will pull through. If the change was started prematurely, you may fail. There will not be enough belief in the vision or enough political support to overcome the opposition to change.

Curiously, the valley of death is essential to most successful change programmes. It is only in the valley of death that people fully realise the scale of the change they will need to make. Opposition to change is the surest sign that they are at last taking the change seriously, that they are engaged. Do not avoid the valley of death: seek it out.

In most major changes I have started, I have alerted the client or the sponsor to the change cycle and the valley of death at the start. If they know it is coming, they worry about it less: they realise it is natural and are ready to work through it. In several cases the CEO has kept on asking, like a child on a long journey, 'Are we there yet? Is this it? Have we got to the valley of death yet?' The valley of death experience is uncomfortable but important. It is the moment when everyone realises that they can no longer continue with the old ways, even if they do not yet know what the future holds. This is when everyone is really grasping reality and is ready to move on.

In the valley of death, followers give up. Leaders look to the future: keep your eyes fixed on the end goal and figure out the way of getting there. At a time when everyone else is seeing problems, you will stand out by offering solutions and actions. In this slough of despondency, people want solutions. The valley of death is your moment of truth: it is when you prove your capability and it will be when you learn and develop the most.

If all this does is to give you some hope next time your change effort hits crisis, then it has at least done some good. Remember, the difference between success and failure is often no more than persistence.

> the difference between success and failure is often no more than persistence

Managing the change network

There is one big catch in setting up change to succeed. Leaders often want everyone to join their jolly bandwagon. Normally, this is not possible. There will always be some diehards who would resist anything. The successful change network consists of those people who collectively have the power, skills and resources to assure the success of the change. In addition, the change leader needs the critical mass of the organisation to be supportive. It is a trap to try to engage the whole organisation. The challenge can be seen in Figure 6.3.

This diagram shows that most people feel pretty indifferent to the idea of change in principle. In practice, their enthusiasm will wax and wane depending where they are in the valley of death. But the bell curve effect will always be present.

There are always extremes at each end of the change bell curve. At one end are the change enthusiasts whom you can recruit as the active leaders and early adopters of change. At the other end, some will always resist. Do not waste time on them. Let them see that the change is succeeding, and let them make up their own minds.

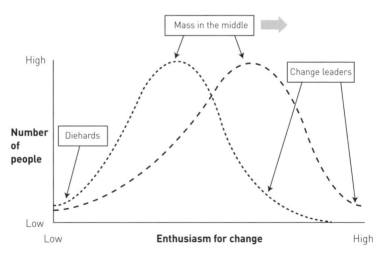

Figure 6.3 Shifting the change bell curve

They will start to feel lonely, left on the platform after the change train moves off. They can decide to leave or get on board. And if they want to protest by lying down on the tracks in front of the train, let them know the train will not stop anyway. The change resisters can consume a disproportionate amount of management time and effort. In practice, management needs to move the mass of people from neutrality to mild acceptance of change. Again, do not expect everyone to become change enthusiasts.

Case Study

Achieving critical mass

At one chemicals company, the plant manager was very frustrated that he could not implement a new set of working practices. We were asked to help. We soon heard loud objections to the whole change idea, expressed very forcibly. They used every reason to object: from cost to work–life balance to health and safety to threats of walkouts. But we found the objections were all coming from a small group of staff and managers in the power plant. Most other people were quietly supportive, but felt overawed by the loud-mouthed middle managers. And the plant manager had let himself become hostage to them – they had secured an effective veto over his plans. Instead of focusing on the objectors, we focused on the supporters. As we started to implement the changes in the more supportive areas, people realised they liked the changes and became bolder about supporting them. We did not need to negotiate with the objectors: one by one they made their own decisions. Some got with the programme, some got out. As a change leader, do not try to please all the people all the time: you will get nowhere.

Aside from the mass of people, you must build the right power network in support of change. Building networks and alliances is essential to your success in the middle of the matrix, and is the subject of the next section.

Acquiring power: the 10 laws of power

The days of command and control are long gone. Power in the modern organisation is the art of making things happen through other people whom you do not control. Things have moved on since Machiavelli wrote *The Prince*. His advice included executing a few people to keep everyone else under control: some managers ritually fire a few people to achieve the same effect. For the most part, acquiring and using power in today's organisations is not about plotting, scheming, betrayal and terrorising your team and your colleagues, although there are some managers out there who like to act that way. Terrorising people over whom you have no control is unlikely to get you far. You need a more subtle set of power skills. Without political skills a potential leader is unlikely to go far in a modern organisation.

A brief history of management

To discover the secret of becoming a successful leader, we will take a short diversion through the entire history of modern management. There are three eras of modern management.

1 From the Enlightenment to the Ford Model T

Isaac Newton is the inspiration for modern management. After he discovered the laws of physics, people wanted to discover the laws of everything. Darwin unravelled biology. Adam Smith tried to unravel economics, and was astounded by the productivity gains that could be achieved by specialisation. A group of semi-skilled workers could produce a hundred times more pins than one skilled artisan. Henry Ford put the specialisation into practice by creating the first car production line for the Model T. This was the start of a trend where the Brits thought up clever ideas (jet engines, computers, world wide web) and the Americans made a fortune from them. This was the world of rational management, epitomised by Frederick Taylor in *Scientific Management*. Being smart and rational went hand in hand with being successful.

2 The rise of humanity

Something went wrong with the rational world. Being a brain on sticks was not enough to succeed.

The workers would have disappointed Marx: instead of rising up, they became educated. They made money, they had choices over where to work and where to spend. They were no longer just factors of production and consumption. To the horror of managers, they had to be treated like, well, human beings. This was perplexing. Eighty years after Freud and Jung had been discovering the humanity in humans, Daniel Goleman became the patron saint of humans at work. Suddenly, managers not only had to have a high IQ, but they also needed a high EQ or emotional quotient.

3 Back to the future

Look around your organisation. You will probably see plenty of people who are smart (high IQ) and good with people (high EQ). And they languish harmlessly in the backwaters of the organisation while people who are not so smart or so nice rise to the top. Something is clearly missing from the leadership formula. The missing element has been recognised since the Renaissance and Machiavelli. What is missing is the political element. As organisations become flatter, so politics increases: you have to make things happen through people over whom you have no control. It is easy to hide but difficult to shine in such an organi-

> the missing ingredient for successful leaders is PQ: political quotient

sation. Wherever there are people, there are politics, and flat organisations are the perfect breeding ground for the most intense politics of all. The missing ingredient for successful leaders is PQ: political quotient.

This short detour through the history of management shows what most practising managers always knew. To succeed you need a combination of IQ (intelligence quotient), EQ (emotional quotient) and PQ (political quotient). The middle of an organisation is where these skills are tested to the full.

Politically adept leaders consistently display 10 types of behaviour. These behaviours give them high PQ or political quotient. High PQ is as important to success as good IQ (intelligence quotient) and EQ (emotional quotient). The good news is that all of these behaviours can be learned: you do not have to be born a politician to acquire high PQ. These 10 behaviours can be thought of as the 10 laws of power (these laws are explored more fully in a sister book to this, *Power at Work*):

1 Take control.

2 Build your network.

3 Act the part.

4 Strike early.

5 Pick your battles.

6 Be (selectively) unreasonable.

7 Go where the power is.

8 Embrace ambiguity.

9 Focus on outcomes.

10 Use it or lose it.

A brief summary of each law follows.

1 Take control

The best book you never need to read is called *Control Your Destiny or Someone Else Will* by Jack Welch, the former CEO of GE. Once you have read the title, you have got the most important message of the book. Gaining control is essential long before you become CEO. You have control if you control the agenda. Controlling the agenda comes down to the ability to tell a very simple story in just three parts:

- This is where we are.
- This is where we are going.
- This is how we are going to get there.

By taking control with a clear agenda, you create clarity and focus for you, your team and your colleagues. Even if they disagree, at least the debate will focus on your agenda, not theirs. The need for clarity and focus is especially important at moments of crisis, conflict and confusion. This is when most people hide. It is when the high PQ manager takes control and stands out from the rest of the herd.

2 Build your network

Standard operating procedure today is to find that your responsibilities are far greater than your formal authority. You cannot tell people what to do: you rely on the support of a wide range of people within and beyond the organisation. The essence of a strong network is trust: if people trust you, they are more likely to help and support you. Building networks of trust is covered more fully in the next section. At this point, simply note that your political power is directly related to the breadth and quality of your network. Network economics come into play: weak networks remain weak because no one wants to join them. Strong networks become ever stronger because everyone wants to be part of the power network. Make sure you are at the hub of a true power network.

3 Act the part

If you want to look and act like a junior manager, your wish will be granted: you will remain a junior manager. If you want to be taken seriously, observe how people two levels above you act and dress. Decode their rituals, values and behaviour. If you don't like them, get out. Otherwise, adapt to the style of power. This can be as shallow as how you dress: people should not be judged that way, but they are. But it can be more subtle. Senior managers do not convince each other with 300-page PowerPoint presentations. Peers persuade each other through conversation. If you go to a senior manager with your big PowerPoint presentation, you will be treated like a subordinate. Instead, discuss the idea with a well-thought-through conversation that allows you to be treated as a peer with the big shot. Act as their partner, helping them work through their agenda and their needs, instead of trying to hard sell them on your idea. This is the partnership principle: act as their partner, not as their servant (unless you want to be their servant).

4 Strike early

Striking early is a very good way of taking control of the agenda. By acting pre-emptively, the high PQ leader sets the terms of the debate. A few examples serve to make the point:

- **Negotiating budgets**. Agree the broad objectives early, before they are dictated to you. Once the framework has been set, you have lost 80% of your room for manoeuvre: you are left arguing over the details of the remaining 20%.

- **Managing crises**. The earlier a crisis is sorted out, the less painful it is. If you have the plan to sort it out, you retain control and minimise the pain and the risk. The longer it goes on, the more likely you are to lose control completely to someone else.

- **Getting the right assignment**. Waiting for HR to announce the latest job opportunities means that you are too late. Your network should alert you to what opportunities are coming up. Some may be the sort of opportunity where you need the Harry Potter cloak of invisibility to avoid the career death assignment. Others you need to grab before anyone else has even heard of the opportunity.

- **Managing meetings**. Meetings should never be used to make decisions. By the time the meeting starts, you should know exactly what the outcome will be. The meeting should simply be public confirmation of all the deals you have already brokered in private. Stay in control and avoid unpleasant surprises.

5 Pick your battles

Organisations are set up for conflict. Conflict is how organisations allocate limited resources between the competing claims of different product, geographic, customer and functional groups. As long as there are not enough resources, bonuses and promotions to go around, there will be conflict. For most managers the real competition is not in the marketplace; it is sitting at a desk nearby. However, many battles are pointless and are ways in which good managers lose friends and alienate people: unnecessary battles destroy the networks of power and influence on which successful managers and leaders depend. It pays to know when it is worth fighting. Sun Tzu, writing the *Art of War* 2,800 years ago, outlined the three conditions for going into battle, which work in today's corporate world:

- Only fight when there is a prize worth fighting for.
- Only fight when you know you will win.
- Only fight when there is no other way of achieving your goal.

Most corporate battles fail at least one, and often all three, of these rules.

6 Be (selectively) unreasonable

Reasonable managers would have understood that it was impossible to take on the might of British Airways, General Motors, the BBC and American TV networks, IBM, the US Postal Service or any other entrenched market leader. Reasonable leaders would never have created Ryanair, Toyota, Sky and CNN, Apple, FedEx, Sony or any of the new upstarts.

Reasonable managers tend to accept the reasonable and logical reasons why something cannot happen. When you accept excuses, you accept failure.

when you accept excuses, you accept failure

High PQ leaders know how to stretch, but not break, their followers. Stretching people develops them and delivers high performance; breaking them leads to long-term breakdown, which may follow illusory short-term success.

7 Go where the power is

If you want money, go where the money is. If you want fame, go where the fame is. If you want power, go where the power is. Of course, when you reach the very top of business, movies or politics you may achieve all three. But in the meantime, you will need to make some choices.

Every organisation has a power core. This is normally a function or career route through which the majority of future leaders are groomed. Staff functions may be important, but they are rarely on the power route. Life in the power centre is often demanding and uncomfortable. But this is where you can best make your mark, learn the real rules of success, influence events and accelerate your career. As with all aspects of PQ, you will find that career acceleration works both ways: you succeed fast or you fail fast. But at least you get to have a stake in the game, which is better than serving in a quiet outpost of the organisation where the risks and rewards are much fewer.

8 Embrace ambiguity

Nature, and business, abhors a vacuum. In business a vacuum often occurs where there is ambiguity, uncertainty or crisis: no one is quite sure what to do or who is in control. The high PQ leader learns to recognise these moments of truth and to take advantage of the right ones by filling the vacuum. These moments include both the predictable and the unpredictable:

- Who is going to take control of the off-site team meeting?
- How shall we respond to the latest competitive move?
- Who should work on this project?
- How can we deal with this crisis?

The high PQ leader who takes control early, takes the high ground. This is your chance to stand out as positive and action focused. Other managers are then left scrambling for smaller roles and responding to the agenda which you have just seized. If you are very smart, take great care to share out all the credit when success is achieved. By doing this, you will earn the gratitude of your followers while also showing that you led the initiative: only the leader is in the position to hand out credit for success.

9 Focus on outcomes

Focus on outcomes should be obvious, but it is not. Many managers find it easier and safer to focus on analysis, processes, procedures and problems. This is safe but gets nowhere. Achieving results means focusing on outcomes, not on navel gazing. Outcome focus enables you to take control, look positive and achieve results. Outcome focus starts by asking some simple questions:

- **Meetings**: what do I want from this meeting (regardless of the formal agenda)?
- **Conflict with another department**: what is the best outcome for both of us and how do we get there?
- **Crises and setbacks**: what is the outcome we need to get to? Looking forward is better than looking back and doing a post-mortem to see who is to blame.

Within an organisation, senior management very quickly spots people who are always driving to action and to solutions, versus those who retreat to the comfort zone of analysis and procedures. The future leaders are the ones with the courage to look forward to action, not backwards to analysis.

10 Use it or lose it

Once you have your hands on the levers of power, use those levers. The more you use your formal authority well, the more formal and informal power you will attract. If you do not use your power well, other people will be more than happy to fill the power vacuum: you will find that you are reacting to their agenda and your own agenda starts to get sidelined. Eventually you will be sidelined as well. Many managers fail to make a difference. In most organisations the best predictor of next year's budget, strategy and performance is this year's budget, strategy and performance. That is a symptom of an organisation drifting with the tide: that works in good times, not when times are hard.

If you want to succeed, you have to make a difference. The simple test is this: 'What will be different next year as a result of my performance in this role?' Answering emails, working late, beating budget by 6% do not count as making a difference. The difference should be big enough to be noticed at least two levels higher up the organisation. And if you are at the top of the organisation, it should be big enough to be noticed in the postroom as well as in the boardroom.

> if you want to succeed, you have to make a difference

What is the network a leader needs to build?

Organisations have formal power structures which are well known. Leaders need to tap into the informal power network, which is at least as important when it comes to making things happen.

In the complicated world of the matrix, it pays to achieve simplicity and clarity. At the risk of being trite and over-simplistic, here is a simple acronym to help figure out the network the leader needs – **GRANTS**:

- **G**atekeepers.
- **R**esources.
- **A**uthorisers.
- **N**etwork nodes.

- **T**echnical influencers.
- **S**ponsors.

To make the simple complicated for a moment, we will start at the end. Each part of the network can offer you different things, and each looks for different things in return. It is worth remembering that this is a business network, not a social network. They are colleagues first. If they are friends, that is useful but secondary. Remember the dictum of Lord Palmerston, the nineteenth-century British prime minister: 'Nations have no permanent friends or enemies. They only have permanent interests.' The business leader rarely has permanent friends *or* permanent enemies.

Sponsors are essential for career survival and success. They are probably not your immediate boss. Hopefully, they are at least one level above that. A good sponsor is a power figure in the organisation who can act as your mentor, coach and occasional political fixer. When you are faced with the potential of an impossible assignment with an impossible boss, this is the time to cash in your chips with the sponsor and find a way of dodging the bullet coming your way. There is an informal psychological contract with the sponsor: you make yourself useful to the sponsor through odd jobs and useful information about what is happening. The sponsor then looks out for your interests in return.

Authorisers are your bosses. The rules of managing up to bosses have been covered earlier in Chapter 1. Ultimately, loyalty is prized above all, and then performance. Although they have authority over you, they do not have the authority to help you achieve all you need to achieve; you need your own network for this.

Resources are the people and skills at your disposal. Again, they are unlikely to represent all that you need to accomplish all your goals. An effective leader will also leverage resources throughout the rest of the organisation by begging, borrowing and stealing them. They will make alliances with other authorisers or resource holders to work on a common agenda. We will cover the process of influence building in the next section. More traditional managers will try to do it by themselves with their own resources: this lack of leverage and support makes achieving the best outcome practically and politically nearly impossible, while also consigning the managers to many late nights and high stress.

Technical influencers are essential to success. They lack much formal authority, although informally they have power of veto over things. The classic technical influencer is the finance department. They look over proposals and check that they are fit and proper. If they are not on your side, they can destroy any proposal you have. Make friends with them early. Comply without complaint with their unreasonable demands. Involve them early on in your proposal and actively seek their advice in shaping your idea; they will be flattered that you value them. Finance are the sheriffs who keep order in town. As any cowboy knows, you can really have fun when the sheriff is on your side.

Network nodes seem to know all the right people. They may have little formal authority themselves. Perhaps a few key executives share a common personal coach. Or there is an old-timer in HR or another staff function whom everyone trusts: they are going nowhere and have no ambition but are seen as absolutely trustworthy. Because they are seen to be above the political fray, these people's views often carry weight. They also tend to be very well informed because everyone talks to them. This naturally makes them even better informed, so even more people talk to them. Find these people, find what makes them tick and bring them on board.

Gatekeepers can be very useful or very damaging. A good gatekeeper can help you gain access to executives who are hard to get to. A poor gatekeeper will promise access and will turn out to be either unwilling or unable to gain you access; you will have wasted valuable time not getting to the right people. The most obvious gatekeepers are secretaries. People tend to mistreat them in at least one of three ways:

- Ignoring them or using them as doormats on the road to power.

- Treating them as servants and ordering them around.

- Condescending to them. Flowers, chocolates and long conversations may be fine for lovers, but most secretaries like to be seen for what they are: skilled professionals doing a good job. Treat them that way, and they will treat you well in return.

Building your network of trust and influence

You build a network the same way you build a wall: one brick at a time. It takes time and care. Each alliance with each individual in the network will be based on a slightly different psychological contract. At the heart of this contract is the Trust Equation. As individuals, we are prepared to support and follow people we trust. Certainly, we do not follow people we do not trust. Trust is the basic currency of any alliance.

The Trust Equation is simple to describe but hard to fulfil. There are four key elements to the trust equation:

1 **T** = Trust.

2 **I** = Intimacy (shared values).

3 **C** = Credibility.

4 **R** = Risk.

Once again risking spurious mathematical accuracy, here is the **Trust Equation**:

$$T = (I \times C) \div R$$

T = Trust. The more mutual trust there is, the greater the degree of mutual influence.

I = Intimacy. But not in the normal sense of the word. Although getting into bed with the boss has a long and ignoble history of success, you make your own decision on that. Intimacy here means having similar values and interests: we both talk the same language, see the world the same way and share some common goals and interests. This intimacy comes from spending time with people and listening to them. The more you listen, the more you understand and the more they will appreciate you.

Executives often leave clues to let you establish common interests, even when you have never met. Photographs are a giveaway. Pictures of houses and cars (ask about them – probably their pride and joy); pictures of football teams (commiserate with them for supporting a team like Spurs); pictures of lakes (ask them about their holidays). Once you have a mutual interest, you have the chance of building mutual understanding. If there are no pictures on the wall or mementoes on the table, you may have a hard ass who just wants to get down to business.

C = Credibility. If intimacy means talking the talk, then credibility is about walking the walk. You have to be able to deliver on what you say. If you are all talk and no action, you are little more than an amusing irritant. Think of it as building up personal equity. Each time you deliver on something which is of interest to the other person, your personal stock rises. Each time you need a favour in return, you are drawing on your equity. It pays to keep a mildly positive balance. If you are always doing things for someone, they may well take you for granted. It needs to be a partnership in which they commit as much time and effort as you do.

R = Risk. Our old friend risk is never far away. We may trust strangers and new employees with trivial tasks. But the more important the task, the deeper the trust has to be. Building trust takes time. We have to earn our spurs and show that we can be trusted on ever more challenging and risky assignments.

Clearly, this Trust Equation will be at different stages of development with different individuals. As a leader, you need some way of accelerating this network development.

A quick way to gain trust is to go to the bank and borrow it. You may need to build trust and influence with someone you do not know well in the organisation. But the chances are that they know someone who knows you. If that person is your strong supporter, then that reference will carry credibility with the other person.

One of the best fundraisers I ever met would spend the first 15 minutes of a meeting with a new prospect just talking about potential mutual acquaintances. Soon enough, the two strangers would figure out that they knew several people in common. They would talk about them glowingly. Inside 15 minutes, they would have got themselves on to the first rung of mutual trust, despite never having met before. Once they had some element of trust, the fundraiser could start to talk about business.

There is one final trick the leader needs to play to build an alliance in a hurry. It is something that all good entrepreneurs know how to do instinctively. They create a sense of inevitability about what they will do. They don't use *if*, they use *when*. They talk up the level of support and commitment they have. If finance are still looking at the proposal with a fine-tooth comb, then they 'are deeply involved with the programme and helping to position it right'. Entrepreneurs create a huge sense of enthusiasm around the vision they have and deliberately make light of the risks and challenges. When I decided to start a bank, with neither the skills nor the money, I approached potential partners with the total conviction that the bank would happen. The only questions were who would be lucky enough to be my partner, and who would lose out on the huge opportunity. If you do not believe in yourself, no one else will.

Chapter 7

Being professional

B y the time leaders finally emerge from the ranks of bright-eyed graduates, they have probably become thoroughly domesticated animals. They have learned the behavioural norms of the organisation. They have learned some craft and trade skills in their industry; they know how to trade bonds or cut code. They have performed well enough to get promoted. They are converting the potential of future leaders into the reality of current leadership.

So it seems unfair to suggest that the matrix professional needs to learn how to be professional. Membership of the matrix implies that a basic standard of professionalism has already been achieved. The situation is like that of the medieval guilds. The apprenticeship has been served, but the apprentice is not yet ready to become the master. In between the apprentice and the master is the journeyman, who hones and develops the basic skills *en route* to becoming the master.

For the matrix leader, professionalism is a mix of behaviours and skills. Professional behaviours are about demonstrating the values of a real leader and being a role model for others. Many people fail both at this level and at the top leadership level because they have failed to develop some of the core behaviours of successful leaders. If you do not develop them at this level, it is too late to hope that they will suddenly emerge at the top of the organisation.

At this point, take a deep breath and sit down. You are going to be asked to emulate the White Queen in *Alice's Adventures In Wonderland* who claimed, 'Sometimes I've believed as many as six impossible things before breakfast.' Below are six impossible things for you to believe before you proceed any further into the leadership journey:

1 We do not know how to **talk**.

2 We do not know how to **listen**.

3 We do not know how to **write**.

4 We do not know how to **read**.

5 We do not know how to **meet**.

6 We do not know how to **communicate**.

The list looks absurd. Of course, we all know how to read, write, talk and listen. We do it every day. So let's take a step back. *You* know how to read, write, talk and listen. But how about your colleagues? How much turgid drivel do you have to wade through in their emails, PowerPoint presentations and Word documents? How often have you been to conferences where some important panjandrum gets on stage and drones on at you, communicating nothing except their self-importance? Have you noticed how colleagues often don't get the message, even when you have communicated clearly with them in writing and in person? There is plenty of evidence that no one else can read, write, talk or listen.

At this point, the leader in the matrix should learn that an essential professional behaviour is humility. Humility is the gateway to self-awareness, learning and improved performance. The humble leader will always seek to improve their core communication skills. We spend most of our day talking, listening, reading or writing. It pays to be good at what you do all day.

We need to recognise that the core skills of reading, writing, talking and listening are fundamentally different in the social and managerial worlds. The ineffective professional recognises this and responds by creating ponderous documents full of management-speak. This is meant to make them look serious. The jargon-filled documents and speeches then fail in their core mission, which is to communicate.

The effective leader learns how to communicate effectively in an organisation. Good communication reflects good thinking, and is the hallmark of many strong leaders, from Churchill to Reagan.

In the following sections we look at the six impossible things we have been asked to believe. For each one, we look at how communicating in the managerial and social worlds is different and at how to become more effective. Each one of these skills areas can take a lifetime to learn. Strong leaders experiment, reflect and develop a style which suits them. The notes that follow are simply a way of helping to structure and accelerate your journey of discovery.

Learning how to talk

The Bambara are the largest farming tribe in Mali. They are largely illiterate. But they regard words as being close to gods. They say: 'Words create whole new worlds in the mind; words make people do things; words separate humans from beasts.' Words are powerful. The Bambara say that words should be forged like a blacksmith, woven like a weaver and polished like a cobbler. Not surprisingly, they value restraint in how people talk – better to talk little and well than to talk for the sake of it.

Words can have as much power in the management tribe as they can in the Bambara tribe. We cover the art of communicating, motivating, influencing and coaching one-to-one in other chapters. Here we will look at the specific challenge of talking to large groups. For emerging leaders these showpiece events can have a disproportionate influence on how they are perceived. Some people are terrified of such events and struggle to shine. The people who think that they are born demagogues often make even worse presentations. Everyone can benefit from learning the basic techniques of presenting effectively.

Effective speaking

> an audience is more likely to remember you than your message; in many ways, you are the message

It is a truism that an audience is more likely to remember you than your message; in many ways, you are the message. So if you are the king of the mumblers, dress like a tramp and slouch like a teenager in full hormonal angst, the chances are that the brilliance of your message will be lost on the audience. In contrast, if you can remember the three *E*s of communication, even a dull message is likely to come across well:

- Energy.
- Enthusiasm.
- Excitement.

It is as hard to fake these three *E*s as it is to rehearse spontaneity. But there are some things that can help. Some of the 'dos' include:

- **Throw away the script**. With it, you will sound wooden or, worse, like a politician. Instead, memorise your opening so that you can make a good start. Memorise your conclusion so that you can make a good finish. Memorise some choice phrases that you want to insert on your way through; each phrase is a waymarker on your speech. You will keep your structure and discipline while sounding spontaneous.

- **Avoid complicated slide presentations**. If you have slides, the principle is to have dumb slides but a smart presenter. The slide might have three or four key words to help the audience anchor where you are – you provide the commentary. The nightmare is to have smart slides which explain everything and a dumb presenter who reads the slides more slowly than the audience.

- **Stand on the front of your feet**, so that a slip of paper could pass under your heel. Weight on the back of the foot encourages slouching and lowers your energy.

- **Try to stand before going on stage**. If you are sitting down before speaking, all your energy is down. You are likely to over-compensate with a sudden rush of adrenalin.

- **Engage the audience**. Look individuals in the eye, rather than gazing into the middle distance. Billy Graham, the great American preacher, did this with devastating effect. Even in an audience of a thousand, he would pick out individuals and catch their eye for a moment or two. No one dared doze off and they felt that they were being addressed personally.

- **Vary your pace and pitch**. Dare to slow down when you come to an important point. Give your key points the space to be heard.

- **Keep it simple**. Focus on one or two messages at most. If you have a large audience, focus on the one or two key executives you want to influence. This will let you focus your message, get rid of excess material and let you tell a simple story.

The three *E*s are greatly enhanced by two more *E*s: expertise and enjoyment. If you are expert at your subject, you are more likely to relax and enjoy what you are saying. If you are enjoying it, your audience is likely to enjoy it as well. If you hate it, do not expect the audience to enjoy it. As an experiment, try telling someone about how the cost allocation system in your organisation works. See if you fall asleep before they do. Now try recounting one of the most memorable events in your personal or professional life. You will naturally display all five *E*s: energy, enthusiasm, excitement, expertise and enjoyment. Such a simple exercise shows that we can all speak well – we simply have to transfer our skills on to the big stage.

Making presentations

1 **Show energy, enthusiasm and excitement**

If you are not enthusiastic about your topic, no one else will be. Enjoy your talk and there is a chance that others will also enjoy it.

2 **Target your talk**

Be clear whom you are talking to, what it is they need to hear and why they need to hear it. This will let you reduce and simplify your message. In a large group, focus your message on the one or two people you most want to influence.

3 **Tell a story**

Show 'this is where we are, this is where we will get to and this is how we will get there'. Make the story clear from the start of your talk. Stick to one simple theme which everyone can remember.

4 **Engage your audience**

At minimum, focus on each individual one at a time and use eye contact; even better, make it interactive, ask and answer questions, and create small group work.

5 **Keep it short**

Your presentation is not complete when you can say no more; it is complete when you can say no less. Focus on your core message for your target audience.

6 **Ditch PowerPoint**

If you must use it, then have a smart presenter and dumb slides: simple slides with few words which you bring to life. Avoid smart slides with lots of data which a dumb presenter then reads slowly.

7 **Seek help in preparation**

Find a coach who can tell you who the audience will be and what they want; get an editor to review your slides; if necessary, get coaching on presenting skills and get help with your script.

8 **Practise, practise, practise**

The more often you present, the better you get. Do the same presentation many times and you build confidence and expertise; you can relax and enjoy.

9 **Arrive early**

Make sure all the logistics work and the room layout is right; have a back-up computer or memory stick; do a final check with the organisers that you have the right expectations; understand what has happened before your talk and be ready to adjust your talk if required.

10 **Start well and end well**

Script your opening so that you start well, however nervous you may feel; script your finish to end on a high (not 'any questions?') and script some choice phrases in between which can mark the start and end of each section of your talk.

Learning how to listen

Good listening is devastatingly effective. Like sincerity and spontaneity, it is difficult to fake. Good salespeople and good leaders, like most normal people, have one mouth and two ears and they use them in that proportion. People like listening to the one person they truly trust and admire: themselves. Give people the chance, and they will talk themselves into submission.

Each of the following three cases includes two approaches. Think about which approach is likely to be more effective in each case.

● **The sales call**. Spend 15 minutes telling your client about the wonders of new miracle Sudso, which cleans up the competition, and then ask for the sale. Naturally, the client will find a thousand objections and, at best, negotiate like crazy on price. Or let the client talk about their competitive situation, and direct your questions to helping them focus on the sorts of challenges that miracle Sudso happens to address. They will discover that they need Sudso and you can be their partner in solving their problem. You have moved from being a salesperson to a partner.

- **The staff challenge**. Your staff bring you a problem. You are the heroic leader who is the fountain of all knowledge, so you solve their problem and tell them exactly what to do. They leave the room feeling that you are clever, but they have no ownership over the solution. And they have learned dependence: it is easier to bring problems to you than it is to solve them themselves. Or you ask questions, let them figure out the answer and let them own both the problem and the solution, to which they are now committed because they feel it is their idea.

- **The performance review**. Tell the staff member that they are under-performing; be clear about what has gone wrong and what remedial action is expected. Watch them retreat, depressed or angry or in denial. Alternatively, let them talk through their performance. Ask questions to make them focus on what they can do better and how they can do better. Watch them leave, feeling cautiously optimistic that they have a way forward. They will also feel grateful and loyal to a boss who has listened and cared.

Listening is much more difficult than talking. Active listening requires acute thinking and acute questioning. There are three fairly straightforward things you can do to develop listening skills, apart from putting tape across your mouth to make you shut up:

> there are three fairly straightforward things you can do to develop listening skills, apart from putting tape across your mouth

1 Paraphrase.

2 Ask open questions.

3 Debrief.

Paraphrase

This is very simple and forces you to listen. When someone has said something and has reached a natural pause, it is tempting to pitch in with your own point of view. Avoid temptation. Instead, summarise in your own words what you heard the other person say. This does not signify agreement – it signifies only that you understood what they said and that you were listening. If you summarise incorrectly, they will correct you quickly and you will have avoided misunderstanding. If you summarise correctly, they will think that you are pretty smart because you have understood them. They will then feel emboldened to embellish what they have said. Paraphrasing builds understanding and respect. As a simple test, try paraphrasing what this section has said. As you paraphrase, you should also find it much easier to remember what has been said. If you say it, you remember it.

Ask open questions

This is a real art form. The right open questions will get the other person to focus and reflect on the right issues the right way. The key part of open questioning is to encourage the other person to give rich answers. The one thing to avoid is a closed question, which results in a yes/no-type answer.

Closed questions invite someone to take a position, which they then feel the need to defend. Avoid boxing them into a corner. Questions which fall into this trap often begin:

- 'Do you agree ...'
- 'Shall we go to ...'
- 'How much is ...'

If you know you will get the 'right' answer to these questions at the end of a discussion, they may be acceptable. If you get the 'wrong' answer, you will find yourself taking opposing positions and you are in a win/lose discussion.

Open questions invite rich answers. They avoid boxing people into a corner too early and allow options to be explored. As you let people talk, you let their trust in you build. Open questions often begin:

- 'Why did they ...'
- 'What happened when ...'
- 'How would you ...'

Inevitably, letting people talk takes more time than simply telling them what to do. The lazy and heroic form of leadership is to tell everyone what to do. The longer and less heroic route is more productive. It teaches people to think for themselves, to own their own problems and to find their own solutions.

Debrief

If there were more than two of you at the meeting, always try to debrief around three questions:

1 What did you hear/observe during the meeting?
2 How were they reacting?
3 Who does what next?

This need only take a few minutes. Inevitably, you will find that two people saw and heard different things. You will get far more value and intelligence out of the meeting by a quick debrief than by trying to take notes in the meeting. Note-taking simply gets in the way. It prevents observation. Writing obstructs thinking about how to manage the conversation. It puts the other people on their guard.

Learning how to write

Good business writing is one of those oxymorons which is up there with military intelligence, social services and head office help.★

★Try also: civil servant, controlled chaos, easy payments, collective responsibility, committee decision, job security, gourmet pizza, non-alcoholic beer, objective opinions and quick fixes.

It is definitely a case of 'Do as I say, not do as I do'. None of us is likely to write as well as our favourite novelist or screen writer. But at least we can save our colleagues from the kind of drivel that they impose on us from time to time.

For many years I was beaten up by an editor who kept on pulling my work apart. Eventually, I figured he caught me consistently on just five rules which I always broke, and still do too often.

1   Write for the reader.
2   Tell a story.
3   Keep it simple and short.
4   Make it positive in substance and in style.
5   Support assertions with facts.

This sounds easy. It is not; it requires real discipline and focus.

1 Write for the reader

Faced with the daily deluge of email, you may occasionally wonder why you are wasting your time on so much trivia. Much of it was not meant for you. You have been copied in on stuff on a just-in-case basis. But some emails have clearly been written for you personally. Even if they are poorly typed, with spelling errors and bad grammar, you are likely to read them. They are relevant to your needs and interests. The good writer thinks themselves into the position of the reader and writes for that person. When this happens, clarity and focus are achieved. You can drop much of what you could write and focus on what the other person needs to read. Avoid the trap of writing for yourself.

2 Tell a story

This does not have to be a literal story, like a nursery story or an adventure tale. Telling a story in business terms means marshalling the facts so that a coherent theme comes out, with a beginning (here's the problem or opportunity), a middle (here's the detail) and an end (so what do we do next?). The story should pass the elevator test: you can summarise it to your boss in a fast-moving elevator going a short distance. The virtue of telling a story is that it helps cut out all the noise that will confuse the message. Think of all the communications you receive every day: you really remember the headlines, not the detail. Focus first on getting the headline right, and then marshal the minimum required to back up the headline.

3 Keep it simple and short

Churchill wrote a long letter to his wife, Clementine, during the war. At the end he added a postscript: 'I am sorry I wrote you such a long letter: I did not have time to write you a short one.' Writing short is much harder than writing long. It requires real mental discipline. P&G used to be home of the one-page memo: young brand assistants had to summarise the entire progress of their brand for two months in one page. It may have been single spaced with no margins, but everyone kept to the same discipline, which forces the writer to focus on what is important and does not confuse the reader with irrelevant detail. Another thing that helps the reader is to keep words and sentences short. Jargon, fancy words and complicated sentences impress the writer more than the reader. Documents, like diamonds, benefit from good cutting. Your document is not complete when you can write no more: it is complete when you can write no less.

> documents, like diamonds, benefit from good cutting

4 Make it positive in substance and in style

People prefer to hear about opportunities and solutions rather than problems and difficulties. Be positive and sound positive. The classic bureaucratic trap is to write passively and in the third person: 'It has been ascertained that the following 27 points were deemed . . . to make your eyes glaze over with tedium.'

5 Support assertions with facts

The alert reader's nonsense detector will start squawking loudly when it encounters vague power words such as:

● important (to whom and why?)

● strategic (important with bells on)

● urgent (not to me it isn't).

Avoid vague power words unless you can back them up. If it is important, show why. Supporting assertions with facts can also include using illustrations, examples and references to support your case. An unsupported assertion is always open to challenge.

Learning how to read

Words

We have a problem – you are reading this. So why on earth do you need to learn how to read when you are already reading?

There is a difference between reading for pleasure and reading for business. I hope you get some pleasure, even if you are not a masochist, from reading this. But I will assume that you are really reading this for business. You have my commiserations. By way of apology, let me tell you a story.

Case Study

Reading with prejudice

We were all sitting together in the old-fashioned partners' office. We all knew what all the other partners were doing; we did not need email because we had ears. Most of the partners were very bright, but one of the partners, Bob, was about 100 watts short of brilliance. And yet the staff loved him and thought that he was brighter than the rest of us. This was deeply irritating to us.

One day I noticed Bob making some notes and I asked him what he was doing.

'I have some associates coming in. They are going to show me a draft of a document. I have not seen it yet. This is their little test to see if I am any use at giving feedback and to see if I am smart enough to understand their brilliant draft.'

I thought about this. I had always thought that associates bringing drafts was our chance to test them. Then I realised that Bob was right: they are also testing our ability as partners to add value to them. I asked Bob why he was making notes if he had not seen the draft in advance.

'Easy,' said Bob. 'I always make a note of three things before seeing a document blind or listening to a presentation. First, I note my own view of the subject. I do not want to be swayed by their internal logic. The better their logic is, the more difficult it is to challenge unless you already have a clear point of view yourself. I do not read openly; I read with prejudice. It makes me a better critic.'

'Ouch', I thought. I always read openly, and I always found it difficult to rise above the brilliance of the internal logic presented to me. I asked him what else he was noting.

'Second, I note down all the topics I expect to see covered. This helps me spot those things which are hardest to spot – things which aren't there. It always surprises them when I see the invisible gaps.'

'And last?' I asked.

'I make a quick note of any coaching points I want to cover with them,' replied Bob. 'It may be about writing style, analytic techniques, data presentation, whatever. They like it when I can give them something practical and positive to go away and work on.'

I suddenly realised that I had never learned how to read. I had read like an empty vessel waiting to be filled with other people's stuff. Socially, this is an enjoyable way of reading a novel. In managerial terms, it pays to read with prejudice and with an agenda:

- Know your point of view.
- Know what you expect to be covered.
- Have some coaching points ready.

Naturally, it is impossible to do this exercise for every email you receive, and you probably do not want to spoil reading for pleasure with this discipline. But if the meeting, presentation or document is important, it pays to go in properly prepared.

Of course, you might discover other things as you review the document or listen to the presentation, but at least you are now reading or listening with focused intent. Naturally, those of you who already read with intent are probably wondering why this reading section is missing one critical element: the art of speed reading. This is because my prejudice is that it is better to read a little well than a lot poorly.

Numbers

> managers use statistics the same way drunks use lampposts – for support, not illumination

Managers use statistics the same way drunks use lampposts – for support, not illumination. Numbers are armies of facts which can be marshalled in support of a business case. Numbers are rarely objective; they can all be spun and manipulated. Politicians know this better than anyone.

The numbers game finds its apotheosis in the spreadsheet. In the days before spreadsheets, senior managers could terrorise junior managers by checking their calculations: the senior manager would quickly add up a few columns or rows and if the number did not come to 100, the inquisition would start. Spreadsheets have destroyed this form of terror. Numeracy is no longer necessary to be very good at analysing spreadsheets. Most spreadsheets add up better and faster than most managers. Although the numbers may be correct, the thinking often is not. Dealing with spreadsheets is about good thinking, not good maths.

Many spreadsheets are constructed backwards from the bottom right-hand corner: that is where the desired outcome usually sits. If the spreadsheet is meant to deliver a 15% margin, or a £10 million profit, then the result is always going to be 15% or £10 million, plus a little bit to be on the safe side. We use the spreadsheet to change the assumptions until the correct answer is achieved.

Reviewing spreadsheets requires challenging the thinking, not the numbers. There are three questions you should always ask, listed below.

1 The venture capitalist's question

Who is behind this spreadsheet? Trust the spreadsheet as far as you trust the person who is behind it. A B-grade spreadsheet or proposal from an A★ manager who always delivers is worth far more than an A★ spreadsheet from a B-grade manager. If you are the person presenting the spreadsheet, it makes sense to have some A★ managers lined up to support you: borrow their credibility.

2 The banker's question

These are the classic 'what if' questions where you get to test sensitivities and assumptions in the spreadsheet. Start with the big assumptions: margins, growth, market size, costs, capital required. Do not bother about detail such as the cost of the coffee machine (unless your business is selling coffee machines): they will not make or break the analysis, even if you can prove yourself very clever by showing that such small assumptions are inaccurate.

3 The manager's question

Every manager of a function or a business will know the key ratios and critical numbers for their part of the business. Philip Green, the British retailing billionaire, can look at a rack of clothes and accurately cost and price them at first glance. You will know the critical budget numbers for your business. Check the spreadsheet to see if the numbers reflect the reality you live with: if the numbers appear to come from a different planet, start asking some probing questions.

None of these questions requires numeracy: they require clear business thinking. Ask the questions well, and people may start to think that you are the king or queen of the spreadsheet, even if you hate numbers.

Learning how to meet

Meetings are a wonderful substitute for work or responsibility. They are also the essence of management. Try explaining what you do to a three-year-old. Saying that you are the Senior Executive Vice President for MegaCorp will simply see all the toys getting thrown out of the window. Explaining that you build CRM databases will not help much either. Whatever leaders do, in practice they spend most of the day meeting people. Even a three-year-old understands that, more or less.

So it pays to have effective meetings. Now think of what proportion of the meetings you have to attend are truly effective. You may be lucky, in which case move on to the next section. You may be like the majority of managers who find too much of a limited day being drained away in ineffective meetings.

> meetings, like Liquorice Allsorts, come in all shapes and sizes

Meetings, like Liquorice Allsorts, come in all shapes and sizes. They range from informal one-to-one meetings to major conferences, from formal decision-making meetings of the board to brainstorming meetings of the staff. For the sake of brevity and sanity, this is not the time or place to explore every flavour of meeting. Effective meetings come down to three principles:

1 Right **purpose**.
2 Right **people**.
3 Right **process**.

Forests have been destroyed describing effective meeting processes. Let us save some trees and concentrate on the right people and the right purpose. If you have these, you are 80% of the way to success. If you do not have them, you are 100% of the way to failure.

The right people and the right purpose

After one particularly mind-numbing all-day meeting Dean, one of my mentors, looked very happy. I asked him what was wrong with him. He should have looked as unhappy as I felt. He explained he had three rules for any meeting. He applied them whether he was leading or attending the meeting, and it always helped him get a good result. Since then, the rules have been a productive guide for me to ensure that meetings have the right purpose and the right people. The three rules for any meeting are:

1 What do I want to learn?
2 What will I contribute?
3 What happens next?

Let's look at Dean's rules as applied to attending a meeting and leading a meeting.

Attending a meeting

Dean went to the all-day meeting with a very clear agenda, which had little to do with the official agenda. There were three people he had wanted to talk to, but they had all been elusive. He wanted to get some information and ideas from them. That was his learning rule. He also realised that the meeting gave him the chance to influence the CEO on one agenda item. He bided his time, and then moved in decisively on the one issue that mattered. Because he talked sparingly, when he did talk he commanded attention. He had fulfilled his contribution rule. By having both a clear learning and contribution objective, he had a series of follow-up actions with the CEO and the three people he had met. Everyone else had left the meeting frustrated because nothing had been achieved in the formal agenda. Dean left happy because he had gone to the meeting with a clear intent and purpose, which he had achieved.

Leading a meeting

Dean applied his three meeting rules to meetings he chaired. He used the rules to decide who should attend. He expected each person to contribute something *and* to do something by way of follow-up *and* to learn something useful. People could contribute by having decision-making power, having expertise or having resources they could contribute.

Resist the temptation to seek safety in numbers. More people reduce effectiveness. Senior people want bag carriers to be present because they have the detail; bag carriers want to be there to get exposure to the senior managers. If the senior people cannot master the detail, they should not be there. They probably should not be senior managers.

You can see the safety-in-numbers mentality even in the executive suite. Normally the discussion dissolves into a series of bilateral discussions between the CEO and individual directors. Each director is a fully signed-up member of the mutual preservation society. The only rule of membership is that 'I will not trample on your turf if you do not trample on mine'. So group discussion does not exist. Instead, each director plays a game of intellectual ping-pong with the CEO while the other directors are spectators waiting for their turn to have a game with the CEO.

Dean refused to let this happen. He would apply his three rules not just to the meeting as a whole, but to each agenda item individually. If an item was best handled bilaterally, he would not bring it to the larger group. This made his meetings small and effective. Also, everyone knew that the meetings were going to be effective and relevant to themselves, so they made a point of attending.

The right process

Having the right people and the right purpose for a meeting is essential. It also helps to have the right process.

We have already considered the parlour game played on the radio called 'Just a Minute'. The object of the game is to speak for one minute on a chosen subject without hesitation, deviation or repetition. It is very difficult. The same principles should apply to the meeting process – to manage it without hesitation, deviation or repetition.

Hesitation is a product of starting late. It is nearly mandatory for senior people to turn up last or late. This shows that:

- they are very busy
- their time is more important than yours, so you can wait.

They may be answering emails or practising the banjo, but they will still want you to wait. It is a common discourtesy that customers visit on suppliers, professionals on their clients, call-centre staff on their callers and managers on their staff. Live with it. Otherwise, putting up a clock in the office at least helps induce some guilt in those who are not shameless. As a leader, you can set an example: be prompt and show that time is valuable and individuals are respected.

Hesitation also comes from a loose timetable. Time the meeting to be as short as possible to force the pace. The Privy Council meets standing up. This is a good way of keeping long-winded politicians short. It was particularly short when the late Queen Mother, aged 98, presided over the meeting. Sitting down is not mandatory.

There are some times never to hesitate. Never be disturbed by interruptions. Leaders should remain totally focused. I learned this in Manila during a period with many electricity outages. The first time it happened the room went pitch black. I hesitated: big error. Next time it happened, I carried on my presentation as if nothing had happened at all. The discussion flowed on in pitch blackness.

Deviation is a common cause of delay. People ramble off the subject or delve into minutiae. A good chairperson should not let this happen. If you set up the 'Just a Minute' rules at the start of the meeting, it becomes easy to challenge deviators; you can even keep score during the meeting. At minimum, make people give the headline before the text, as in a newspaper column. The headline tells people whether it is worth listening to or reading. It forces the speaker to think about what they want to say before they launch into a ramble.

Repetition normally happens when someone thinks they are not being heard properly. So they keep on coming back to the same point time and again, and again, and again. The rolling of eyeballs and looks of disbelief from everyone reinforces the repeater's belief that they are not being understood. Do not roll your eyeballs at repetition. Paraphrase the speaker to check you have heard what they are saying; this shows them that you are listening and they may shut up. If they raise the same point, repeat the paraphrase. Even the most obtuse participant should figure out that they have been heard and they are being repetitive.

The right process is helped by the right context. Dark, stuffy rooms do not help. The seating layout in the room does not have to be taken as given. I have become an expert furniture mover over many years of arranging meetings. How people sit affects the dynamics of the meeting. Having tea and coffee available is great, but the smell of hot food arriving at the back of the room loses an audience fast. Figure out the logistics that will make the meeting work for you and the attendees.

Learning how to communicate

The previous five sections have all been about communicating. But they have also been about something more subtle and more important – learning how to think and behave as a leader. The leader's mindset in communication has two main characteristics:

1 Being proactive.
2 Decentring.

Being proactive

For many people, reading and listening are naturally reactive processes. Being called to a meeting is a reactive event. If you want to lead, do not be led by other people's agendas. Proactively think of your own agenda, your own point of view. As a result, you will have a much more productive and insightful interaction with the person who thinks they are leading the meeting, presenting or writing the report.

Decentring

Communicating well is not about clearly stating what you think. Good communication requires thinking your way into the head of the other person. If you can see the world through their eyes, you can start to communicate effectively with them. Your end goal remains the same: you still want to influence them. But the starting point is radically different. You start from where *they* are, not from where you are. Two journeys with the same destination will be completely different if they have different starting points.

good communication requires thinking your way into the head of the other person

Naturally, different people feel comfortable with different styles and forms of communication. Some like face-to-face communication; some prefer email. Some play hard-to-catch behind a defensive secretarial wall. Adapt your way of communicating to what works.

As a leader, you do not have to be a literary giant or a brilliant orator. But you must communicate well. This requires focus, discipline and clarity. These are good disciplines for any leader to acquire.

Part 3

Mastering leadership

Chapter 8

Leading from the top

S trange things happen to people when they get to the top of an organisation. They suddenly find that their jokes become funnier, their taste becomes impeccable and their judgement becomes excellent. Everyone starts being nice to you. And everyone wants a slice of your time and a chunk of your support for whatever their interest is. Staff, suppliers and customers cluster around you like moths drawn to an artificial light at night. Watch the CEO walk down a corridor. Staff more or less genuflect and walk backwards as their entourage sweeps by. It is like watching a medieval king at court.

This can be alarming. You make a casual suggestion to someone and suddenly find they are doing it: they have justified their idea on the basis that 'the boss says so ...'. You come into the office and you are having a bad hair day. You find that your little personal cloud of gloom has spread like a major depression over the entire office.

This newfound power can go to people's heads. Until now they have had plenty of people competing with them for promotion and plenty of bosses to remind them, gently, when they are being daft. These disciplines disappear, because few people choose to challenge the CEO.

With the previous disciplines of competition and honest feedback disappearing, things can start to go wrong quickly. Typical traps include:

● **Diving into the trough of status and entitlement**. This is not just about becoming a greedy fat cat, despised within and beyond the organisation. It is also about all the small signs of not caring: not sharing the pain of cost cutting, retreating to the comfort of the CEO's office and enjoying the status symbols of reserved parking, nights at the opera and golfing parties at the weekend.

● **Under-estimating your influence**. Everyone picks up their cues from you in terms of behaviours and direction. Innocent comments can get blown out of all proportion. Role-modelling the values of the organisation becomes a challenge of never letting your professional guard slip. The CEO lives in a goldfish bowl and is always being watched.

● **Riding the momentum of the organisation**. Many CEOs become stewards and custodians of a legacy they have inherited. This is a recipe for a quiet life. Leaders need to create a legacy, not live off one. They need a clear vision and direction.

● **Over-estimating your own capabilities**. Some leaders become dictators who enjoy command and control and try to decide everything. This is often portrayed as heroic and brilliant leadership. It is more likely to be highly ineffective leadership; no one person has a monopoly on wisdom. In a changing and complicated world, you have to recognise your limitations. Build a team which complements your strengths and weaknesses.

> recognise your limitations and build a team which complements your strengths and weaknesses

At this point, it is worth reminding yourself what people truly value in a leader at the top of an organisation:

● Ability to motivate others (people focus).

● Vision (positive focus).

● Honesty and integrity (professionalism: values).

- Decisiveness (professionalism: skills).
- Ability to handle crises (professionalism: skills).

Take a moment to think honestly about how well you score on each of those criteria. The list below shows the percentage of our respondents who were satisfied with their senior leaders on each of these five criteria:

1	Ability to motivate others	37%
2	Vision	50%
3	Honesty and integrity	54%
4	Decisiveness	50%
5	Ability to handle crises	47%

Most of our respondents felt their leaders had self-confidence (72%). The confidence of leaders in themselves is not mirrored by their followers. There is a large perceived leadership gap. What people say to your face and what they think is not the same thing. You will be the last person to find out that people think you suck.

If you do not have a coach whispering in your ear, the danger is that the first piece of honest feedback will come from the chairperson when they fire you. With the career expectancy of a FTSE-100 CEO now below five years, tolerance of sub-par performance is evaporating fast. Everyone who becomes a leader thinks that they will succeed – the evidence is that an increasing number fail.

We will look in this section at how you can deliver against the top five leadership criteria. Some of them, like honesty and integrity, look absurdly simple. As we talked to our leaders, it became clear that this is a high hurdle to jump. Other criteria, like vision, look daunting; we cannot all be visionaries. But here we found some reassuringly practical and simple things you can do to create and communicate a vision.

The challenge for senior leaders is that they are often very poor at learning. Old dogs do not learn new tricks. By the time you reach the top you will have 20 years of success behind you. You will not take kindly to someone coming along with a theory which says that your practice is no good. It is easier to stick with a tried and tested formula. The only problem is that at the top of the organisation you need new skills. So instead of offering a theory of top leadership, this section is based on the experience and practice of top leaders from across industries and continents.

The mindset of a leader

1 **Start at the end**

Focus on where you want to get to; be clear about the outcome you want to achieve, the impact you will make and the difference you will leave.

2 **Take responsibility**

Take responsibility for your performance, for the performance of your team and for your career, your conduct and your feelings.

3 **Raise the bar**

Set challenging and stretching goals for yourself and others; force business not as usual; dare to achieve.

4 **Drive to action**

Focus on what you can do, not on what you cannot do; prefer action to analysis; look to the future, not to the past.

5 **Be positive**

Find a role where you can flourish; you only excel at what you enjoy; maintain energy, excitement and enthusiasm for what you do.

6 **Always deliver**

Accept no excuses; setbacks are a reason to learn, not a reason to scale back; be inflexible on goals but flexible on how to get there.

7 **Work hard**

Be prepared to go the extra mile; take on new opportunities.

8 **Work through others**

Build a loyal and committed team around you; invest time to build your team and build your network of trusted allies.

9 **Act the part**

Be a role model to those around you; live up to the standards of the role models you most admire.

10 **Keep on learning**

Push your limits; stay curious; try new roles and experiences; always reflect on what works and does not work; adapt your way of working; be open to feedback.

Before you relax into the CEO's suite and congratulate yourself on reaching the top of your profession, it is worth knowing what success really looks like. We have already established that leadership and title is not the same thing. Being CEO does not mean you are a successful leader. Followers have their expectations of what a good leader looks like, but what should you expect to achieve as a top leader?

There is no single answer to the question, 'What is leadership?' It may help to offer three tests which many practising leaders have found useful and challenging in roughly equal proportions.

1 The Kissinger test

Henry Kissinger defined leadership as the art of 'taking people where they would not have gone by themselves'. This is a good test for leaders at all levels. Most organisations have an in-built momentum. They are always seeking to improve costs, quality and sales and to win the one race of the corporate Olympics: better-faster-cheaper. If your main claim to success is that you did these things, then you may well be a very good steward of your organisation. But you have not taken people where they would not have gone by themselves: you will have failed the Kissinger test.

2 The legacy test

Try this test on yourself. Try to name the leaders of your nation since the Second World War (or as far back as you dare to go). Now try to remember what they did. As a Cambridge history graduate, here is what I remember, and I may be wrong in several cases:

- Attlee: the welfare state
- Churchill: in peacetime, not much
- Eden: Suez debacle
- Macmillan: 'You never had it so good'
- Wilson: raincoats, pipes and unions
- Heath: sailing and going into the EU
- Wilson again: giving peerages to cronies
- Callaghan: strikes, power cuts and general disaster
- Thatcher: bashing unions and Argentines, Thatcherism
- Major: what was the point of Major?
- Blair: Iraq?
- Brown: financial crisis?
- Cameron: ???

It is hard to remember them for much, and even then they are not remembered the way they would like to be remembered. There is one prime minister who is so forgettable that he is not on the list and no one notices. Now repeat the exercise for the CEOs of your company, for as far back as you can remember. They were all giants of their time, dominating staff newsletters and annual reports: what did they achieve? And now repeat the exercise for yourself: how will you be remembered? If nothing else, this is a humbling experience in discovering our own limited relevance. Beating budget will not get you remembered, although it is worthwhile. To make an impact requires raising the bar greatly.

> to make an impact requires raising the bar greatly

3 The memory test

This is a softer form of the legacy test. Try to remember what was special for you for each of the last 10 years (or even 20 years, if you can go that far back). Hopefully, you will remember each year for one or two special things that you have done or achieved. But there are also some years where I can remember nothing of note: all that I achieved was to get one year closer to death. Salaries, bonuses and budget battles are all quickly lost in the fog of the past. Lost years are not worth having. It is better to live life with the 'Record' button on than with the 'Delete' button on. It may take three years to bring about a special outcome in one year, but however long it takes, make each year worthwhile. As a leader, how will you make this year memorable?

As a top leader you are likely to be your own toughest critic. You will have learned to challenge and stretch yourself. Use the three tests above to set yourself meaningful challenges, and the chances are you will find top leadership worthwhile and memorable.

Chapter 9

Focusing on people

The old adage says that it is lonely at the top. Objectively, you are never lonely at the top. Casual observation of any leader's day will show that it is a never-ending procession of meetings. Some may be formal, many are informal. Leaders want to find out what is really going on. They trust people much more than paper. The carefully crafted written word is there to make a case, not to tell the truth. Talking to trusted people gives a chance to test ideas, see reactions and get slightly closer to reality.

John Kotter, the HBS professor, studied how top leaders really spend their time. On average, less than 25% of their time is spent alone: thinking, writing, reading or attached to emails. Many leaders spend less than 10% of their time alone. Face time with others is not just in formal meetings. A large amount of the leader's time is spent informally with a vast array of people covering a vast array of subjects. A 10-minute meeting might easily cover five topics.

All of this runs counter to the received wisdom that the leader should structure each day for greatest efficiency – tightly scheduled and well-planned meetings together with scheduled reflection and thinking time. Of the leaders I interviewed, the closest one of them came to having personal thinking time was on his bicycle to work and in the toilet. The mobile phone was invading both of those sacred spaces in the day.

Leaders and the people paradox

If leaders spend so much time with people, how come they fancy they are lonely?

Lonely in a crowd: people as issues, not humans

It is possible to be lonely in a crowd. As a leader you suddenly discover that everyone wants a slice of you; they want a slice of your time, your energy, your power, your resources, your insight. Some bring problems to deal with. Some bring solutions for which they want approval and authority. Everyone wants something from you. For them, talking to you as the leader has high stakes. You rarely have a genuinely casual conversation.

> the loneliness of the leader comes from the changed nature of relationships with the rest of the organisation

The loneliness of the leader comes from the changed nature of relationships with the rest of the organisation. You find that every person and every conversation comes with an issue attached.

To counter the pressure of dealing with issues attached to people all day, many leaders create a kitchen cabinet – a group of trusted staff and advisers who can help you see through the issues and the people effectively. One CEO recruits a graduate entrant in their mid-20s as a PA. The graduate is on the fast track, is no threat and can be the eyes, ears and hands of the CEO as needed. You may have a personal coach. One way or another, you need a source of objective and impartial advice.

The leader alone: in search of a peer group

As a leader you will be lonely for another reason: suddenly, you will have no peer group with whom to interact regularly. A salesperson frequently sees lots of other salespeople and has a sales manager who knows all about the sales job. At every level of the organisation you have a peer group that is facing similar challenges. It is possible to learn from their successes and failures. At the top, you have no one else to observe as a peer on a daily basis. You have no one to tell you if you are messing up. No one has the courage to be honest with you or to criticise you to your face. The first thing you will hear about it is when the chairperson sits down to discuss your severance package.

It was striking that most of the leaders interviewed on video were very keen to see the results. This was not just vanity of wanting to see themselves on video. Most can have that as much as they want. They really wanted to see what their peer group thought and how they would have handled the situations we talked about. They wanted to reach out to their peer group in a meaningful way. The attraction of conferences such as the World Economic Forum is less about the speakers and more about the chance to meet a peer group.

Leadership and the pinnacle of people practice

At the top, some things change, some do not. Perspectives certainly change at the top of the mountain. You can see for ever on a clear day. The people at the bottom of the mountain will see the trout in the stream, the cat in the garden and the flowers by the road. None of this will be visible to the leader at the top, gazing across the distant ridges into the future. Neither view is right or wrong.

Some things do not change. The people skills, acquired *en route* to the top, do not change. The skills previously covered remain important:

- coaching
- influencing
- giving feedback
- handling conflict
- motivating.

These skills remain unchanged. The way leaders deploy these skills remains unchanged. The tough nut remains a tough nut; the tree hugger remains a tree hugger. They will not change a winning formula because some clever book or consultant says that there is a better way. They may adjust at the margins, especially if something goes wrong. But their underlying style will remain the same.

You learn your style of people management on the way up, not at the top.

The good news is that as a leader, you will now be spared any more theory telling you that you have been coaching, influencing and motivating the wrong way for the last 20 years.

The bad news is that there is yet more to be learned. All the leaders I interviewed had the humility and self-confidence to say that they are still learning as leaders. There are always new situations and new opportunities.

There are three new people-based skills that you have to acquire at the top:

1 **Creating** the top leadership team.
2 **Leading** the top leadership team.
3 **Working** with the board.

We will look at each in turn.

Creating the top leadership team

It is a truism that great teams achieve great things. Marry a great team to a great strategy and anything is achievable. Money need never be the constraint; talent is the constraint. Before we offer any instant recipes for talent success, let's look at some of the typical traps that leaders fall into:

● **Too much self-confidence**. Self-styled heroic leaders want to do it all themselves. They trust no one else. By making decisions themselves or overriding their team they demoralise and weaken their team. This is a vicious circle where the weaker the team becomes, the more the heroic leader believes in taking personal control. Even if the heroic leader succeeds for a while, they leave behind a weakened organisation with no effective succession in place.

- **Too little self-confidence**. Not all leaders have the self-confidence to know and admit their own weaknesses. Instead, they look for people like themselves to fill the leadership team. The result is an inbred, dysfunctional, unbalanced team of yes-men who feel very happy in the leadership club. There is nothing to balance the leader's weaknesses, and their strengths are echoed redundantly by the rest of the team.

- **Excess humility and power loss**. Some leaders let themselves get captured by the power barons that reside in any organisation. The barons make themselves indispensable. Dangerous power barons are budding heroic leaders. They take complete control of their part of the business and deliver results; it becomes impossible to see past them or manage through them. In investment banks, the barons threaten to take their teams across the road to a rival.

- **Excessive reason**. Some leaders fall in love with the logical side of business. They start to believe in drawing up organisation charts with lots of boxes and putting people in the boxes. You should only put people in boxes when they are dead. Especially at the top, you need to deal with people, not boxes.

Principles of the effective leadership team

If we can turn these negatives around into positives, we find that the effective leadership team is based on four principles:

1. Power.
2. Purpose.
3. Balance.
4. Shape.

1 Power

John Major, the former British prime minister, was famously attacked by one of his colleagues, Geoffrey Howe, for 'being in office, not in power'. Major did not survive much longer in office either.

Just because you have a big title, it does not mean you have power as well. You have to acquire power.

One of the easiest ways to seize power from the power barons is to reorganise. This has nothing to do with the logic of improving the structure or strategy of the organisation. It is about making sure that your power is recognised and respected. Move some power barons away from their fiefdoms so that they become dependent on you, not vice versa. If you lose a power baron or two, the rest will be cowed. Ritual executions have always exerted a strong fascination on the mob.

The dark side to reorganising is obvious. There is also a more positive side. Reorganisation is a chance to reset the psychological contract with each member of the leadership team. Working with one CEO on reorganisation, we designed all the predictable stuff about job descriptions, titles, roles, responsibilities and goals for each member of his leadership team. By far the most important part of the discussion was what the new psychological contract should be: working styles, mutual expectations and needs, risks and opportunities. This was the first step to creating a functioning team that existed in reality, not just on paper.

2 Purpose

A team without a purpose is as useless as a leader without followers. You must create an agenda which is greater than the sum of the parts of the leadership team. There needs to be a shared purpose. The purpose of the team will help inform the required balance of the team; globalising businesses need global capabilities.

Leadership vision is dealt with at length in Chapter 10. From the people perspective, it is the vision or purpose that transforms a collection of talented individuals into a leadership team pulling in the same direction.

3 Balance

It takes great self-confidence and self-knowledge to acknowledge your own weaknesses. This is your first step towards creating a balanced leadership team. Some of the weaknesses are obvious. Non-financial leaders need good financial support. Great strategic leaders need great operators at their side, as much as the great operator needs a great strategist nearby. You also need balance in terms of style – a team of yes-men is as destructive as a team of prima donnas.

it is better to have a slightly messy structure than a slightly dysfunctional leadership team

This sounds obvious, but it is not. You may be tempted to design the ideal organisation and then create the team to fit the design. It is better to do it the other way round: start with the people and then shape the organisation around your team. It is better to have a slightly messy structure than a slightly dysfunctional leadership team.

4 Shape

Architects, at least those who exist in the pre-postmodern world, have always held that 'form follows function': the design of a building should reflect its purpose. What works for architects does not work for leadership.

the structure, or form, of the organisation follows from the people and the purpose; it does not precede it

For leaders, the motto should be: 'People perform purpose'. In other words, figure out the purpose and the vision then assemble the right mix of skills and styles to achieve that purpose. The structure, or form, of the organisation follows from the people and the purpose; it does not precede it. Putting people first annoys consultants who want neat and tidy organisation charts. That is why you are the leader and they are not.

Hiring and firing: hiring

When you know the desired power, purpose, balance and shape of the team, you are still left with the question of making sure you have the right people. Hiring decisions are possibly the most important decisions you make. The 'A' team will make mountains into molehills; the 'B' team will make molehills into mountains. The 'A' team will over-achieve and let you sleep easily at night, whereas the 'B' team will simply give you nightmares.

Hiring decisions are often made on the basis of someone's experience and skills. This is natural, necessary and often catastrophic. Experience and skills are clearly necessary, but they often cloud judgement around the other, vital ingredients for a successful hire.

Crucially, people skills become more important for more senior people. In the words of one CEO: 'I find I hire most people for their technical skills and fire most for their people skills.' At junior levels, you do not need huge interpersonal skills to do a stock check for an audit, to trade some bonds or to do some desk research. If you aspire to leadership you have to look beyond doing stock checks. In doing so, you will find that more and more of your time is spent persuading, coaching, influencing and dealing with people. You have to move beyond the technical skills track. As a leader you need to surround yourself with people who have both technical and people skills.

> if you aspire to leadership you have to look beyond doing stock checks

Even managers with great people and technical skills can still fail. The likelihood of failure increases with seniority, especially where the hire is made from outside the organisation. There are two reasons for hiring failures at a senior level.

First, when you hire someone from another organisation you remove them from their power networks, their established ways of working, their alliances and proven success models. They lose the entire infrastructure which helped them succeed in the past: even the best induction programme will not give them a new power network overnight. Essentially, they have to start all over again. Some succeed, some fail.

Second, even if they can create a new power network, they may not have the same values as the rest of the organisation. These values do not have to be high-minded values about respect, diversity, integrity and all the other stuff that goes into the corporate values statement. The values that count are the daily values which mark out those who succeed, survive or struggle. The values might be things like 'make your numbers at all costs', 'stay in line and don't mess up', 'take initiative or take a hike'. These values are rarely articulated but are critical. Putting a 'stay in line' person into a 'take initiative' environment (or vice versa) is an invitation to watch a slow motion career crash. It is painful for all concerned.

Be prepared to hire for that and people skills: technical skills and experience do no more than put a candidate into the race.

The consequences of this approach are not good for diversity. By hiring people to a common set of values, an organisation shows that it prefers intimacy to diversity. There may be diversity of sex, faith and race but there will be less diversity of thinking and approach. This is the reality of how most organisations work in practice: they need intimacy of values because decision making and implementation are speeded up hugely when everyone shares a common language, approach and set of values. If everyone has completely different assumptions, values and operating styles, then you have a recipe for chaos. Gurus will shriek with outrage at this: they will advocate diversity to encourage innovation and other funky stuff. That is why they are gurus, not practitioners.

Hiring and firing: firing

There is no good way of firing people, even if you call it 'letting people go', 'rightsizing' or any other euphemism. Firing someone can seriously mess up that person's life, and the person doing it knows it. The least bad way of doing it has three characteristics which can conflict with each other. Firing should be:

1 **Legal**. Make sure you follow whatever insane legislative requirements are in place. Use your legal and HR staff to make sure you follow the right process.

2 **Fast**. There is little worse than seeing an increasingly demoralised person edge closer and closer to the career cliff. Kindness can be cruel in firing people. By giving people one more chance, one more deadline, one more set of deliverables while waiting for one more set of excuses, you simply prolong the agony for everyone. Move fast to get the misery over for all involved.

3 **Fair**. This is different from being legal, and occasionally at odds with legal procedure. When you fire someone, they should not be surprised and should feel that they have been respected and given a fair chance. Clearly, overdo this and you can face the problem of letting the process run on too long and missing the 'Fast' principle.

Ultimately your responsibility is to your organisation: the survival of the organisation takes precedence over the survival of the individual. Having the wrong person in the wrong place puts many other jobs at risk. You have to make the difficult decision and change people who are not in the right post. But this also means that your firing decision must be seen to be right and fair, not just a personal vendetta: fair process is essential to maintaining morale.

> the survival of the organisation takes precedence over the survival of the individual

Firing people assumes you know when it is right to fire someone. There are plenty of poor reasons for firing people which I have seen:

- needing a scapegoat when things go wrong
- personal vendetta
- making a statement about your power as the new boss
- punishing a one-off failure or setback
- making room to promote a favourite
- eliminating a potential rival.

All of these reasons get noticed in the organisation, even when they are denied. They breed a culture of politics, mistrust and fear which are not good starting points for a high-performing team.

You need to know how to read genuine distress signals around individual performance. Failing to meet numbers or any other under-performance is not necessarily a distress signal: there are many legitimate reasons why a setback might occur. Few leaders can claim to have never had a setback. The task is to differentiate between a one-off problem and a pattern of failure. The typical career death spiral has some classic patterns:

- Repeated failure to meet deadlines or goals, followed by pleading to change deadlines or goals and denial that they were fair, achievable or clear in the first place.
- Failure to take responsibility: blaming others.
- Unclear communication leading to a 'he said/I said/she said/I said/they said' discussion when things go wrong.
- Becoming invisible: in its final stages often marked by increasing sick leave and other absences from the office.
- Increasingly direct complaints from colleagues.

In contrast, someone who has a setback but takes responsibility, communicates clearly, maintains visibility and sorts out the problem is more likely to be a success than a failure. But when the death spiral is set in motion, there is rarely a way back for the individual. You need to move fast and put everyone out of their misery.

Leading the top leadership team
Achieving clarity, focus and alignment

It is not easy to lead leaders. Exert too little control and they become power barons. Exert too much power and you become a caricature of the heroic leader, demoralising and disempowering your team. Whatever your personal style may be, it will not suddenly change once you arrive at the top. As a leader, you will still find yourself inundated with managerial tasks such as monitoring performance. All the numbers have three or four more noughts on the end, but the basic task remains the same.

As a leader, you need to decide where you are able to make a difference and add value to the team. In essence, there are three things that the leader of leaders can deliver:

1 Clarity.

2 Focus.

3 Alignment.

Clarity

Clarity is not about the answer. Plenty of experts claim to know the answer. For the leader, the real challenge is to *know the problem*. In any organisation, there are myriad challenges and opportunities. But there are limited resources and only 24 hours in the day. Your job is to cut through the fog of internal competition and turf wars, and cut through the deluge of daily detail to see the few opportunities and challenges that make the difference.

Focus

I have yet to meet a leader who wants less focus. Once you have clarity about the problem, then it should be possible to focus the organisation on two or three must-win battles. If you have four must-win battles, the chances are that people cannot focus on them all. They will pick and choose and one or two must-win battles will be lost.

Alignment

Most leaders I interview have great clarity and focus. They talk passionately about exactly what they must achieve. There is just one problem with this. Different leaders in the same organisation often have clarity, focus and passion around completely different things. They can be pulling energetically in different directions.

Achieving alignment is not just about strategy papers and aligning reward and measurement systems, although these are important. You also have to create a common vision. This is best done through the much derided off-site meeting. Away from the all-consuming trivia of daily management, your leadership team needs time to reflect and achieve common clarity, focus and alignment. If the vision is visual, a map of the future, so much the better: it avoids details, focuses on what is important and is more memorable than a long and worthy set of words.

The art of unreasonable management

Achieving clarity, focus and alignment sounds reasonable and rational. Effective leaders learn to be selectively unreasonable.

All leaders know the world is not getting any easier. Suppliers do not cut prices voluntarily, staff want more money and fewer hours, competition does not go to sleep and there are always regulators and tax officers who want another slice of your action. The result is that the performance baseline for an organisation is not a steady state – it is faster or slower decline. All the profit improvement programmes promise more profit; in practice, they only keep your organisation from decline.

The reasonable leader understands these constraints. There are always good reasons why targets may be difficult to hit.

How to drive performance

1   **Focus on impact**
    Deal with matters that are important and urgent, and which have visibility and impact across the organisation. Make a difference.

2   **Be unreasonable**
    Set stretching goals; force business not as usual; take people beyond their comfort zone so that they can grow and develop.

3 Be flexible about the means

Do not micro manage professionals. Believe in your team. Let them come up with a better approach than the one you first thought of. If they want help and guidance, let them ask for it and then provide it.

4 Empower and support your team

Set your team up for success; give them the right budget; give them air cover from politics, interference and administrative grief; ask them what they need and make sure they get it. Pre-empt any excuses.

5 Be specific and detailed about your expectations

Be precise about your goals. Specify what good looks like in detail, be clear on timings and milestones. Avoid any vagueness or ambiguity, and check your team understands your expectations. No surprises.

6 Manage By Walking Away (MBWA)

Do not solve all their problems for them: help them learn to step up to each challenge by coaching them, not instructing them.

7 Monitor appropriately

Trust your team and they will respond. Do not over-monitor. Review progress early on so that you can take corrective action in time and coach as needed. Break large tasks into bite-sized chunks which can be achieved, monitored and delivered.

8 Accept no excuses

When you accept excuses, you accept failure. But be generous in your praise and do not hog the limelight. Give recognition; motivate your team.

9 Deal with setbacks promptly

Setbacks are an excuse to work better and more creatively, not for delay or scaling back ambitions. Create an open culture where setbacks are recognised early, and you learn from them and drive to action fast. Avoid the blame game.

10 Drive to action

Avoid analysis paralysis. Be clear about what happens next and do it now.

Case Study

Biting the bullet

One electronics company was heading for bankruptcy. The president ordered a 20% cut in working capital and in headcount, across the board. Each division head had an excuse:

'We just cut 20% from costs last year; we can't do it again.'

'Our benchmark costs are already best in class; you can't beat that.'

'You can't cut a business which is growing.'

The reasonable leader would have accepted these excuses, and the company would now be bankrupt. The unreasonable response was to insist on the 20% cut, and if it wasn't achieved, the division heads would become part of the 20%. Occasionally, the leader has to be unreasonable.

The art of unreasonable management is not confined to crises. Anyone who was sane would have told Fred Smith that his idea for FedEx, a nationwide overnight delivery service, was insane. Legend has it that he got a 'C' grade from his tutor at business school for the idea. Branson and O'Leary were nuts to take on British Airways. Soichiro Honda was clearly deranged to think he could take on the might of the Big Three US auto manufacturers. Reasonable people do not create great empires. We all remember Alexander the Great. Who has ever heard of Alexander the Reasonable?

there is a fine line between unreasonable and intolerable

There is a fine line between unreasonable and intolerable. The unreasonable leader will stretch the team; the intolerable leader will break the team. To make the goal more realistic, you need to split the challenge into stretching, but achievable, targets. Do not ask everyone to score a hole in one every time. Let them take as many shots as they need to get to the target. The important thing is to get to the target. Tackle it in bite-sized chunks, give support and be flexible about the means. But do not bend on the goal.

Working with the board

Operationally, the CEO needs to work out how to manage the board. In theory the chairperson should do this. But by the time you become CEO, you will have many years of experience of managing upwards. The same tools and techniques still apply at this exalted level:

- Avoid surprises: pre-warn, pre-wire, and prepare the ground in advance.
- Agree expectations about working styles, roles and goals.
- Involve appropriately.
- Never lie or shade the truth.
- Deliver results.

As CEO, your trickiest relationship may be with the chairperson. It is the chairperson who hires the CEO and fires the CEO. There is, rightly, some tension in a good relationship here.

Part of the problem is that the CEO and the chairperson often want to perform each other's roles. The chairperson, especially if they have been kicked upstairs from the CEO role, finds it difficult to let go. The chairperson suffers the 'leader in the locker room' problem that first-time managers suffer. They want to play the game. This means they interfere too much and get in your way.

In contrast, the CEO can acquire delusions of grandeur. It can be very appealing to be the spokesperson for the organisation – talking to the media, romancing the financial analysts, and joining the ranks of the good and the great by becoming committee and commission person. Some of these things the CEO can do. Leave the rest to the chairperson to keep them happily occupied and out of harm's way.

The real problem for the chairperson is that they cannot see into the organisation. Financial results are a lagging indicator of performance. By the time the financial results head south, it is too late to do much. CEOs, as Kotter discovered in his study, spend a disproportionate amount of time walking the corridors and finding out what is really going on. This is not a luxury that the board is allowed. They do not have the time, and they would get in everyone's way if they acted as an alternative leadership team.

In practice, the relationship will work where there are the following:

1 Performance.
2 Clear expectations.
3 Trust, stories, quick wins and no errors.

Performance

Your power as a CEO is directly related to your performance. The better your performance, the more the board will feel unable to question or challenge you. With the career expectancy of FTSE-100 CEOs falling below five years, as previously noted, there is a strong indication that CEOs are not performing to expectations and that boards are prepared to use their muscle.

The key word here is *expectations*. Managing both board and investor expectations is an essential art form.

Clear expectations

You will have learned to manage expectations from the earliest days of your management career. If you set the baseline as low as possible, it is easy to show you are making progress. If you accept the lunatic growth and profit projections you have inherited, you will be set up to lose. It is no surprise that when a new CEO is appointed, there is a fairly predictable clearing out of skeletons from cupboards. The resulting write-offs set a low financial baseline and give some possibility of later write-backs.

Trust, stories, quick wins and no errors

Trust builds up over time, but as CEO you do not have time on your side. You need quick wins to show that you are in control and that you can be trusted. As much as anything else, you need to sell the board a story. You can call the story a strategy, to impress the board. But, in practice, it is normally a very simple story which even a non-executive board member can remember when being entertained at the opera. The stories which work are as simple as:

● We will focus on the basics (no strategy, just operational excellence).

● We will grow internationally.

● We will refocus on our core business (i.e. sell non-core assets).

● We will be number one or two in every market in which we compete (e.g. GE).

● We will leverage our brand into similar markets.

● We will concentrate only on major, global brands (e.g. Unilever).

These simple stories may be built on deep strategic analysis and insight. This is where management consultants like McKinsey and Monitor are useful; board members want their stamp of approval. They outsource their thinking to consultants. But it all comes back to something simple.

Equally, the consequences of your story can be dramatic and give rise to early wins:

● Reorganise the top team.

● Sell a business or two.

- Drop an expensive project.
- Drop an under-performing product line.

These early wins help you buy time. The non-executive can now go to the opera and recall that you not only Have A Plan, but you are also Doing Something. They can now relax and enjoy the opera.

For the board, financial performance is their main indicator of how well you are doing. But as already noted, it is a lagging indicator of performance; once the results are in, there is nothing they can do about it. The only other evidence they have of your performance is how you operate in board meetings. This means that you have to spend a perhaps disproportionate amount of time in engineering the board meetings for success – late, missing or faulty papers are corrosive of trust. Attention to detail may not be your strength, but it is the detail the board notices. Equally, the board likes to feel involved in the business; you need to throw them the right bones to chew on. Put practically, the more the board members are involved in crafting and approving your strategy, the harder it will be for them to distance themselves from it if it goes wrong.

As CEO you will find that all the old disciplines of building trust and commitment, selling ideas, influencing people and building networks apply at board level as much as they ever did in the past. It is a case of back to the future.

Chapter 10
Being positive

All leaders inherit a position and a legacy in terms of an organisation, strategy, resources and performance. This is good news and bad news. The legacy gives you something to build on. But the legacy can also be a prison. Organisations assume a life and a momentum all of their own. It is easy to be trapped by the existing legacy and momentum. This is the low-risk option: if it ain't broke, don't fix it. If you do try to change things, you will find the inertia of the organisation is against you. Neither organisations nor individuals enjoy change or risk.

Leaders who simply maintain the inherited legacy are more like stewards of a business and less like leaders. Stewardship is respectable. If you are the CEO of the Grosvenor Group, which is 350 years old, you have to have enough humility to recognise that your primary role is to be a great steward of the business. You do not need the arrogance of a leader who decides to change the old property business into a funky new-age dot.com bankruptcy.

You need to navigate between the two extremes of being passive and being revolutionary. You need a positive vision of where the organisation is going and how it is going to get there, and the vision also needs to be communicated positively.

Speed readers will have missed that. So to reinforce the point, your positive agenda will have three elements:

1 **Creating** the vision.

2 **Communicating** the vision.

3 **Enabling** the vision to happen.

We will look at each of these elements below.

Creating the vision

The vision thing can be pretty daunting. It sounds like we have to be able to lead our people out of the desert and into the promised land.

I tried the vision thing once. I got as far as 'I have a dream . . .' and gave up. My last dream had been about a cloud of intergalactic flying teacups. This might have inspired some shrinks and amused the staff. But it would not have helped the organisation achieve its goals.

> some visions take you to the promised land; others take you straight back into the desert

Visions and visionaries can be dangerous. Mao, Pol Pot, Marx and Hitler all had visions which collectively killed hundreds of millions of people. Some visions take you to the promised land; others take you straight back into the desert.

Despite this, the best leaders have visions, but they are not necessarily visionary. All you need to do is tell a story, in three parts:

- This is where we are and why we must change.
- This is where we are going and what it means for you.
- This is how we will get there and how you can help us get there.

This is pretty simple stuff. The simpler it is, the better. In today's world we suffer a surfeit of choice. The resulting complexity and confusion are impediments that we cannot afford. A good vision creates clarity and helps people at all levels make better decisions.

The vision must be simple enough that it can be interpreted and made relevant for shareholders, trustees, staff, suppliers and customers.

The need for a simple direction becomes more important as the world becomes more complicated and change happens at least as fast as ever. In practice, it takes either genius or courage to create simplicity out of complexity.

It's time to look at some effective visions in practice.

Good visions give everyone a very clear idea of where they are going, what they are meant to do and what they should not do. They can come in many shapes and many fashions. Here are two examples:

1 The Red Arrows: the perfect show.
2 Ryanair: the low-cost airline.

These are mind-numbingly simple and obvious statements. They do not take long to understand. They provide total focus on what is important. In both cases the vision drives the organisation.

The Red Arrows

The Red Arrows are the air display team of the RAF. They have a clear vision – to achieve the perfect air show. They do not try to mark themselves against other air show teams. The only measure of success is perfection.

The search for perfection pervades everything they do, from careful selection of team members, to planning of each mission and detailed debriefing of each mission afterwards to see what they need to do better to reach perfection. They have total clarity and focus on what is important to them.

Ryanair

There are many ways for airlines to compete: in-flight service, loyalty schemes, convenient schedules, route network, legroom, on-board entertainment, quality of food and wine, airport lounges, sleeper beds, punctuality, choice of airport, or quality of connections.

Michael O'Leary, the founder of Ryanair, has a simple response to all these competitive challenges: low cost, low cost, low cost, low cost, low cost, low cost, low cost, low cost, low cost, low cost.

This is very simple, very focused and very effective. Everyone, including the customer, understands what this means for them. Everything flows from the low-cost focus:

- Aircraft: one type to minimise costs.
- Marketing: cut out travel agent, minimise costs.
- Ticketing: electronic confirmation, no costly paper.
- Punctuality: high to maximise fleet usage, minimise costs.
- Airports: secondary airports, low landing fees, quick turnarounds.

As a low-cost carrier, they have a different market and different model from the flag carriers and are best positioned to survive the shake-out of the low-cost carrier market. In contrast, the staff of flag carriers find themselves confused by serving different markets (budget travellers and premium business travellers) with different messages and different needs. The difference is visible to all: on British Airways you see businesspeople in suits. A suit is rare on Ryanair.

Testing your vision

In 1962 President Kennedy promised to put a man on the moon within 10 years and bring him back alive again. To deliver the mission, he created NASA. The vision was compelling and eventually successful, even though at the time no one knew if it would be possible. The power of the vision can be seen by what has happened to NASA since the moon landings. It has had some successes (Hubble) and some failures (Challenger), but it has lost its original focus and drive. Kennedy's vision was inspired by the need to catch up with Russia (the old Soviet Union) in space. Yuri Gagarin was the first man into space and the USA did not want to give control of space to its cold war enemy. **RUSSIA** gives you a simple way of testing the power of your vision:

- **R**elevant. Is your vision relevant to your needs? America faced losing the space race, so Kennedy's vision was highly relevant.

- **U**nique. Could you apply your vision ('be world class') to another company? If so, it is not good. NASA's vision was unique.

- **S**imple. If no one can remember your vision, they will not act on it. Fifty years later, Kennedy's vision is still powerful and memorable.

- **S**tretching. Leadership is about taking people where they would not have gone by themselves. That means stretching them. NASA's vision was certainly about going where no one had gone before.

- **I**ndividual. Is it clear what each person is meant to do to achieve the vision? NASA's simple vision gave everyone very clear direction about what they were meant to do and where they were meant to focus.

- **A**ctionable. Your vision must be actionable and measurable; it should help staff decide priorities and make clear what they should do and what they should not do.

How does your vision fare against the RUSSIA test?

Communicating the vision

CEOs like to read the company newsletter and annual report. There are normally lots of flattering photographs of the CEO looking magisterial behind a desk, looking dynamic at a company site, looking important with a royal or a government minister and looking generous and sociable at a company awards event. Generally, the role of company newsletters is to confirm to the CEO that they are a wonderful person.

Now think back to when you started work. How often did you read the company newsletter or believe what it said? Sadly, some CEOs still think that a few elegantly written articles, a couple of inspirational emails and a lavishly produced video supported by an equally lavish company conference will build excitement and commitment to the new vision. Think again.

Staff and other stakeholders have other things to think about besides your vision, like mortgages, shopping, holidays, bills and the weekend. Your vision probably comes somewhere below buying the cat food. The cat will survive without your vision but will not survive without some food. It takes real effort to make people take notice, let alone take action, as a result of your vision.

Communicating the vision is a combination of broadband (one-to-many) communication and narrowband (one-to-one) communication.

Communicating the vision in broadband

Successful communication comes down to three elements:

1 One consistent message.
2 Constant repetition.
3 Multiple methods of communicating.

Look back to the successful visions. They could be summarised in one sentence or just a phrase. If you have a clever and complicated vision, throw it out. Make it simple and you have a chance of its being remembered.

> Constant repetition gets the message home.
>
> Constant repetition gets the message home.
>
> Constant repetition gets the message home.
>
> Constant repetition gets the message home.
>
> Constant repetition gets the message home.
>
> Constant repetition gets the message home.
>
> Constant repetition gets the message home.
>
> Constant repetition gets the message home.

Constant repetition gets the message home.

Constant repetition gets the message home.

Do not try to be subtle. I will confess to being guilty of creating some Daz advertising. Over 40 years the basic message has not changed: Daz is great for whiteness. It is not subtle, but at least people seem to remember the basic message. Even if you have repeated the message many times to the same group, do not assume that you can move on to other messages. Repeat it again.

Finally, use multiple methods of communication. Some are obvious – newsletters, emails, company conferences, meetings, training events, the website and walkabouts all give the chance to hammer home the message. The more you talk about it, the more challenge and feedback you will receive and the better you will become at communicating the message and refining it for each audience.

Celebrate successes and war stories. When you find someone who has done something that embodies the vision you are creating, recognise them and reward them in public.

Communicating the vision in narrowband

Ultimately, leadership is an engagement sport. You cannot lead by remote control. As John le Carré wrote: 'A desk is a very dangerous place from which to view the world.' This is as true of leaders as it is of spies.

You need to create a team and a network of people who have faith in your vision. Clearly, your top team needs to buy in. If they do not buy in, they need to move on. A team which is playing against itself is unlikely to succeed.

Less obviously, you need to engage a specific network of individuals across your organisation. You need to get the informal grapevine of the organisation working for you. Relying on broadband media to get your message across is not enough.

Newsletters tend to have the style and credibility of *Pravda* in the days of the Soviet Union. You need to get up close and personal with the owners of the grapevine.

Some of this will happen in the natural, semi-random process of meeting different people in different situations. In practice, there are a few individuals who are likely to carry informal influence out of all proportion to their formal position in the organisation. They might run a social club. They might be the crusty old-timer who has seen it all many times before and has seen CEOs come and go with regularity. These people can spread poison, but they can also spread hope. Because they are outside the formal hierarchy they are trusted, and because they have wide networks they are influential. These are the people who feed the grapevine; if they say the new vision makes sense to them, people listen.

One chief executive reviewed the first three years of his tenure and estimated that over half of his time was spent on communicating the vision. People do not get it easily. You have to be creative about how you communicate.

John Timpson owns and runs a chain of 650 shoe repair shops. This is potentially one of the dullest, smallest and most dead-end industries that anyone could inflict on themselves. But he has made his business a success, and his employees are proud to be part of his firm. To succeed, he realised that he was as much in the customer service business as the shoe repair business. Good service meant more custom. He also realised that it was easier to hire good people and train them to repair shoes than to hire grumpy cobblers and train them to be happy and service-focused staff. He realised he needed a revolution.

Timpson trained his area managers to select staff on service aptitude, not technical skills. They listened and they did not get it. They still hired cobblers, albeit slightly less grumpy cobblers.

Eventually, Timpson changed the hiring assessment form. All the words went out. In came pictures of 'Mr Men'. Mr Neat, Mr Happy, Mr Prompt, Mr Smart and Mr Reliable all were on one side of the form. Mr Messy, Mr Late, Mr Dirty and Mr Lazy pictures were on the other side of the form. The area managers had to circle which of the Mr Men each recruit most resembled. This was not good on diversity. But it worked. Area managers understood it and started to hire the right people. Timpson's pulled away from all the traditional cobblers by offering great service from great staff who kept the customers happy and loyal.

Enabling the vision to happen

There are many people with lots of great ideas. And you will never lack for advice. Everyone will have a view on what you should do and where you are messing up. If you want ideas, read the newspapers. From the features pages to the horoscopes there are endless ideas about what people should do.

The hallmark of the leader is the ability to make things happen. Virtual visions are daydreams. They need to move from virtual reality to reality.

> virtual visions are daydreams, they need to move from virtual reality to reality

Enabling the vision to happen is not easy. Prime ministers come with great hopes of what they will do once in power. But even prime ministers find it difficult truly to change society the way they want. As in Chapter 8, think back for as many prime ministers as you can, and think what they are remembered for. Few of them are likely to leave much more than one major legacy to history.

In reality, both nations and organisations assume lives of their own. No one person controls the whole organisation. No one can know exactly what is happening everywhere all the time, let alone change it all. There are a limited number of things that you can, in practice, control. You have more levers of power than anyone else in the organisation. But, unlike the Pope, you are not infallible. Unlike God, you are neither omnipotent nor omnipresent.

How to take control

1 **Set expectations before you start**

Set yourself up for success: right goals, right budget and right strategy; use discretion to shape your team and set the agenda.

2 **Have a plan**

Be clear about what will be different under your leadership; show where you are going and how you will get there. Do not blindly accept the plan you have inherited. Make a difference; don't drift.

3 **Shape your team**

Move people in, out and about as required for what you want to achieve. You do not have to live with the team you inherit.

4 **Find the money**

Ensure you have the right budget. Plans without money are pipe dreams.

5 **Move to action fast**

Show some early wins and build confidence; the longer you live with the plan and the team you inherit, the harder it is to change and the more it is your problem.

6 **Build your coalition**

Make sure you have a trusted network of allies and supporters at all levels; identify the key stakeholders who can affect your performance and gain their backing.

7 **Over-communicate**

Set the agenda and craft the story about what you are doing: do not let others spin the story about what you are doing or not doing. Stay ahead of events and manage the message.

8 **Set your style**

Show how you want to manage; use symbolic events and moments of truth to demonstrate your values, beliefs and way of working. You can change style when you change role, especially in a new organisation: reinvent yourself if you want to.

9 **Protect your territory**

Your team, your budget and your agenda are yours: do not let others interfere. Manage the politics and do not let yourself or your team be derailed: fight the right battles.

10 **Deliver the results**

You only stay in control as long as you deliver.

In practice, as a leader, you have five levers of power at your disposal:

1 Strategy.
2 Resource allocation and management.
3 Reward and measurement systems.
4 People: team formation.
5 Structure.

All five power levers are closely connected. The degree of change you achieve depends on your ability to pull these levers of power. You do not have to be a revolutionary. No organisation can survive by going through constant revolution. For decades P&G held the humble, evolutionary vision of doubling in size every 10 years. That calls for 7% real growth every year. Double in size every 10 years, and after 150 years you will be 32,000 times bigger than today. That is a lot of detergents and personal-care products for the world.

1 Strategy

This flows directly from your vision. There is a nice philosophical debate about the difference between a vision, the mission, a strategy, goals and objectives. Get it wrong and your business school professor may have you burned at the stake for heresy. Risking the *auto-da-fé*, we will assume that strategy provides the framework for realising the vision. The vision shows where we are and where we will go. The strategy shows how we will get there. It provides the framework for setting appropriate goals, allocating resources and priorities, and going to market the right way.

A good strategy helps your organisation focus in the right areas and make the right trade-offs in all the ambiguous decisions that departments face. It will help people decide what not to do, as well as what they should do.

2 Resource allocation and management

This is one of the two major ways in which your strategy finds expression in the organisation. For good reasons, the annual budget cycle in most organisations follows close on the heels of the strategy review. The strategy review sets the framework and the priorities; the budget review makes the priorities real.

It is in the resource allocation process that you have to be unreasonable. There are always reasonable reasons for budgets to be increased as salaries and supplier costs increase. Turning a deaf ear to reason and turning on the pressure is standard operating practice in this cycle.

Resource management represents much of the weekly and monthly grind of management and leadership. Budget variances are rarely positive; dealing with the consequences of negative variances is time consuming but critical.

Leaders rarely rely on just the formal resource management systems. Reports and spreadsheets give a version of the truth, and it is often the version that the reporter wishes to present rather than the one the leader needs to hear. Spreadsheets ensure that the maths are right. They do nothing for the logic or assumptions.

You can compensate for the deficiencies in the formal reporting systems in two ways:

- Develop an intimate knowledge of the key numbers. This has been styled as tuning a very sensitive garbage detector. You should know the numbers and trends well enough that an odd number looks, well ... odd. It merits further investigation by the garbage detector.

- Spend time wandering around the organisation, talking to people at all levels and in all areas. This lets you get behind the numbers and the formal reports. You need an insatiable appetite, or paranoia, to find out what is really happening in your organisation.

3 Reward and measurement systems

These systems are the second way in which strategy finds expression in the organisation. They frequently go wrong. The two major problems are:

- setting the wrong incentives
- misaligning incentives.

Wrong incentives abound. The first edition of this book noted that loan officers were rewarded on the size of their book, not on loan quality. That was before the financial crisis. When the crisis hit, banks discovered the eternal truth that lending money is easy; getting it back is hard. Poor-quality incentives led to poor-quality loans and to meltdown.

Misaligning incentives is an even more common problem because it is genuinely difficult to achieve. It is natural that sales, IT, operations and HR should have different objectives. This leads to different priorities and to conflict where neither side is objectively right or wrong. They both have goals to defend. In theory, you should be able to design goals which are perfectly aligned across the organisation. In theory, anyone can win the lottery if they enter.

> in practice, it is through the process of conflict and disagreement that the priorities of the organisation are effectively established

In practice, it is through the process of conflict and disagreement that the priorities of the organisation are effectively established. Where there is conflict between groups, it pays not to listen too closely to the rational arguments. Look instead at how each group is being measured and rewarded. They are going to be eloquent and rational in defending what may be irrational goals. Changing the goals and measures is often the best way of cutting through irreconcilable differences between departments.

4 People: team formation

Case Study

What you see is what you get

The partners of a consulting firm did a test at their summer retreat. Each partner led a team on one common problem that the Brazilian office faced. No one knew the details, other than those written up for the case. There were five teams. Five different answers came back, suggesting the client should:

- cut costs
- merge with another company (be acquired)
- acquire another company
- open new distribution channels
- restructure the top team.

Each answer reflected the strengths and interests of the partner concerned: the cost-cutting partner suggested cost cutting; the marketing partner suggested the new distribution channels.

The answer was not a result of the problem; it was the result of the person looking at the problem.

There are several potential lessons from this case study, such as be careful of consultants and of unfamiliar Brazilian organisations. The most important lesson is that the strategy you get for the organisation will be a function of the top team you put in place. You will not get great market-led growth from a restructuring and cost-cutting team.

No leader can control a large organisation single-handedly. Leadership is a team sport. The hallmark of good leaders is that they create good teams around them to push their vision and strategy into the organisation. As we have seen, good is not an absolute term. Good is about fit, not perfection. An organisation in crisis may well need a team of experienced cost-cutters; an organisation intent on rapid growth may seek to make their leadership team more professional and introduce more disciplined, market-focused capabilities.

5 Structure

Restructuring is a favourite of management. It is easy to do – shuffle the boxes around on pieces of paper. It is highly visible. It shows that you are doing something. In practice, there are two forms of restructuring, with quite different motives and impact.

Restructuring the top team

This is essentially a political act which new leaders often undertake. It is a way for you to gain power over the organisation: removing power barons who need to be removed, and opening up positions for the sorts of people whom you want in the team. In other words, the restructuring is more about people than it is about structures. This makes the restructuring no less valid, except in the eyes of middle managers. They have seen it all before: the carousel goes round. Centralisation and decentralisation; shifting the matrix from geography to clients to functions and back again. What goes round, comes round. Rarely does restructuring itself transform the prospects of the organisation, however much hot air is expended in selling the relative merits of one structure over another. But restructuring as a vehicle for putting the right leadership in place is essential.

Restructuring the business

This is, again, highly visible and shows that you are doing something. It is loved by investment bankers (fees), consultants (fees), lawyers (fees), accountants (fees) and PR people (fees). Once they have helped you build an empire and saddled you with debt, they will help your successor dismantle the empire, collecting their fees a second time around.

Restructuring the business can have a dramatic effect on the fortunes of the business, for better or for worse. In each case, the challenge is to make sure the restructuring is driven by the strategy, not by the advisers. Research shows that acquisitions destroy value for shareholders in about 80% of cases; all the value is transferred to the shareholders of the acquired organisation. This misses the political reality of acquisitions: the acquirer gets to play with a bigger toy. The acquired has lost the game.

> the political reality of acquisitions: the acquirer gets to play with a bigger toy

Crafting a leadership agenda

Besides the five generic levers of power above, each leader will normally choose two or three initiatives which they will control personally. These will reflect the main priorities of the organisation. In many organisations this will be some form of change programme. But some leaders look for much greater focus, for instance:

1 The insurance company (brand, technology, people).
2 The systems house (deal making).
3 The consulting company (key clients and IP).
4 The non-profit (external constituencies).
5 The bank (people, systems, property).

We will look at the first three of these in more detail below.

The insurance company

Insurance is a technical industry; actuaries make rocket science look simple. For many years, this industry was led by actuaries. As a result, the industry became a museum of management malpractice – high costs, internal focus, customers coming last and opaque profits and reporting. As life insurance clients signed up for 25-year contracts, there was not much pressure to perform. So the way was open for new insurance companies to come in. They did not need to be excellent to win. They needed to be less incompetent than the incumbents. Direct insurers such as Allied Dunbar (life insurance) and Direct Line (general insurance) started to take real market share away from the incumbents.

The incumbents had to enter the world of twentieth-century management fast.

Case Study

Changing the locus of power

One leader came in to turn around an ailing insurance company and focused on just three items:

1 Brand.
2 Technology.
3 People.

There was nothing about actuarial work, complex product development and all the traditional concerns of insurers. This was about efficiency, effectiveness and market presence. Branding was a new language to the company. It was not a matter of putting a few marketing types into an obscure office; it was about changing the locus of power from actuaries to the marketplace. This clearly required new people, new skills and new processes. The technology need was driven by the desire to lower costs and improve customer focus dramatically. It resulted in redesigning processes to support the new brand and service orientation.

▶

Within such a revolution there are countless challenges. The leader realised he only had 24 hours in a day: he picked the battles where he could have the biggest impact and delegated as much of everything else as possible.

The systems house

Systems companies do things like integrating systems and outsourcing the technical infrastructure of an organisation. So it is natural to think that leaders should perhaps support the occasional client megadeal and be technically focused.

Acquiring expertise

One leader realised that this was not where he could add most value. He did not focus on clients or on technology; he focused on deals. He realised that there were many sub-scale systems houses doing good work. But they could only serve small, local or regional clients. These clients could not or would not pay top dollar. Billing rates were about half what the major players like IBM or EDS charged. By pulling the smaller systems houses into a large international network, he gave them brand power and pricing power, while he got access to skills and technology.

So the CEO went shopping. He gained a black belt in shopping for systems houses and then integrating them into the network. He built a deal team which always negotiated well on price. It was a winning focus: buy a company which is charging out its staff at £100 an hour, and raise billing rates over three years to £150 an hour, which is still cheaper than the £200 an hour being charged by the competition.

This is a strategy which has been replicated with varying degrees of success by both accounting and legal firms. The degree of success is directly related to the capability and focus of the leader in deal making and management. The leader does not need to be a professional lawyer, technologist or accountant. The leader needs to focus on those activities where they can best add value to the rest of the organisation.

The consulting company

If you are ever given the chance to run a consulting company, don't. It is full of prima donnas who are good and know it. They are not keen on being managed. They know exactly how much economic value they have added to the partnership and are keen to extract at least that much value back again. No leader in the industry can escape the grind of herding the cats at the top of the organisation. It goes with the territory. But an effective leader needs more.

Most leaders in most professional firms enjoy their profession too much to want to go into management roles. They want to lead by example.

Case Study

Leading by example

James led by example. He decided to build the group's global presence outside the United States by doing it himself. So he left the security of an established office and clients in the United States, bought a plane ticket to Europe and set up shop. His partners bade him 'adieu', not 'au revoir': they did not really expect to see him back again.

He focused on three things:

- **Key clients**. He took personal responsibility for acquiring and serving key clients. No clients, no revenues, no office. A key client at the start was anyone who would pay for a meal. It soon became anyone who would pay over £100k, then £500k, then £1 million and beyond.

- **Hiring great staff**. He hired ahead of the demand curve, which is dangerous. He was building costs without revenues. He figured that if you attract and retain great people, they will attract and retain great clients.

- **Intellectual property**. The defining difference of the company was its network of business school faculties that helped keep clients at the leading edge of management thinking and practice. He built this network outside the United States.

▶

Within five years, the international business was larger than the American business he had left behind.

There are two common features in each of these cases. They have implications for all leaders. The leaders in each case focused on activities which:

1 Supported the distinctive vision of the company – they did not represent business as usual.

2 Represented a way of the leader adding value to the organisation – they were not doing things which other people could do.

Ultimately, you have to create your own role. This freedom can be unnerving. It is tempting to do what you have done before, but on a larger scale. This probably means that you are simply replicating some skill set which is already abundant in the organisation. If other people can do something as well as you can, let them do it. If you do the same as them, you add no value.

Freedom gives you the ultimate challenge of showing where you can distinctively add value to your organisation.

Chapter 11

Being professional

I t is a brave person who would dare to accuse a leader of being unprofessional. In extreme cases the brave person turns out to be the public prosecutor who accuses some leaders of various forms of kleptocracy.

Aside from the extreme cases, most leaders are professional. Professionalism takes many forms. The way in which the leader is professional is vital. It shapes the culture of the entire organisation. In this chapter we will take a tour of four aspects of the professional leader:

1 The must-have personal and professional values.
2 Alternative styles of leadership.
3 Creating values for the organisation at large.
4 Making the values real.

For leaders in the middle of the organisation, professionalism is focused mainly on core skills, especially communication skills. For leaders at the top, professionalism concerns the values and style of the leader and the organisation.

The must-have personal and professional values

After interviewing the leadership group it became clear that there are as many different styles of leadership as there are leaders. Each leader has created a unique leadership DNA which works for them in their current situation. Copying the DNA is an exercise in futility;

it is impossible to achieve and irrelevant. What works for one leader in one situation may not work for you in another situation.

In the interviews, each leader talked about different values. Words like *courage*, *empathy*, *decisiveness*, *respect for the individual* and *determination* all cropped up. But only two words came up consistently, both from the leaders at the top of the organisation and from people lower in the organisation. Both words came as a surprise. The two key words were *honesty* and *humility*.

Honesty

The leaders' constant calls for honesty implied that they were less than happy with the levels of honesty they observed in other leaders. This implicit criticism was echoed explicitly by the followers who saw that there was insufficient honesty among their leaders. Only 54% of followers said that they were satisfied with the honesty of their leaders. This should be a wake-up call to leaders who tend to be self-confident individuals: 72% of followers thought their leaders were highly self-confident.

Perhaps to the disappointment of the prosecutor, lack of honesty was not about finding leaders with their hands in the till or in other improper places. Expectations of honesty were much higher than that.

Followers all want leaders they trust. Put simply, they do not trust a leader who is less than totally honest with them. This strong-form honesty (having the courage to tell the truth even when it is painful) was more than the mere absence of lying. Examples of strong-form honesty included:

> followers all want leaders they trust

- Being open about performance problems. A person who is not performing wants to know early enough to do something about it. They do not want a nasty surprise in the form of zero annual bonus, or worse.

- Sharing information. If you suddenly cancel all meetings for a week and disappear into closed meetings with advisers, people get nervous. They want to know what is happening.

- Admitting mistakes. Avoid creating a blame culture. It stops the organisation from recognising and rectifying mistakes before they do too much damage.

Strong-form honesty takes both courage and self-confidence. But if you want to have willing followers, followers have to trust you. If they do not trust you, they will not follow willingly.

At this point, the honesty challenge disappears off the optional ethics course at business school. It becomes part of the mandatory survival course for leaders.

Humility

Humble leadership brings us back to the curious world of the oxymoron. All the leaders used the word in the same way. They did not mean that the leader had to drive a second-hand car, wear old clothes and do menial jobs to set an example. They meant that the leader had to have acute self-awareness.

You need to know what you don't know. Recognise your limitations, weaknesses and errors. If you have the self-awareness and self-confidence to do this, a series of benefits will flow:

- You can build an effective leadership team which complements your strengths and weaknesses. Arrogant leaders believe that they can do it all themselves; this puts an impossible burden on them. Groups have greater wisdom than individuals. In the TV programme *Who Wants to Be a Millionaire?*, the phone-a-friend option gives the right answer 67% of the time. The option of asking the audience of amateurs and unknown strangers yields the right answer 91% of the time. There is an old Chinese saying: 'The person who is right half the time is clever. The person who is right three-quarters of the time is clever and lucky. The person who is right all the time is a fool.' The humble leader is not so foolish as to believe they are infallible. Leaders build their teams, not their egos.

- You can rectify errors fast, before they cause too much damage. Having the humility to recognise mistakes and act on them is essential.

- You create a positive environment for progress. The infallible leader will naturally blame setbacks on ineffective staff and managers, who then all play the game of 'pass the parcel'. This parcel of blame has the habit of exploding when the music stops. No one wants to take responsibility; fingers start to be pointed at each other; politics and the blame game take over. Fixing the underlying problem plays second fiddle to allocating blame.

Alternative styles of leadership

Much has been written about different leadership styles. The essence of this book is that each leader creates a unique leadership DNA based on begging and borrowing bits of leadership DNA from all the other leaders and role models they have observed over the years. All this book does is to help you accelerate your journey of discovery by helping you observe and reflect on the different ways in which leaders can succeed. If you are thinking that this is just a long apology for not giving you the single, brilliant theory of leadership which will transform your life, you are right.

Having made my apologies, it is possible to identify four-and-a-half broad types of leadership. Most leaders sway between all four major types of leadership. A few leaders focus exclusively on the half-type of leadership.

Here are the four-and-a-half types of leadership:

1 Autocrat.

2 Bureaucrat/technocrat.

3 Aristocrat.

4 Democrat/meritocrat.

$4\frac{1}{2}$ Kleptocrat.

Take a quick look at the summary below. Decide where you are and where your peers and bosses are.

	Key driver	Preferrred habitat	Strengths	Kryptonite/ weaknesses
Autocrat	Success, achievement, recognition	Entrepreneurs, crises	Decision making, drive	Scale, complexity, succession
Bureaucrat/ technocrat	Control, accuracy, perfection	Large, complex organisations	Fair, thorough, safe pair of hands, good process	Rapid change, uncertainty
Aristocrat	Title, status	Any non-executive role	Won't rock the boat, pliable	Harmless verging on useless
Democrat/ meritocrat	Excellence, performance	Wherever the other tyrannies are absent	Flexible, balanced, progressive	Needs right habitat to survive
Kleptocrat	Money, perks, privileges	Where's the money?	Money	Disaster for everyone else

Let us deal with each of them. Hold your nose while we dispense quickly with the half-type of leadership: the kleptocrat.

The kleptocrat

The great kleptocracies of the world are alive and kicking. They are as destructive of businesses as they are of nations, and they share many similar traits. In both cases a small elite engineers a takeover from the inside and proceeds to treat the assets of the business or the nation as their own. During the dot.com boom, 25 executives from six of the most spectacular bankruptcies awarded themselves a cool $2.6 billion for their collective failure. That is over $100 million each as a bounty for bankrupting their businesses and wasting other people's money. The credit crunch revealed that the kleptocrats are alive and well in financial markets. Having enriched themselves in good times, they require trillion dollar bailouts by the taxpayer in tough times. Kleptocrats do not create value: they transfer value from others into their own bank accounts. It is a route to wealth, but not to respect.

The kleptocratic tendency exists in milder form in many organisations. The golden hellos and golden parachutes, the performance-linked bonus which is virtually guaranteed, the repriced options, the perks and privileges of office are all hugely tempting. If they are clearly seen to be earned and deserved, most people do not begrudge them. When it is seen to be riding the gravy train of entitlement and privilege, it erodes trust and respect. The leader lands up looking the wrong way – at their bank account, not at their organisation.

It is easy to express moral outrage, tinged with a little envy, at the antics of the kleptocrats. As leaders, we have a decision to make about how we want to be remembered. As followers, we have a decision about whom we are prepared to work for.

> as leaders, we have a decision to make about how we want to be remembered

The autocrat

The autocrat can do great things and good things. They can also be a disaster. The autocrat is often held up as the ideal model of leadership. The autocrat is seen as the all-powerful, all-wise leader who single-handedly leads an organisation to the promised land. This is a popular media myth: it is much easier to write about colourful personalities doing flamboyant things than it is to talk about a leadership team quietly working to make an organisation succeed.

Most entrepreneurs are instinctive autocrats. Because they have a deep passion for their creation, they understand it inside out. They want to keep on top of every detail. They have a track record which tells them that they have a successful way of leading. If you become an entrepreneur, you will become familiar with the following routine:

- When you start out, you will be told that you are bound to fail and what you are trying to do is impossible.
- As you start to succeed, all sorts of hangers-on try climbing on board and claiming a slice of the action.
- After you have succeeded, everyone tells you that you got lucky.

Given this experience, successful entrepreneurs have a right to feel a little superior and to trust their judgement more than those of all the experts and hangers-on. Within more established organisations, people who have succeeded against the odds often have the same tendency. And some people are just plain arrogant and bossy.

The autocratic form of leadership works where the organisation is small enough that one person can get their hands and their intellect around it. It also works where the organisation is in crisis and needs fast decisions.

Autocracy fails in the face of complexity and size. The autocrat finds it difficult to build an effective leadership team. There is simply no one else who comes up to the standards of wisdom, performance, enthusiasm and excellence that autocrats believe they have. And yet the organisation becomes too big for one person to manage. Slowly, the autocrat loses touch and control and the business spins off track.

Autocratic leaders also typically fail to build strong teams or strong succession. Because the autocrat controls everything personally, followers are not entrusted to make decisions and to lead themselves. They do not get the opportunity to develop their skills; they do not get leadership experience. When the great leader leaves, there is a vacuum. Naturally, this confirms the opinion of the autocrat that they were the only person capable of leading the organisation; no one has been able to fill the autocrat's boots. This failure is the lasting legacy of the autocrat. The autocrat is the last person to recognise that they caused the failure.

The bureaucrat/technocrat

The bureaucrat is much maligned, and sometimes rightly so. A good bureaucratic machine is one that manages huge complexity fairly and efficiently. It is something of a technocracy – a rational world where rational decisions are made under the twin guiding stars of efficiency and fairness.

The technocratic leader is often quite self-effacing. They recognise that success lies with the strength of the machine they run, not with the operator of the machine. They are often hugely trustworthy people. They typically care more about fair and efficient processes than about achieving great outcomes.

As leaders, the technocrats are good at maintaining and enhancing a legacy. Do not look to the technocrat to create a new legacy. Rapid change, uncertainty, risk and ambiguity are like kryptonite to them. They are not comfortable in start-ups or in rapidly evolving crises. They are more comfortable in the public sector and in industries which are usually more stable like retail banking and insurance.

The technocrats will never change the world, but they will probably run the world before and after it has been changed.

The aristocrat

Aristocratic and wannabe aristocrats are everywhere. Try asking someone what they do. If they reply, 'I am a partner/vice president/ senior manager/ director at …', they are not telling you what they do. They are telling you about their title and position. This is what is important to them. Work and achievement are unfortunate, grubby barriers they have to jump on the way to title and status. You will see young wannabe aristos proudly displaying their gold cards from airlines. They will happen to drop into conversation that they have just got back from LA/shooting/fishing/skiing/the Grand Prix/meeting the PM. One such wannabe exploded with anger when I made fun of his platinum card from BA: he had wrapped his whole meaning into flying first class frequently. It made him feel important. In practice, he was going to irrelevant internal meetings at huge expense to feed his ego. The platinum card was a measure of just how much money he had wasted.

The ultimate goal of the aristocrat is the non-executive position, or chairing a government commission with a view to getting a knighthood. Both roles give prestige but require no responsibility. In their quest for status, the aristocrats become very pliable. They will find what the government wants them to find on the commission; they will nod through the CEO's outrageous compensation package. There is no need to bribe them. They are so hungry for status that they happily corrupt their judgement for you.

The best that can be said of the aristocrats is that they are largely harmless. Like the French aristocracy before the Revolution they are also largely useless. They gently corrode the values of their organisation; they represent the triumph of froth over substance and create an 'us versus them' culture. The aristo turns left on entering the plane, the proles turn right; they have separate lifts, dining rooms and parking spaces. It is a class system which undermines the whole organisation.

Many good leaders are narrowband leaders: they succeed in one context. Success goes to their heads. They believe in their own greatness. They get invited to sit on boards where they know nothing of the business or the organisation in the mistaken belief that their narrowband success can be replicated everywhere else by turning up on one or two days a month. Narrowband leaders need to stick to what they are good at. The temptation to go broadband, to join the aristocracy, is overwhelming. Few resist this final twist to their careers.

The democrat/meritocrat

A democratic leader sounds like a weak leader. But try telling Pericles, Washington, Lincoln, Churchill or Thatcher that they were weak. History shows that democracy thrives where the other tyrannies can be defeated or avoided. History also shows that democracy is advancing. As people become wealthier and better educated, they have more choice and they expect to have more say in whatever affects their lives.

The democratic leader has to combine three qualities:

1 **Ability**. The leader needs to have a proven track record.

2 **Support**. The leader needs to be recognised, trusted and supported by peers.

3 **Circumstance**. History is littered with nearly-leaders. They might have been great, but the conditions were wrong. Even Churchill suffered his 'wilderness years': it was war that made him.

The democratic leader will try to balance the need for excellence and fairness (the bureaucrat) with the need for decisiveness and speed (the autocrat). They will try to build commitment through inclusiveness and consultation. But they will balance that with the need for clarity, responsibility and accountability. They discover that there is no simple formula for leadership. Instead, there are endless trade-offs and balancing acts that need to be managed daily.

Many democratic leaders are narrowband leaders. They succeed in one particular industry, organisation or set of circumstances. The leader who has made their career building the top line will not know how to react when there is a bottom-line crisis that requires radical cost surgery. Great bankers do not make great retailers. This creates a challenge for the board as it seeks a new CEO. The new CEO is not just a leader. Each candidate is a different solution in search of a problem. The finance-focused candidate will not suddenly be transformed into the customer champion when entering the CEO's office. The board has to know what problem they are trying to solve before they look at any candidates.

So what?

By the time the leader emerges from the middle of the organisation into the top leadership position, the die is already cast. The leader has developed a set of skills and a style that will not change. In Shakespeare's words:

'There's a divinity that shapes our ends,
Rough-hew them how we will.'
– Hamlet V, ii

From this point on, the leader's career follows Shakespeare's plays. It turns out to be tragedy or comedy before becoming history. All leaders hope that their script is *All's Well That Ends Well*.

If your die is cast before you emerge at the top, there are two major implications.

The first is that you need to manage your values and your style from an early stage in your career. Early role models are decisive. It is natural to copy someone who is successful. This book says that there are many different ways in which you can succeed. You have a choice to make about the sort of person and the sort of leader you want to become. You need to be aware of that choice all the time, rather than blindly following role models. Most people do not make a conscious decision about who they want to be as a leader – they drift into a style. Sometimes they are lucky, sometimes they are unlucky. This book gives you a choice.

The second implication is that the established leader can have a huge impact on future generations of leadership. Emerging leaders watch you: they see what you do, whom you reward and why, and how you work. Your legacy is not just the business you leave behind, it is the values you leave behind.

Creating values for the organisation at large

Leaders create a legacy which future generations of leaders can build on and enhance. Part of your legacy will be your results – the size, scope and strength of the organisation. Another part of your legacy are the values you leave behind. These are likely to last longer than your results. Anyone who has been through a merger will recognise how long it takes for values and cultures to change. Even 10 years after the event, individuals will identify each other as coming from side A or side B; the merged group C is simply a veneer that is applied to the underlying cultures of the two old organisations.

> leaders create a legacy which future generations of leaders can build on and enhance

In this section we will look at the *what* and the *how* of creating effective values. We will start with looking at *what common values are effective and ineffective*.

Look at the values statement from one company in the box opposite. But don't look too long. It is tedious and irritating in equal proportions. It is a typical agglomeration of worthy words. In essence, their values aspire to sainthood. If you can identify the company or the industry in which it operates, you are doing very well. In fairness to them, their values statement is neither worse nor better than much of the twaddle that passes as values statements in other organisations.

A good values statement will achieve the following:

- Everyone can remember it. If people can't remember the values, they can't act on them. Twelve words maximum.

- It helps staff decide what to do in ambiguous situations. Do I give a refund or make margin? Do I confront improper behaviour or let it go?

Typical values statement

Delivering on our mission

The tenets central to accomplishing our mission stem from our core company values:

A global, inclusive approach

Thinking and acting globally, enabling a diverse workforce that generates innovative decision making for a broad spectrum of customers and partners, and showing leadership in supporting the communities in which we work and live.

Excellence

In everything we do.

Trustworthy

Deepening customer trust through the quality of our products and services, our responsiveness and accountability, and our predictability in everything we do.

Great people with great values

Delivering on our mission requires great people who are bright, creative and energetic, and who share the following values:

- Integrity and honesty.
- Passion for customers, partners and technology.
- Open and respectful with others and dedicated to making them better.
- Willingness to take on big challenges and see them through.
- Self-critical, questioning and committed to personal excellence and self-improvement.
- Accountable for commitments, results, and quality to customers, shareholders, partners and employees.

- It relates to the particular needs of that organisation – customer service, attention to detail, fairness, innovation, whatever.
- It lasts. Values, like dogs, are not just for Christmas.
- It is enforceable and actionable. Thinking globally is tough for a cleaner.

Using the criteria listed, try scoring the values statement on page 279.

Great care needs to be taken in building the right values for an organisation. There are many popular buzz words that are thoughtlessly included in values statements. Passion is very much flavour of the month – pizza boys are meant to be passionate about pizza and cleaners are meant to be passionate about toilet bowls. It is relatively easy for the founder or leader of an organisation to feel passionate about their 'baby'. They should avoid projecting their own passion on to everyone else. Demanding passion as one executive did – 'I want to see our logo emblazoned on the hearts of all our staff' – is not helpful. The same executive then wondered why they employed a majority of women, but none made it to the executive suite. Not everyone wants to become a fully signed-up member of a cult: some have lives outside work as well.

What it takes to be a leader

Leadership is not for everyone. Decide if you really want to become a top leader. Here is what it takes:

1 **Have endless self-confidence**

The worse things are, the more the leader shines. Build resilience. When disaster looms, take control, take responsibility, move to action.

2 **Be unreasonable**

Dare to set stretching goals for yourself and for others. Escape the comfort zone: push yourself and others to over-deliver and to learn new tricks.

3 **Be ambitious**

Have clear goals for yourself and have a plan on how to get there. Do not hope to get lucky in your career: hope is not a method and luck is not a strategy. Control your destiny.

4 **Manage time ruthlessly**

Focus, focus, focus on what matters. Delegate all you can. Schedule assertively: manage your diary.

5 **Work the politics**

Build your influence and informal power. Find the right boss, role and assignment. Manage how you are seen, control the messaging. Defend your territory. Fight the right battles. Wise up.

6 **Work anywhere, anytime**

Queues, delays and public transport were not invented to frustrate you: they were invented for you to deal with email and other noise of life. Work or sleep on planes. Leadership is hard work: there are no short cuts. You need never endure the rush hour as a leader: you will arrive before and leave after it.

7 **Sleep anywhere, anytime**

Learn to rest and relax when and how you can. Manage your diet: avoid conference death food of cookies and more; decide if you really need to put your liver on the line to succeed.

8 **Speak well**

Speaking to small groups, large groups and individuals is what you do all day. Learn to do it well.

9 **Be endlessly positive and constructive**

Learn to deal with stroppy colleagues, customers, receptionists, bosses, check-in clerks, crises, conflicts. Wear the mask: what you think behind the mask is for you alone.

10 **Find your context**

Marry your strengths to the sort of firm, function and role where you will flourish. You only excel at what you enjoy, so enjoy it.

Making the values real

You have the values statement. You have the bronze plaques and motivational posters to go with it. You have even recorded a piece on camera for the annual meeting and for all new-hire inductions. Nothing happens. All those hours spent arguing over the nuances of each carefully crafted word have come to nothing.

A large ocean separates the hope of the official values from the reality of the unofficial values within the organisation. There are two steps to bridging the gap between hope and reality: communications and action.

Communicating the values

Endless communication of the values is an essential, but exhausting, part of building the values of the organisation. It is also very dangerous.

You have just come up with some great new values for the organisation. You want to embed a new set of behaviours to carry the organisation forward. You get on stage, wave your arms and enthusiastically communicate the new vision. The response sounds nearer to mutiny than adoration. What went wrong?

To tell people you are going to change the culture of the organisation is toxic:

- Cultural revolutions do not have a good history. Think Mao and tens of millions of deaths.
- Telling people you are going to change the culture is like telling them that you are going to mess with their heads and change the way they think and behave. Not everyone gets excited about this.
- Changing values is an implicit attack on the past. It is like saying the way you have been behaving is no good. Not many people like to be told they have spent the last 20 years getting it wrong.

● The brave new world sounds exciting to you, but dangerous to them. Can they succeed in this alien world you have described?

If you want to build a new culture, do not attack the old one. It simply invites a battle. Instead, act like a crab: tackle the culture sideways on. Continue to celebrate and reinforce those parts of the old culture that are still useful; emphasise one or two new things that will be important in the future; ignore and let wither some of the old values that are less useful.

> if you want to build a new culture, do not attack the old one; it simply invites a battle

Once you have the right message you will find yourself having to communicate it endlessly, and for years. It will need constant repetition through all the media. It is a war of attrition. But even more than your words, people will believe your actions.

Enacting the values

In practice, followers learn the right and wrong sorts of behaviour from three vital influences:

1 Pay, performance and promotion systems.
2 Tough decisions.
3 Personal behaviour of the CEO and symbolic acts.

Pay, performance and promotion systems

In many instances, pay, performance and promotion systems are still not properly aligned with the values or objectives of the organisation. The telecommunications company trumpets customer service, but rewards its call centre staff on the number of calls they process. The result: incomplete and dropped calls, and hurried customers as the call centre staff try to meet their hourly call targets. A consulting company values professional integrity and teamwork. It promotes to partner the manager who has acquired some big accounts. The manager has also tested the limits of the expense system and been highly political. Everyone understands the real rules – sell big or die.

The pay and promotion systems are the acid test of the values a leader really believes in.

Tough decisions

As a leader, you need to think through the logical consequences of the fine words you talk about, and then see those consequences through to their conclusion.

Case Study

Actions speak louder than words

The school head decided, with the staff, that respect for the individual was going to be the central value of the school. The staff had some idea what this might mean, but no one was really sure.

One day, a teacher mentioned that they were going to give a class detention to Year 6. There had been some cheating, and the teacher wanted to make the point that cheating was unacceptable. The head teacher was horrified. You cannot give group detentions to the guilty and innocent alike; you have to respect the individual. The teacher had to go back and do more work to separate the guilty and innocent.

The PE teacher in the same school was a traditionalist who believed everyone should aspire to high standards of fitness. If you did not have high standards and ability, you suffered. The teacher seemed to believe in ritual humiliation of the fat, unfit and asthmatic. The head teacher observed that this did not amount to respect for the individual. The PE teacher could either change or change schools. He changed schools.

The staff learned what 'respect for the individual' meant not through speeches, but through practical, hard decisions.

Personal behaviour of the CEO and symbolic acts

New CEOs are often surprised to find out how much power they really have. They expected and understood the nature of the formal authority they would inherit. They are often more surprised by the informal authority they have. People take their cues from the leader, who is the ultimate role model.

Case Study

Walking the talk

How not to do it

One leader of an organisation which employed many low-paid staff realised he needed to cut costs dramatically to meet profit targets. He announced the plan at a company meeting of area and regional managers. He told them to beware of tough decisions on pay and redundancies. Everyone would have to make sacrifices. He had personally ordered the air conditioning in the boardroom to be turned off. This all sounded great. He left the event in his chauffeur-driven Bentley to attend a big corporate hospitality event. He lost all credibility with his managers and was later fired.

How to do it

Another CEO decided he wanted to create a more open culture. He announced a new open-door policy. He had an open door, but it was on the thirteenth floor, accessible only through the special executive lift. He knew the thirteenth floor was referred to as 'death row' by staff. They were summoned there sometimes to be promoted, but more staff were summoned there to get fired.

The CEO realised that an open door behind a closed elevator made little sense. He decided he should show that he was more open. He summoned up his courage and went to the alien world of the seventh floor. Staff were in shock. They had never seen a director, let alone the previous CEO. They all made themselves busy and tried to avoid eye contact. Eventually, the CEO found one unlucky clerk to talk to. There was nowhere for him to sit. ▶

Instinctively, he took an empty waste basket, turned it upside down and sat on it to get down to the level of the clerk. They talked about nothing very much. But news of the revolution spread like wildfire: he was a boss whom anyone could actually talk to.

Being asked to walk the talk on values is irritating and unhelpful. It is not really clear what you are meant to do or how you are meant to do it. In practice, you can walk the talk if you focus on the three basic ideas outlined above.

Part 4

The leadership journey

Chapter 12

The leadership journey

Anyone can lead, and everyone can learn to lead better. There is no great secret to learning the skills of being positive, professional and people focused. But if you want to succeed on the leadership journey, there is more you have to do. There are three elements to your leadership journey:

1   **You have to perform**. As a leader, you have to take people where they would not have gone by themselves. That means you have to make a difference, whatever level of the organisation you may be at.

2   **Find your context**. Even the greatest leaders struggle out of context: think of Churchill and his 'wilderness years'. The wartime hero was forgettable in peacetime. Find the context in which you will flourish.

3   **Keep on learning and adapting**. The rules of survival and success change at each level of the organisation. Your recipe for success becomes a recipe for failure at the next level up of the firm.

We have already explored what good performance looks like at each level of the firm, and how you can learn to lead. Now is the time to discover the context in which you can succeed.

Leading across sectors: find your context

Leaders are creatures of context. If you look at leaders today, very few succeed across sectors. The great CEO is a one-trick pony. When they step down there is rarely a second trick: none of them go on to become great entrepreneurs; few of them go on to lead other sorts of organisation with great success. Most of them disappear into the irrelevance of committee and commission land where the good and the great deal with the mad and the bad.

> the great CEO is a one-trick pony

If you are to succeed as a leader, you have to choose the right context. This is very hard to do. The right context means finding a fit between your signature strengths and the strengths which different sorts of organisation require from their leaders. This means that you have to discover two unknowns: most people do not discover their true strengths until they have been working for several, or many, years. And knowing the rules of survival and success in different sorts of organisation is nearly impossible to divine from the outside. They all talk about the same sorts of things: teamwork, initiative, results, leadership. But the words and the emphasis mean different things. Leadership is like a piano: the notes are the same for everyone, but you can play endless different tunes. And we can all learn to improve our basic skills.

This section demystifies some of the differences of context which leaders have to choose from. Differences within a firm can be as great as differences between sectors and between countries. So choose well.

1 Differences between functions

Each function within a firm is a different tribe with its own rituals, beliefs and rules. These will not be written down, but they are fundamental to your success or otherwise. The skills you need to flourish differ depending on which function you choose to work in.

Most organisations look for some combination of the following: people skills, organisation, analytical skills, action focus and initiative. There is also an unwritten rule about risk appetite. Take a look at the grid below to see how strong you need to be to succeed in each sort of function.

	Finance	Operations	Sales	IT
People skills	4	8	8	4
Organisation	8	8	6	6
Analytical skills	8	5	4	8
Action focus	3	7	7	5
Initiative	3	7	8	5
Risk appetite	2	3	6	3

These are clearly crude comparisons: IT covers a wide range of tasks all the way from cutting code through to dealing with customers on a help desk. So the differences within each function can also be great. But each of these functions has some inbuilt biases about what 'good' looks like. A good salesperson is rarely mistaken for a good finance person and vice versa: they are different sorts of people. The grid above shows the signature strengths which you typically need to get ahead in each function.

The scores in the grid above are out of 10, where 10 shows that the relevant skill is in very high demand in that function; 1 shows that there is very little demand for that skill. The shaded boxes show the sorts of signature strength which successful leaders demonstrate in each function.

2 Differences between levels of the firm

The rules of survival and success change as your career progresses. One of the most dramatic examples is in the consulting industry, where they even have a motto to describe the different levels: finders, minders and grinders. Finders are the partners who go and find (sell) the work; minders are the managers who oversee delivery of the work; and grinders are the people who actually do the work. Naturally, they all have fancy titles, but finders, minders and grinders describe what they really do. In addition, large firms have a mysterious group of 'binders' whose job is to manage the whole firm and to pay themselves lots of money.

Here is how the skills requirements vary by level of the consulting firm; with some variation, it reflects how skills needs vary in all firms. Remember, the grinders are the most junior leaders and the binders are the top leaders.

	Grinders	Minders	Finders	Binders
People skills	3	6	9	10
Organisation	5	8	6	5
Analytical skills	9	8	7	6
Action focus	6	7	7	7
Initiative	5	6	7	8
Risk appetite	4	5	6	6

In a consulting firm, as with most firms, your skill set changes over time. You start out needing strong technical (analytical) skills; you then need good organisational skills. As a finder you need very good people skills to manage clients and to sell to them. Meanwhile your technical (analytical) skills become less and less important. You simply no longer need to do detailed analysis because there are other people who can do that for you. Instead, you need to have insight. This is obvious, but explains why so many people turn from heroes to zeros when they are promoted: they simply have the wrong skill set to succeed at the next level. If you want promotion, make sure you are building the skills you will need at the next level now. When you are in the post, it is too late to start building those skills.

many people turn from heroes to zeros when they are promoted

3 Differences between type of career

Much career advice varies between the poor and the abysmal. Dating agencies have a much better track record because they are able to get a much better profile of both parties. In practice, most people find out the hard way: by experience. The data bear this out. Older people stay with employers longer than younger people. Over 75% of 23- to 27-year-olds change employer within two years of starting; the 'first bouncer' syndrome is a classic for graduates who discover that their first employer is different from what they had hoped.

Each career is unique, as a very basic comparison of three careers in the grid below shows:

- a trader dealing bonds in an investment bank
- a teacher in an inner city school
- a civil servant working in a central government department.

	Trader	Teacher	Civil servant
People skills	2	9	4
Organisation	4	8	8
Analytical skills	8	6	6
Action focus	8	6	3
Initiative	6	6	3
Risk appetite	9	4	1

The trader has to be very comfortable taking and managing risk, which also means having a quick, analytical mind that is unafraid of acting on analysis. This is the opposite of the civil servant, to whom risk is anathema. Instead, the civil servant needs to be very good on process, organisation and risk avoidance. Driving to action is not the most important skill a civil servant needs. In contrast, the teacher will need to have superb people skills, good organisation and confidence in making things happen in the classroom. These are three different careers with completely different signature strengths for the successful leader.

4 Differences between sectors

The private sector likes to caricature the public sector as a bunch of pampered and useless idlers who make tea all day. And the public sector likes to caricature the private sector as a bunch of greedy, heartless pigs who would sell their grandmother's ashes to make a quick buck. These caricatures are universal. In Costa Rica they have two-fingered and three-fingered sloths. They also claim to have the five-fingered sloth: civil servants.

Beyond public and private sectors, there is the voluntary sector which has challenges all of its own.

But we have already seen that differences between functions and between levels are as great as any possible differences between sectors. Nevertheless, there are profound differences between the three sectors, as shown below.

	Public sector	Private sector	Voluntary sector
Risk appetite	Very low	Medium to high	Medium to low
Goal clarity	Unclear	Very clear	Medium
Motivation focus	Good terms, conditions and job security, modest pay at senior levels	Demanding work–life balance, high pay potential, poor job security	Modest pay at all levels, high intrinsic rewards
Budgets	Use it all (or lose it next year)	Cut where you can and invest where it makes money	Watch every penny
Organisation focus	Process compliance, plus some outputs	Profit focus, plus some other outcomes	Mission focus

To highlight the differences, see how each sector reacts to under-performance by an individual.

The public sector finds it very hard to fire anyone. In one organisation I found that staff were 50 times more likely to die in service than to be fired, and this was an organisation with very low occupational health hazards. In practice, weak staff get sidelined into areas where they can do least harm. In the private sector, under-performance is confronted more directly. Staff will be given a choice: shape up or ship out. Some firms explicitly weed out the bottom 10% of their management staff each year, to keep standards high. The public sector pays to keep under-performers; the private sector pays to get rid of them.

The voluntary sector has perhaps the toughest challenge in people management. Most charities find that their ambition exceeds their means. Every penny counts, which means they cannot afford to have any under-performers. Unlike the private sector, they cannot pay under-performers to go away. Equally, they cannot afford to keep them and they cannot afford the legal bills that come with a case for unfair dismissal. Anyone who thinks that managing in the voluntary sector is a soft option is deeply mistaken.

Although the differences between sectors appear great, they are becoming increasingly blurred. The private sector is taking on more and more of what used to be public sector work; the public sector is contracting out its delivery obligations to the private sector. Equally, many charities are increasingly dependent on government contracts and have to act like private sector firms to get those contracts.

> the differences between sectors are becoming increasingly blurred

We can choose to believe or disbelieve the caricatures of each sector. In practice, aspiring leaders need to look at the organisation and the function as much as they look at the sector they want to join.

5 Differences between employment and self-employment and entrepreneurship

Moving from employment to being your own boss is a one-way leap. You will find it very hard to jump back into the gilded cage of employment. Once you have tasted the freedom and responsibility of working on your own account, it is hard to go back. The gilded cage of perks, benefits and regular pay cheques has its attractions. But from the outside it looks more like an iron prison: you may work for a boss you do not respect; you are demeaned and constrained by information systems which monitor your every move and show that you are not trusted; your future is in the hands of other people who may or may not care for you.

But as you make your leap to freedom, you discover that with freedom comes responsibility. When things go wrong, the only person to blame is yourself. You discover that cash flow is not some arcane report which that useless finance function produces and you do not understand: it is what tells you whether you can pay your mortgage at the end of the month. You make other discoveries:

- You can turn right, not left, when getting on a flight.
- Taxis are not the only means of transport around town.
- Flowers in the office are not essential to productivity.
- When your computer crashes, there is no IT department to call: you have to fix it yourself.
- Weekends are for wimps.
- Customers do not call you out of the blue: you have to fight for every one.

Most entrepreneurs find that there is an inevitable cycle of success. When you start out, people will help you by pointing out all the risks and hazards. At best they will quietly smirk behind their hands and wait for you to fail. There will also be about 20 people who give you some very nebulous advice and demand 10% of your firm in return for their brilliance, insight and contacts. When you start to succeed, they will start to condescend to you: you are still nothing compared to the prestigious firm they work for. When you are finally sailing around in your mega yacht and they are still stuck in the traffic commuting to work, they will remind you (and everyone else) how they were 100% central to your success.

Then people wonder why entrepreneurs can be a bit arrogant and chippy. Entrepreneurs have done it the hard way and deserve everything they get, even if they get jealousy more than respect for what they have achieved.

> entrepreneurs have done it the hard way and deserve everything they get

Completing the journey

Most books and gurus like to give you The Answer. Ideally, The Answer is simple. It will contain three points and can be summarised in a snappy phrase or acronym. You read the book, remember The Answer and then you become a leader. Except, of course, that real life is not like that.

Life is becoming more complicated, more stressful and more time constrained. In this world we want quick, easy answers. So if anyone promises The Answer, it is very seductive. But once we have been let down a few times, our cynicism tends to grow about all such answers. We are left groping through the fog in search of leadership.

> the Answer in this book is that leadership is not a destination – it is a journey

Leadership is not some far distant objective that is all about a rare breed of human which controls the fate of nations and organisations. Leadership is here and now. We can all take part in the leadership journey. We may never lead the nation or a multinational organisation. We can be leaders of a project team, a club, an expedition or a department. We can develop our leadership skills from the first day we start work.

Because most people focus on The Answer and the destination, they never focus on the journey.

Each person's journey is different. We all have different starting points, and we all have different leadership destinations. We will lead different types of organisation in different situations and with different styles. If the start and finish of a journey are different for each person, the journey in between will also be different.

For many people, the leadership journey is a random walk. Like a snakes and ladders game, we sometimes achieve the right situation and rise rapidly; then we find ourselves working for a snake of a manager and fall back rapidly.

The journey does not have to be random. Although we cannot say, 'Turn left after six months and do this', we know that there are consistent sets of behaviours and skills which leaders tend to have. These skills and behaviours can be learned. They do not guarantee that anyone will become a leader or that they will become a heroic success as a leader. But they will load the dice heavily in favour of success.

We also know that leaders can exist at all levels of the organisation. You do not have to wait to get the top job before you can demonstrate that you are a leader. In fact, you cannot afford to wait that long. Leaders practise and demonstrate their skills from a very early stage.

What this book has shown is that the expected skills and behaviours of the leader change at each level of the organisation. These skills and behaviours are cumulative. In the past, people have talked vaguely of the importance of 'experience' for leaders. This does not help. It simply frustrates ambitious people by implying that they are going to have to wait 30 years before they can succeed. We have peeled away the mysteries of leadership to show what leaders need to do and what they need to learn, at each stage of their individual leadership journey.

With this road map to leadership, you do not have to become a heroic leader in the mould of the famous people who litter the pages of history books and business magazines. You cannot succeed by trying to be someone else. Equally, coasting along as yourself and hoping that the world will recognise your innate excellence will not work either. To succeed as a leader, you have to be the best of who you are. This book is not just a road map to being a leader. It is a road map to helping you become the best of who you are.

> whatever your journey is, enjoy it

Whatever your journey is, enjoy it.

Index

alignment 233–4
aristocrats 269, 274–5
assignment
  obtaining right one 170
  process 28
attributes required for effective
    leader 280–1
autocrats 97–8, 269, 271–3
'awkward squad' 135–40
  characteristics 135
  emotional response 136–9
  political response 139–40
  rational response 136

barriers to success
  autocrat 97–8
  'boffin in the box' 96
  'boy scout' 96–7
  'cave dweller' 97
  matrix leaders 95–8
  'politicians' 96
Begg, David 71
behaviour
  CEO 285–6
  emerging leaders xviii, xxii
  personal 76
  senior leaders xviii, xxi, xxii
blame culture 267
board of directors, and CEO 237–40
'boffin in the box' 96
bonuses as motivators 106–7
boss

influencing see boss – influencing
and network building 175
relationship with 31
shows interest in my career 117–18
boss – influencing 25–32
  delivering right results 29–30
  finding right boss 27–9
  guidelines for success 27–30
    summary 30–1
  right behaviours 31–2
'boy scout' 96–7
Branson, Richard 44
budget negotiation 170
bureaucrats 269, 273
business literacy 196–8
business numeracy 198–200

career death spiral 232
career as a noun and a verb 72–4
'cave dweller' 97
CEO 211–86
  analysis of time spent 221
  art of unreasonable management
    234–7
  creating top leadership team 224
  expectations 238–9
  firing decisions 230–2
  hiring decisions 228–30
  Kissinger test 215
  leadership agenda 258–62
  leading top leadership team 232–7
  legacy test 216

CEO (*continued*)
  loneliness 222–3
  memory test 217
  peer group 222–3
  people focus 212, 221–40
  people skills 223–4
  performance 238
    driving 234–5
  personal behaviour 285–6
  positivity 212, 244–62
  power – identifying and using
    253–8
  professionalism 212, 213, 265–86
  qualities required 212–13
  relationship with chairperson
    237–40
  resource allocation and
    management 254–5
  and restructuring 257–8
  reward and measurement systems
    255–6
  self-confidence 213, 224–5
  strategy 253–4
  taking control – summary of
    guidelines 252–3
  team formation 256–7
  trust – building 239
  value creation 278–81
  values
    communication 282–3
    enacting 283–6
  vision 244–62
  working with board 237–40
chairperson, relationship with CEO
  237–40
change management 158–65
  capacity to change 160
  change network 164–5
  FUD factor 159, 160–1
  managing process 161–3
  need 160
  political and emotional
    consequences of change
    161–3

risks and costs of change 160–1
  'valley of death' 162–3
  versus project management 151–2
  vision 160
clarity 233
closed questions 131, 192
coaching journey 129, 133–5
coaching relationship, requirements
  for successful 133
coaching session 129–32
  case study 132
  closed questions 131
  goals 133–4
  objectives 129
  obstacles 130
  open questions 131
  options 130
  outcomes 130
  overview 130
coaching for success 128–34
communication 83, 184, 185
  being proactive 205
  decentring 205–6
  effective 205–6
  skills 76
  three *E*s 187
company newsletter 247–8
conflict management 144–6
consensus building 59
context – finding 292–9
  difference between functions
    292–3
  differences between levels of firm
    293–4
  differences between sectors 296–7
  differences between type of career
    295–6
control 168–9
  taking, summary of guidelines
    252–3
courtesy 88
credibility 178
crisis, handling 213
crisis management 146–9, 170

data
  finding 47, 54–6
  review and analysis 47, 57–8
data structure creation 47, 51–3
  Pareto's 80/20 rule 51
debriefing 193
decentring, communication –
      effective 205–6
decision-making 52–3
  guidelines – summary 52–3
  and values 284
decisiveness 46, 213
delegation 84, 115
  and time management 62
democrats 269, 275–7
development assessment 124
deviation 64
disloyalty 26–7
dress codes 77
dysfunctional behaviour from peers,
      dealing with 84–5

emerging leaders
  behaviour xviii
    effective xxi
    ineffective xxii
  what bosses look for in 26–7
emotional objections 21–2
  dealing with 22
emotional quotient (EQ) 167, 168
energy 80–1
entrepreneurs 151, 272, 298–9
EQ (emotional quotient) 167, 168
etiquette 85–9
  courtesy 88
  focus 87–8
  Japan 86
  personal touch 88–9
  promptness 87
  responsiveness 88
evaluation, formal 122–4
expectations 29
  CEO 238–9
  delivering 122

experience 42
  learning from xxvi, 72–4

failure 43
fear 113, 114
feedback 122–6
  formal 122–4
  informal 124–5, 128
  negative 122, 124–5
  SPIN 125–6
firing decisions, CEO 230–2
flattery 15
focus 233
Ford, Henry 166

gatekeepers 176–7
goals 236–7
gossip 40
greed 113, 114

Herzberg's two-factor theory 106–9,
      110
hesitation 64
hiring decisions, CEO 228–30
history of modern management
      166–7
honesty 79, 118–19, 212, 266–7
humility 267–8
hygiene factors 107

idleness 113–14
influencing people
  boss 25–32
    analysis of and adaption to
        boss's style 9–11
    one to one basis 11
    public meeting 11–13
information sharing 267
inspiration, compared with
      motivation 104
integrity 212
intelligence xvii
intelligence quotient (IQ) 167, 168
interpersonal skills 76

intrinsic rewards, as motivators 107
IQ (intelligence quotient) 167, 168
issue tree 53

Japan, etiquette 86

Kissinger test 215
kleptocrats 269, 270–1
knowing yourself 6–13
    Myers-Briggs Type Indicator 6–9
Kotter, John 221

leader, attributes required for
        effective 280–1
leadership agenda 258–62
leadership journey 299–301
leadership styles 268–77
    aristocrat 269, 274–5
    autocrat 269, 271–3
    bureaucrat 269, 273
    democrat 269, 275–7
    kleptocrat 269, 270–1
    meritocrat 269, 275–7
    technocrat 269, 273
learning to lead 70–6
    from experience 72–4
    from role models 71–2
    from structured observation and
        discovery 74–6
    methods xxv–xxvi
        experience xxvi
legacy test 216
listening 184, 185
listening skills 16–17, 24, 190–3
    closed questions 192
    debriefing 193
    open questions 192, 193
    paraphrasing 192
loneliness 222–3
loyalty 26–7, 79, 118, 121
luck 41–4

McGregor, D., X and Y motivation
        theory 105–6

Major, John 226
Management By Walking Around
        114
Management By Walking Away 114,
        235
management skills 76
Maslow, A., hierarchy of needs
        111–15
matrix leaders
    barriers to success 95–8
    change management 158–65
    conflict management 144–6
    crisis management 146–9, 170
    motivation 103–40
    network building 169, 174–9
    people focus 98, 103–40
    performance 99
    positivity 99, 143–79
    power acquisition 166, 168–74
    professionalism 98, 183–206
    project management 151–8
    rewards 150
    risk management 149–51
meeting – learning how to 184,
        200–4
meetings
    attending 201–2
    deviation – preventing 204
    leading 202–3
    management 170
    prompt attendance 203
    repetition 204
    right people and right purpose
        201–3
    right process 203–4
    timetable 203
memory test 217
menial work 40
mentoring 128
meritocrats 269, 275–7
middle organisation leaders
        see matrix leaders
mindset of leader 214–15
money, and motivation 117

Morita, Akio 39
motivation 103–40, 120–6, 212
    boss shows interest in my career
        117–18
    compared with inspiration 104
    description 103–4
    feedback 122–6
    guidelines – summary 115–16
    Herzberg's two-factor theory
        106–9, 110
    intrinsic rewards as motivators
        107
    Maslow's hierarchy of needs
        111–15
    and money 117
    pay and bonuses as motivators
        106–7
    in practice 116–20
    public sector 106, 108
    and recognition 120
    and trust 118–19
    and vision 119
    worthwhile job 119–20
    X and Y theory 105–6
Myers-Briggs Type Indicator (MB/
    TI) 6–9

names 89
needs, Maslow's hierarchy 111–15
network building 169, 174–9
    authorisers 175
    gatekeepers 176–7
    network nodes 176
    resources 175–6
    sponsors 175
    technical influencers 176
    trust 177–9
    Trust Equation 177–8
numbers – reading 198–200

objections, dealing with 19, 20–2, 25
O'Leary, Michael 44, 246
open questions 131, 192, 193

organisations, changing,
    disadvantages 28–9

paraphrasing 192, 204
    and effective persuasion 16, 17
Pareto's 80/20 rule 51
    and time management 61
partnership principle 170
pay as motivator 106–7
pay system, and values 283–4
people focus xix, xxi, 5–32
    CEO 212, 221–40
    decentring (knowing yourself) 5,
        6–13
    effective behaviour xxi
    ineffective behaviour xxii
    influence see influencing people
    influencing the boss 25–32
    managing upwards 5, 25–32
    matrix leaders 98, 103–40
    persuading people see persuasion –
        effective
performance xix, 291
    driving 234–5
    matrix leaders 99
    reactions to under-performance
        297
performance system, and values
    283–4
persistence 42–3
personal behaviours 76
personal touch 88–9
perspective 43
persuasion – effective 13–25
    adaption of style to that of other
        person 16, 24
    agreeing challenge from their
        perspective 17, 24
    giving story and a win 19–20, 24
    listening skills 16–17, 24
    move to action 23, 25
    objections – dealing with 19, 20–2,
        25
    paraphrasing, use of 16, 17

persuasion – effective (*continued*)
  positive commitment 23
  preparation 13–14, 24
  rapport and trust – building
    14–16, 24
  'size the prize' 17–19, 24
  suggesting idea and showing how
    it works 19, 24
  summary of steps 24–5
political quotient (PQ) 167, 168,
    169, 170, 172, 173
'politicians' 96
positivity xix, xxi, 35–65
  CEO 212, 244–62
  change management 158–65
  conflict management 144–6
  crisis management 146–9, 170
  defining 36
  demonstrating 39–40
  effective behaviour xxi
  ineffective behaviour xxii
  matrix leaders 99, 143–79
  power acquisition 166, 168–74
  and problem solving 46–59
  project management 151–8
  risk management 149–51
  sustaining 37–9
  time management 59–65
  versus being smart 45–6
  vision 244–62
power
  levels – identifying and using
    253–8
  10 laws of 168–74
  top leadership team 226
power acquisition 166, 168–74
  acting the part 169–70
  and ambiguity 172–3
  control 168–9
  network building 169, 174–9
  outcomes – focusing on 173
  picking right battles 171
  striking early 170

  and unreasonableness 171–2
  'use it or lose it' 173–4
PQ (political quotient) 167, 168,
    169, 170, 172, 173
practice 41–2
presentations, effective speaking
    186–9
private sector
  reaction to under-performance
    297
  skills required 296–7
problem solving 46–59
  data
    finding 47, 54–6
    review and analysis 47, 57–8
  data structure creation 47, 51–3
  hypothesis – creating 47, 50
  identifying problem 47, 48–50
  issue tree 53
  Pareto's 80/20 rule 51
  recommendation – making 47,
    58–9
  traps
    problem-free analysis 49
    problem-free solutions 48–9
    symptoms versus causes 49
problems, handling 126–8
professionalism xix, 69–89
  business survival etiquette 85–9
  CEO 212, 213, 265–86
  communication 184, 185, 205–6
  effective behaviour xxi
  honesty 266–7
  humility 267–8
  ineffective behaviour xxii
  learning local rules 77–8
  listening 184, 185, 190–3
  matrix leaders 98, 183–206
  meeting 184, 200–4
  reading 184, 185, 196–200
  speaking 184, 185, 186–9
  universal lessons 78–85
  value creation 278–81

values
 communication 282–3
 enacting 283–6
 view from the bottom 83–5
 view from the top 78–83
 writing 184, 185, 193–6
project management 151–8
 basics 152–8
 governance 158
 identifying real problem 154–5
 outcomes – defining 157
 process 157–8
 sponsor 155–6
 team 156–7
 versus change management 151–2
promotion, over-promotion xx
promotion system, and values 283–4
psychological contract 118
public sector
 reaction to under-performance
  297
 skills required 296–7
 staff motivation 106, 108

rapport, building 14–16, 24
reading 184, 185, 196–200
 case study 196–7
 numbers 198–200
 words 196–8
recommendation, making 47, 58–9
Red Arrows 245
reliability 80
reorganisation 226
resource allocation and management
  254–5
responsibilities 40
responsiveness 88
results, delivering right 29–30
reward and measurement systems
  255–6
rewards, matrix leaders 150
risks 178
 management 149–51

taking 40, 43
role models, and learning to lead
  71–2
rules, learning local 77–8
Ryanair 44, 245–6

Scientific Management 63, 166
self-confidence 213, 224–5
self-employment 298
senior leaders
 behaviour xviii
  effective xxi
  ineffective xxii
seniority xvii
Serligman, Martin 37
'size the prize' 17–19, 24
skills
 communication 76
 essential 81–2
 interpersonal 76
 management 76
skills required 292–9
 differences between functions
  292–3
 differences between levels of firm
  293–4
 differences between sectors 296–7
 differences between type of career
  295–6
skills-based approach xxiv
solutions 80
speaking 184, 185, 186–9
 effective 186–9
sponsor 28, 175
spreadsheets 198–200
strategy 253–4
 resource allocation and
  management 254–5
 reward and measurement systems
  · 255–6
structure
 restructuring business 258
 restructuring top team 257–8

style 29
style of leadership
  analysing others 10
  boss's – analysis of and adaption
    to 9–11
  discovering own 6–13
  Myers-Briggs Type Indicator 6–9
success, recognising 120

talking *see* speaking
Taylor, Frederick 63, 166
Teach First 109–10, 148
team
  formation 256–7
  see also top leadership team
technical influencers 176
technocrats 269, 273
time, CEO analysis of how used 221
time efficiency 63–5
time management 59–65
  and delegation 62
  guidelines – summary 62–3
  Pareto's 80/20 rule 61
Timpson, John 250–1
top leadership team
  balance 227–8
  creation 224
  power 226
  principles of effective 225–8
  purpose 226–8
  restructuring 257–8
  shape 228
  see also under CEO
top, leading from *see* CEO
trust 26, 115, 266
  building 14–16, 24, 239
  developing 121–2
  and motivation 118–19
  network building 177–9
Tzu, Sun 171

under-performance – reaction to,
    comparison of various sectors
    297
unreasonable management, art of
    234–7

value creation 278–81
values
  communication 282–3
  and decision-making 284
  enacting 283–6
  and pay, performance and
    promotion systems 283–4
values statement 278–80
Virgin Atlantic 43
vision 115, 160, 212, 244–62
  communicating 247–51
  enabling 251–62
  and motivation 119
  testing 246–7
voluntary sector
  reaction to under-performance
    297
  skills required 296–7
volunteering 40

walking the talk 285–6
when, use of term 179
Wiseman, Eichard 42
words – learning to read 196–8
writing 184, 185
  developing skill 193–6
    simple and short 195
    substance and style 195
    supporting assertions with
      facts 196
    telling a story 194–5
    writing for reader 194

X and Y motivation theory 105–6